T0334895

Epidemic Disease in Mexico City, 1761–1813
An Administrative, Social, and Medical Study

Latin American Monographs, No. 3
Institute of Latin American Studies
The University of Texas

EPIDEMIC DISEASE IN MEXICO CITY
1761–1813
An Administrative, Social, and Medical Study

by **DONALD B. COOPER**

published for the
INSTITUTE OF LATIN AMERICAN STUDIES *by*
the UNIVERSITY OF TEXAS PRESS, AUSTIN

Copyright © 1965 by Donald B. Cooper
First paperback printing 2015

All rights reserved

Requests for permission to reproduce material from this work
should be sent to:
  Permissions
  University of Texas Press
  P.O. Box 7819
  Austin, TX 78713-7819
  http://utpress.utexas.edu/index.php/rp-form

Library of Congress Catalog Number 65-23161

ISBN 978-1-4773-0575-1, paperback
ISBN 978-1-4773-0576-8, library e-book
ISBN 978-1-4773-0577-5, individual e-book

THIS BOOK IS FOR

ELLEN

FOREWORD

EPIDEMICS are a phenomenon of ancient and universal occurrence. Hundreds of successive generations have witnessed their devastating effects; the incalculable mortality that they have caused can never be known. Indeed, it cannot be doubted that epidemics have always constituted one of the chief enemies of human kind. In earlier days the threat that they posed was far more terrible than it is today. There was rarely, if ever, any effective defense against them, and young and old, rich and poor, alike fell victim to their power. And in recent times not even the progress of modern medicine has succeeded in completely freeing mankind from the threat of epidemic disease.

The study of epidemics and their effect on human life is but one of the innumerable fragments in the totality of history, and even this one fragment is very unevenly known and understood. Only portions of it have been studied in reasonably full and fruitful detail, as, for example, the epidemics of the United States and Europe. But the outbreaks of many other regions, including those of Latin America, have at best been imperfectly studied. Historians seem to be licensed to section history into fragments so that each may be studied in depth. Such a methodology is both essential and inescapable, but we may hope that in time the various portions will be so clearly understood that their relations to each other will be obvious. When the time comes that the complicated mosaic of world history can be fitted together, the fragment on epidemics could have no fixed place unless studied in its entirety—both in time and in space. The present study is intended to be a modest contribution to the sum of the parts.

The purpose of this volume is to set forth clearly and fully the story and significance of five major epidemics that attacked the people of Mexico City between 1761 and 1813. In those years Mexico City was the major metropolis of the New World, and the capital of New Spain, the largest colony within Spain's far-flung world empire. Much has been written about the political, economic, and military history of this great city and the provinces that she ruled, but much less has been said about the social history of the time—and of epidemics and public health almost nothing at all. The present volume is more a historical study of public-health administration and social history than medical history per se, and professes to be a contribution to the study of Latin American history in an area where almost nothing has been published previously, particularly in English.

The five epidemics that are emphasized occurred in the years 1761–1762, 1779–1780, 1784–1787, 1797–1798, and 1813. In terms of loss of life these were probably not the most devastating outbreaks of disease in the history of New Spain. But they are the only ones for which a substantial body of primary-source materials has survived, and consequently the only ones for which a detailed historical reconstruction is feasible. Most of these primary sources are in the form of original manuscripts, of which the great majority are housed either in the Archivo General de la Nación or in the Archivo Municipal del Ex-Ayuntamiento, both of Mexico City. A few pertinent primary sources have been published, usually in fragmentary form. Various secondary works are cited, but only the excellent articles of Sherburne F. Cook proved to be of major value.

ACKNOWLEDGMENTS

IN THE preparation of this study I received invaluable assistance from various individuals and institutions, and I wish to express my appreciation for their support. The following persons read the entire manuscript and each made helpful suggestions: Dr. John Duffy, Dr. Charles Gibson, Dr. Lewis U. Hanke, Dr. Thomas F. McGann, Dr. J. Lloyd Mecham, and Dr. Max Moorhead. Dr. Nettie Lee Benson gave useful bibliographical suggestions. Dr. Richard E. Greenleaf verified several references after my departure from Mexico City. Dr. Kenneth W. Newell and Dr. Stephen W. Bennett, both of the Division of Epidemics of the Tulane University School of Medicine, offered helpful criticism. Father Ernest J. Burrus, S.J., facilitated my work in Mexico City in a number of different ways. Above all I am very much indebted to the directors and staff of the Archivo General de la Nación and the Archivo Municipal del Ex-Ayuntamiento for numerous courtesies.

I thank the following institutions for major financial support: The Woodrow Wilson Foundation, The University of Texas, The Henry L. and Grace Doherty Charitable Foundation, and the Public Health Service of the National Institutes of Health of the Department of Health, Education, and Welfare. In addition, the Latin American Institute of The University of Texas provided funds for microfilming documents, and the University Council on Research of Tulane University provided funds for typing the final copy of the manuscript. My parents furnished additional financial aid, and my father, Professor Charles D. Cooper, Department of Engineering Drawing, The Ohio State University, through his own outstanding successes as a teacher and author, did more than he realizes to inspire me to pursue a career of teaching and research. My wife, Ellen Hutchins Cooper, has unfailingly lent me her interest and support, and besides rendering the service of typing the manuscript during several early drafts, her professional experience as a Public Health nurse saved me from some errors and provided certain valuable insights.

D. B. C.

New Orleans, Louisiana

CONTENTS

PART I

THE BACKGROUND

Introduction

THE NATURE of this study divides it into three parts of unequal length. Part I, which includes Chapters One and Two, deals with certain carefully selected background material which was thought to be important to a clear understanding of the various problems posed by the five epidemics. Chapter One describes in brief form the physiographical features of the Valley of Mexico, and attempts to relate them to the recurrence of disease in the area. Mexico City is located in a large valley virtually encircled by high mountains. Consequently the valley comprises an independent and self-contained drainage system, and most of its rainfall is retained locally. Historically this fact caused the creation of several large semisaline lakes; it also spurred the construction of the numerous canals which crisscrossed the capital city at the time of our story. Contemporaries believed that the valley's unusual aquatic environment, especially the recurrent floods, adversely affected the healthfulness of the area.

Chapter Two outlines the administrative machinery devised by the colonists to meet the challenge of mass outbreaks of disease. An epidemic was in fact everybody's business, and consequently all administrative levels, both national and local, secular and ecclesiastical, were involved in varying degrees. The purpose of Chapter Two is to set forth and to differentiate the diverse responsibilities of the various overlapping and interrelated authorities, and to indicate the procedures used to enforce sanitation.

The heart of the volume is Part II, "The Five Epidemics," which includes Chapters Three through Seven. Each of these chapters is devoted to the discussion of a separate epidemic, and describes—insofar as the sources permit—the facts relevant to all aspects of these terrifying events. The aim is to present in expository fashion a full picture of the course of the five epidemics—their inclusive dates, the mortality which they caused, and their impact upon the community. It will be seen that an epidemic invariably produced a time of crisis, and that the attendant problems were too serious, prolonged, and costly to be dealt with effectively by the normal administration of the city, province, or colony. Consequently many officials and agencies, some of them not usually closely, or primarily, involved with matters of public health and disease, such as the viceroy, the Church, or the courts, were suddenly called upon to provide both resources and leadership.

In the early stages of an epidemic many things needed to be done all at once. First, attention had to be given to efforts to prevent a further spread of the infection, a measure frequently involving a proclamation of quarantine and the establishment of provisional treatment centers, or lazarettos. Funds had to be raised very quickly, and major reliance was placed on contributions which were solicited—often demanded—from nongovernmental sources, such as the Church, certain wealthy corporations, and private citizens. This money was spent, as the epidemic progressed, for food, medicine, clothing, shelter, and on occasion burial services and sites for the thousands of indigent poor whose usual standard of living was marginal, and who, in a time of economic crisis, were utterly destitute. The right of these disadvantaged persons to such assistance as would keep them alive was never disputed, but social lines were clearly drawn. The poor were often thought to be chiefly responsible for their own misfortunes, and the elaborate relief measures which were devised for their benefit reveal a curious admixture of Christian concern and callous contempt.

The conclusions that have been drawn from the study of the background and occurrence of the five epidemics are set forth in Part III, or Chapter Eight. Chronology is abandoned in this final section, and the material presented in earlier chapters is, at that point, considered as essentially an integrated body of data from which certain observations may be made. Part III, therefore, is not intended to be a mere summary of the preceding chapters, but additional analysis of the fact content, presenting on a fresh basis and with new meaning the total view, and cutting across the material from a new angle to give a different and revealing cross section.

chapter one

A Menacing Natural Environment

IN ALL THE vast expanse of New Spain no spot was more coveted, and few were more favored, than was the wooded, watered, and verdant Valley of Mexico. Ringed by encircling mountains, the valley is an elliptical depression some thirty miles east and west, and fifty miles north and south. But though locally depressed, the valley is much higher than most of that great region which lies at this latitude between the Pacific Ocean and the Gulf of Mexico. Its elevation of more than 7,000 feet above sea level gives it the great advantage of cool and mild climate in a tropical land. Historically its attractions were many, and for several thousand years waves of migrant Indians climbed the mountain slopes leading to the rim of the valley and gazed in wonder at the awesome sight below. Here was a valley full of promise, so unlike the hostile northern desert regions which heretofore had been their home.

The waters of the valley, and especially the lakes, have played a vital role in the history of the region. Long ago nearly the entire floor of the Valley of Mexico was covered with water, a result of the fact that the valley's encirclement of lofty mountains gave its rivers no outlet to the sea, and most of the valley waters were trapped within the basin. When the Spaniards came two great lakes existed, one salt and one fresh, but by the eighteenth century only five smaller fragments of the larger ones remained, called Texcoco, Zumpango, Xaltocan, Chalco, and Xochimilco. The lakes are nearly gone today, but for centuries before, in sickness and in health, the valley people's lives had been wedded to the lakes. Jean Chappe d'Auteroche, a famous French astronomer who visited Mexico in 1769, wrote: "Mexico [City] ... is situated on the banks of a lake, and built upon a fen, crossed by a multitude of canals, consequently the houses are all built upon piles. The ground gives way in many places, and many buildings are observed to have sunk upwards of six feet."[1]

The valley lakes have passed through many changes. This is a natural thing since in general lakes are among the most ephemeral of geologic features. But many of the changes came about from man's unthinking acts, as time and time again the lakes and their surroundings were defiled and abused. Unlike the Indians, whose ties were close to nature, the Spaniards ravaged the natural world about them when they settled in the valley. At their command, and largely to serve their needs, the vegetal cover of the valley's mountains was stripped away. Trees were felled to supply charcoal, firewood, and lumber to the populous capital of New Spain. With the plants uprooted, rain water was no longer slowly absorbed by the soil, but rushed over bare rocks through gutted forests to swell the rising level of the valley lakes. Newborn mountain streams carried the eroded topsoil to the bottom of the shallow lakes, where it caused a further spilling over of their shore lines.[2]

---

[1] Jean Chappe d'Auteroche, *A Voyage to California, to observe the transit of Venus. By Mons. Chappe d'Auteroche; with an historical description of the author's route through Mexico, and the natural history of the province. Also, a voyage to Newfoundland and Sallee, to make experiments on Mr. Le Roy's time keepers. By Monsieur de Cassini*, pp. 40–41. "The former portion of this work was drawn up by Cassini from the journal and papers of Chappe." See *Dictionary Catalog of the History of the Americas. The New York Public Library Reference Department* (28 vols. Boston: G. K. Hall & Co., 1961), XV, 14102. Chappe arrived in California only to lose his life. He died on August 1, 1769, at La Rada de San José del Cabo, which is at the southern end of Lower California. See Santiago Ramírez, "Don Joaquín Velázquez Cárdenas y León, primer Director General de Minería," *Memorias de la sociedad científica "Antonio Alzate,"* I (1887), 237. Chappe is thought to have died of typhus *(matlazahuatl)*, and, if so, it would seem to be his distinction to have been the most celebrated of all the many thousands of persons who have died in Mexico of this dread disease. See Francisco de las Barras de Aragón, "Viaje del astrónomo francés [Jean] Chappe a California en 1769, y noticias de J. A. Alzate sobre la historia natural de Nueva España," *Anuario de estudios americanos,* I (1944), 767.

[2] Gonzalo Blanco M., "El abastecimiento de agua a la ciudad de México: Su relación con los recursos naturales renovables," *Boletín de la Sociedad mexicana de geografía y estadística,* LXV (March–June, 1948), 204, 207.

The lakes were ravaged in other ways as well. The improvident capital city used the largest of them as a natural cesspool. The following was written in 1873, but it describes a venerable custom of Mexico City: "The lake [Lake Texcoco], which is situated to the northeast of the city, is the receptacle of all its refuse. As one knows, . . . the waters which have served the public and domestic uses of the city flow into this. Into this vessel are dumped the fecal materials which are transported in special carts, and to this same lake comes the organic leftovers from the tanneries which are carried by the canal of Santo Tomás."[3]

The life within the lake could not long survive this formidable onslaught. As late as the end of the eighteenth century, José Antonio Alzate refers to the importance of fishing and hunting in and about Lake Texcoco.[4] But a writer of 1873 comments upon what was certainly in large part a legacy from much earlier times:

The flora of this lake is very scarce, although a kind of water lily grows around the springs of sweet water. The fauna is a little more numerous: there is a quantity of small fishes, such as the *cyprenas*, viviparous [creatures] which comprise the greater part of those sold with the name of *meztlapiques*. [There are] some mollusks, and a great quantity of insects, such as the *pulesos* (popularly called *mosquitos*) and ducks. . . . The feathers of the wings of some of these birds have been destroyed by the alkalinity of the waters; they cannot fly, and they are gathered up by the Indians on the outskirts of the lake.[5]

In former years the lake had truly been the Indians' guardian and provider. Many years before the Conquest the Aztecs had built a great city, Tenochtitlan, in the Valley of Mexico. As a defensive measure it was built on islands in Lake Texcoco, whose banks and waters also

[3] Gustavo Ruiz y Sandoval, "¿Cuál es la influencia patogénica que tienen los lagos sobre la ciudad de México?" *Gaceta médica de México*, VIII (May 1, 1873), 67. Unless otherwise indicated, all translations in this book have been made by the author.

[4] José Antonio Alzate, "Proyecto para desaguar la laguna de Texcoco y las de Chalco y San Cristóbal," *Memorias de la sociedad científica "Antonio Alzate,"* III (1889), 199.

[5] M[anuel] Pasalagua, "Algunas observaciones higiénicas sobre la ciudad de México relativamente a los lagos que la rodean," *Gaceta médica de México*, VIII (April 15, 1873), 50.

gave the Indians food. But the Spaniards came and destroyed Tenochtitlan, and upon its ruins they built their capital, whose imperial buildings and great churches suggested to the conquered tribes the mighty
power of the victors. The small lacustrian islands were inadequate for
the large and splendid city of the Spaniards, and many of its buildings were crowded close against the water's edge. But the lake itself
was never fully mastered, and while for three hundred years the
Spaniards held the city, the lake about it remained at best a silent foe.
There were times when its placid stillness suddenly disappeared. The
waters rose—it seemed as if in vengeance—and the proud buildings
and imposing churches were reduced to curious little islands in the
center of an inland sea. And then the waters went away, leaving be-
hind their heritage of destruction and disease.

It was widely believed by residents of the capital that the city's
proximity to water, to say nothing of the recurrent floods, was highly
contributory to the spread of disease. This view was not universally
accepted, however, and in 1777 José Antonio Alzate (1737–1799)
denied that the city's nearness to water was a necessary cause of disease. Alzate's opinions were usually respected by his countrymen, as
he was one of the leading scientific and literary figures of late eighteenth-century New Spain:

> The terrain of this city is not as unhealthful as one might suppose, be-
> cause it is known that the number of births well exceeds the number of
> deaths. If the closeness of the lake was harmful to this city, so much more
> so must be those of the seaports of Europe, and many other cities which
> are close to lakes, such as Mantua [Italy], etc., and yet the contrary is
> what is experienced. It is true that many of the ports of Spanish America
> are unhealthful, but this depends upon causes other than their closeness
> to waters. The city of Philadelphia, capital of Pennsylvania, which is situ-
> ated between two navigable rivers, is one of the most healthful which the
> English have in North America; therefore one knows that the proximity
> to lakes or rivers does not make the terrain of such places as unhealthful
> as one might think.[6]

[6] Alzate, "Proyecto para desaguar la laguna de Texcoco," *Memorias de la
sociedad científica "Antonio Alzate,"* III (1889), 200. This was written before
the terrible yellow fever epidemic of 1793 in Philadelphia.

Alzate was speaking, of course, about the ordinary relation between the city and its lakes, and not about the unusual, but hardly rare, times of flooding, when the link between the valley's waters and disease, though indirect, was nevertheless obvious:

A flood in Mexico City is a terrible thing: the greater part of the population emigrates, commerce is paralyzed, traffic is suspended, the food supply of the valley is reduced even after the flood has departed. . . . [A] multitude of various objects are destroyed, numerous buildings are gradually worn away, while others are left in ruins. The sicknesses multiply and feed upon an indigent population overwhelmed by water, while those who were not able to emigrate, and who survived the catastrophe, are always found in a worse state of fortune, and frequently of health, than before the inundation.[7]

As the city straddled the lowest portion of the valley, the threat of floods was constant. During the incumbency of the second viceroy of New Spain, Luis de Velasco (1550–1564), great dikes were built astride the lowlands.[8] These failed to solve the problem, and in 1607 another viceroy, the Marqués de Montesclaros (1603–1607), commissioned the celebrated cosmographer Enrico Martínez to study the matter. He suggested the construction of a tunnel through the mountains at a site called Nochistongo, which would in part drain the waters of the valley. Construction started in November of that same year, and in eleven months some fifteen thousand Indians had cut a gash in the mountains for a distance of six kilometers.[9] King Philip III of Spain, unconvinced that this measure had solved the drainage problem, in 1616 ordered that Mexico City be abandoned and be rebuilt on higher ground. But ninety years of prideful building could not be quickly set aside, and nothing was done to move the city.[10]

In 1623, another viceroy, the Marqués de los Gelves (1621–1624),

[7] Juan N[epomuceno] Adorno, *Memoria acerca de la hidrografía, meteorológica, seguridad hidrogénica y salubridad higiénica del valle, y en especial de la capital de México*, p. 24.

[8] Archivo General de la Nación, "Desagüe," Vol. XV, Exp. 6, fols. 2v, 6v (archive cited hereinafter as AGN).

[9] Ramírez, "Don Joaquín Velázquez Cárdenas y León," *Memorias de la sociedad científica "Antonio Alzate,"* I (1887), 251–252.

[10] AGN, "Desagüe," Vol. XV, Exp. 6, fol. 4v.

suggested that perhaps the danger of flooding might well have been exaggerated. He ordered that as an experiment the waters of the valley be allowed to seek their natural level. When the rains next came none of the great dikes was to be closed. Enrico Martínez ridiculed this scheme as dangerously absurd, and so he went to jail. The Viceroy insisted that if the experiment was carried out it would clearly establish the true level of the lake. Indeed it did. On September 21, 1629, a thunderstorm of such force struck the city that forever after it has been honored with a designation of its own—The Cloudburst of San Mateo.[11] One of the few places in the city not flooded was the central plaza, which also won a short-lived title of its own—"Island of Dogs," after the hundreds of these animals that took refuge there from the rising waters.[12] Enrico Martínez was speedily released from jail, but there was little he could do. The city remained flooded for five years, or until an earthquake, which some called providential, split the encircling mountain wall and freed the city from its torments.[13] Gelves' experiment of allowing the waters of the valley free rein had failed to pacify them, and more than a century later watermarks three feet above the ground were still clearly visible on the city's older buildings.

In 1637, after King Philip had revived his scheme to relocate the city, it was decided that only a drainage project of gigantic size could stop the chronic threat of floods. One phase involved the construction of a drainage ditch (*desagüe*),[14] which would divert away from the city the waters of three small rivers which rose to the east of Mexico City near the volcanoes of Río Frío. Work began on this project in 1630 at the village of Amecameca at the foot of the volcanoes. The ditch passed through the mountain village of Otumba, and ultimately it carried the waters of the three rivers down to the semitropical lowlands beyond the valley. The ditch was successful, but it was not maintained. By 1754 it was ruined and abandoned, and once again the

[11] *Ibid*, fol. 3; J. A. Calderón Quijano, "Ingenieros militares en Nueva España," *Anuario de estudios americanos*, VI (1949), 9.

[12] Adrian Téllez Pizarro, "Apuntes acerca de los cimientos de los edificios en la ciudad de México," *Memorias de la sociedad científica "Antonio Alzate,"* Vol. XIV (1899–1900), Pt. I, pp. 104–105.

[13] Ramírez, "Don Joaquín Velázquez Cárdenas y Léon," *ibid.*, I (1887), 252.

[14] In the interest of simplicity and appearance Spanish terms normally italicized appear in italics at first usage and in text type thereafter.

waters of the three eastern rivers afflicted the capital of New Spain. A second, and considerably larger, drainage project had also been started in 1637. This ditch passed through the village of Huehuetoca to the north of Mexico City and took its name from this village. Nine streams were diverted by means of this project. At the village of Tula they joined forces with the Teperi River, flowing as one body of water to Tampico on the coast where they joined "the sea of the north."[15]

The construction and maintenance of this great ditch had cost millions of pesos through the years. Still the floods continued, particularly in the years 1648, 1675, 1707, 1732, and 1747–1748.[16] But by 1753, although the ditch of Amecameca lay in ruins, as did also many of the dikes, the King was of the opinion that no further money should be spent on draining the valley. In a royal order (*cédula*) of March 24, 1753, he canceled a tax on meat whose revenue had been applied to the operation of the ditch. Domingo Trespalacios y Escandón, the superintendent of the project, endeavored to persuade the King to change his mind. He prepared a detailed history of the various efforts to drain the valley, and offered his opinion on the dangers of future neglect of this matter. He reported that in past years the King's engineers "had tried to divert the waters of those rivers which might be diverted, to dam up others, and to hold back the little streams and freshets of various hills and mountains . . . because they knew that if all [these waters] should come together at one time flooding was inevitable."[17] Trespalacios urged the King to continue to make funds available for the drainage projects, especially that of Huehuetoca, because if "any change whatsoever [was to be made] in what has been established and decreed, the inconveniences which would follow are [such] that all that has been done until now [1754] in one hundred and thirty years would be lost, and this city, and its surrounding farms and haciendas, would all be ruined and lost."[18] The tax on meat was

---

[15] AGN, "Desagüe," Vol. XV, Exp. 6, fols. 3v–4v, 7v–8v. For more information on the physiographical features of the Valley of Mexico and the efforts to control flooding, including the desagüe, see Charles Gibson's outstanding volume, *The Aztecs Under Spanish Rule: A History of the Indians of the Valley of Mexico, 1519–1810,* esp. pp. 1–8, 236–242, 303–307.

[16] Adorno, *Memoria acerca de la hidrografía,* p. 14.

[17] AGN, "Desagüe," Vol. XV, Exp. 6, fols. 2v–3.

[18] *Ibid.,* fol. 15.

retained, and in 1794 Viceroy Juan Vicente de Güemes Pacheco de
Padilla, the second Conde de Revilla Gigedo (1789–1794), advised
that it be continued, since he did not believe that the capital was yet
free of the threat of floods.[19] In 1798 his successor, Viceroy Miguel de
la Grúa Talamanca y Branciforte, the Marqués de Branciforte (1794–
1798), said that the security of the capital of New Spain depended
upon maintaining the Huehuetoca ditch.[20]

The recurrent floods were a constant menace to the health of the
city. In 1795 Mexico City suffered another of its periodic floodings,
and on this occasion the flood, specifically blamed for having caused
the death of nine nuns from the Convent of Jesús María, triggered
some direct action. The mother superior of the convent informed
Cosme de Mier y Trespalacios, the superintendent, or leading official,
of the city government, that the convent suffered from "frequent
floods which cause grave damage not only to its physical structure . . .
but also to the health and lives of the nuns."[21] She reported that "almost any thundershower" was sufficient to flood the convent. The situation was aggravated by an open drainage ditch that lay to one side
of the convent. Since the ditch was usually so clogged that its waters
did not circulate, each time flooding occurred fetid materials were
carried from the ditch to the lower parts of the convent. This had the
effect of "infecting the air" and causing an epidemic of "putrid
fevers" within the convent.[22] The convent's physician, Juan Joseph
Bermúdez de Castro, confirmed that nine nuns had died in the latest
outbreak within the convent.[23]

Within two weeks the city sent an official inspection party composed of, among others, Judge Mier and the two city architects, Ig-

---

[19] [Conde de Revilla Gigedo], *Instrucción reservada que el Conde de Revilla
Gigedo dió a su sucesor en el mando, Marqués de Branciforte, sobre el gobierno
de este continente en el tiempo que fue su virey*, p. 60, par. 256.

[20] Archivo Municipal del Ex-Ayuntamiento, "Actas de Cabildo (1796–1802),"
Vol. 380, p. 33, session of January 18, 1798 (archive cited hereinafter as Ex-
Ayun.).

[21] *Ibid.*, "Historia: Inundaciones," Vol. 2272, Tome I, "Expediente [unnum-
bered] formado a instancia de la Madre Avadesa, Vicaria, y Definidoras del
Real Convento de Jesús María sobre ha verse inundado dicho convento," fol. 295.

[22] *Ibid.*

[23] *Ibid.*, fols. 301–301v.

nacio Castera and José del Mazo. They reported that as soon as the gates were opened one was greeted by an "intolerable stench." Three feet of water lay in the porter's lodge, and the walls of the nuns' cells all sweated water.[24] Architect Castera said the basic problem was the fact that since nearly all of the convents of the city dated from the sixteenth century, they had settled groundward in relation to the level of the streets. The ideal solution would be to raise the floors of the convents, but this would be so costly as to be impracticable. A more feasible solution would be to clean up the cluttered canal which lay to the side of the convent. This canal was used by the Indians to bring foodstuffs in canoes from outlying villages for sale in the capital. Unfortunately the Indians also used the canal as a depository for all manner of rubbish and human waste. Several years previously—in 1787—the government had ordered that a large section of the canal in the center of the city be closed to canoe traffic, "because the fetidness of these interior canals . . . carries the very grave threat of the pest."[25] Castera lamented that the law had not been enforced.

Dr. Bermúdez de Castro endeavored to give a "scientific" explanation of the disease which had killed the nine nuns:

Physicians know from a series of observations which have been continued for many centuries that the cause of many sicknesses, whether endemic, or epidemic, is the dampness [of any given] site, which would be even more unhealthful if it were found adjacent to swamps, or stagnant waters. Consequently a physician who is in possession of this knowledge can easily recognize the poor state of its inhabitants, and also determine the sicknesses which ought to be more frequent among them. Actually a ground floor is nothing but a receptacle for excess waters which might be in the vicinity: a source of dampness and vapors, which fill the air with an infinity of miscellaneous small bodies [*cuerpecillos heterogéneos*], which are putrid and very harmful to health. Once this has happened those who breathe in such an environment are very disposed to suffer putrid and fatal sicknesses . . . [such as] diarrheas, hydropsies, [and] rheumatic pains.[26]

[24] *Ibid.*, fol. 298.
[25] *Ibid.*, fols. 299–300.
[26] *Ibid.*, fols. 302–302v.

He insisted that this condition could not be prevented unless the offending canal was cleaned, and two months later, after appropriate deliberation, the city agreed to have the canal dredged.

In numerous other minor and usually unrelated ways the periodic flooding of Mexico City unfavorably affected the health and well-being of the people. For example, floods often blocked the commercial routes over which supplies and foodstuffs were brought to the city. In 1769 an alderman of Mexico City reported: "The causeway which leaves this city for the village and sanctuary of Nuestra Señora de Guadalupe is impassable on the lower part on both sides because of the multitude of waters which have been experienced in these last years. The result is that they bring many hindrances to the passengers who carry the provisions to this capital."[27] In another instance, a time of high waters threatened to curtail the ministrations of the priests of the Convent of San Diego: "Because of the rains the street . . . is so impassable that nobody is able to pass by there without obvious danger. . . . And if nobody remedies [this situation] the priests will find themselves in the sad, painful, and bitter necessity of not going to the sick to hear their confessions."[28] In 1785, a year in which Mexico City experienced a major epidemic, Father Miguel Gaviola reported certain unusual difficulties in treating the sick: "The Hospital de San Juan de Dios of this city, especially the infirmary for women, finds itself in grave danger of being flooded with water."[29] The priest reported that water had been standing in the hospital courtyard throughout the year. In 1810 the *Guardián* of the Convent of San Francisco solicited money for the purpose of raising the ground level of the convent cemetery as a defense against the "annual floods."[30] The church itself —at the heart of the city—frequently suffered serious damage from floods. Years earlier, in 1766, the city had sought the aid of San Gre-

[27] *Ibid.*, Expediente (unnumbered), "Diligencias practicadas para que estén represas las aguas en la calzada de Nuestra Señora de Guadalupe," fol. 63.

[28] *Ibid.*, Expediente (unnumbered), "Don Francisco Riofrío sobre el mal estado en que se pone con las llubias la calzada," fol. 124v.

[29] *Ibid.*, Expediente (unnumbered), "Fray Miguel Gaviola sobre los perjuicios que causa al Hospital de San Juan de Dios con la agua," fol. 135.

[30] AGN, "Bienes Nacionales," Leg. 185, Exp. 59, fols. 1–2.

gorio Taumaturgo. He was one of the city's patron saints, and was thought to be attentive to appeals for protection from the chronic threat of floods.[31]

It can be seen that in many ways the special environment of the Valley of Mexico closely affected and indeed menaced the lives of its people. While the relation between the physical setting, especially the lakes, and the susceptibility of the people to disease and epidemics is inexact and sometimes speculative, it appears to have been much too important to be ignored.

[31] *Ibid.*, "Audiencia," Vol. XII, no Exp. number or title, fols. 322–322v.

chapter two

Public-Health Administration

IN COLONIAL Mexico City the responsibility for initiating and implementing policies relating to sanitation and public health rested with a wide range of overlapping and sometimes competing authorities. Indeed, the entire hierarchy of governmental authorities, great and small, was involved in varying degrees, ranging all the way from the viceroy, representing the king, to a junior employee of the city government (*alcalde de barrio*). However, certain officials were chiefly, or routinely, involved with the public health, while the others exercised only occasional, or supplemental, control. In the first category would be included the municipal council *(ayuntamiento)*, and the Royal Board of Medicine (Protomedicato). In the second category would be included the viceroy, the high court (*audiencia*), and the Church.

This chapter outlines the degree of involvement of these various authorities in the general area of public health. It is useful to have a clear understanding of the routine duties of these officials as they dealt with the problems of public health on a day-to-day basis. Such information provides a framework, or perspective, which enables one to grasp the impact of a major epidemic in the area of public-health administration, for a time of crisis invariably forced a temporary reshuffling among those authorities who in calmer times enjoyed a preponderant influence in the area. Primary attention is, therefore, given to their regular and ordinary responsibilities, or, in other words, to that rather loosely defined area which today would be called "preventive medicine." But, as will be seen in later chapters, during an outbreak of epidemic disease the roles of the viceroy and the Church as health agencies were suddenly magnified, while, relatively speaking, the role of the Protomedicato was temporarily overshadowed.

The Ayuntamiento

In colonial Mexico City the ayuntamiento was clearly the chief authority routinely concerned with public health. Its involvement was so deep it could almost be said that its every action had some connection, direct or indirect, with the health and well-being of the citizenry. In 1787 Hipólito Villarroel reported as follows its function as it related to public health:

'[The ayuntamiento should ensure] the abundance of provisions; the equity of weights and measures; the good quality of foodstuffs; the cleanliness of the streets; the lighting [of the streets] so that the disorders and infamies might be averted which darkness and obscurity tend to produce; . . . prompt attention to fires; the comfort, tranquillity, and security of the citizens; and above all, the gathering up of vagabonds, harmful animals, and the many matters of this type from which harm might result.'[1]

In view of the complexity of the ayuntamiento's role in public health, no attempt has been made to exhaust this very broad subject. For the purposes of this study it is more important to concentrate on the three primary areas which are representative: municipal sanitation, the water supply, and the health menace generated by inadequate and poorly situated cemeteries.

Municipal Sanitation: The need for regular cleaning of streets, plazas, and canals had been recognized by the Indians even before the arrival of the Spaniards. The sixteenth-century friar, Toribio de Benavente, better known by the name of Motolinía, commented favorably on the cleanliness of the Aztec capital, Tenochtitlan.[2] In Mexico City the first municipal ordinances formally addressed to the problems of sanitation were the *Ordenanzas de Policía*, approved by the Audiencia

[1] Quoted in [Hipólito Villarroel], *México por dentro y fuera bajo el gobierno de los vireyes. O sea enfermedades políticas que padece la capital de la N[ueva] España en casi todos los cuerpos de que se compone, y remedios que se deben aplicar para su curación*, p. 69. Villarroel does not disclose the original source of this borrowed quotation.

[2] José Alvarez Amézquita *et al.*, *Historia de la salubridad y de las asistencia en México*, I, 29.

in 1612.[3] They were written by Archbishop Francisco García Guerra, who served as interim viceroy of New Spain for eight months in 1611–1612, and later they were incorporated in the various editions of the laws of Mexico City. Technically they remained in force throughout the colonial period.[4] The ordinances of García Guerra established a Junta de Policía, composed of the local royal commissioner (*corregidor*),[5] an alderman (*regidor*), and a justice known as the *ministro togado*, who cannot be precisely identified but who was probably a judge of the audiencia. The size and composition of the Junta changed from time to time. In 1728 an attorney representing the city (*promotor fiscal*) was added to the membership.[6] In 1797 the Junta de Policía consisted of nine aldermen, the corregidor, the constable (*alguacil*), and a notary (*escribano*).[7]

From the beginning, the Junta de Policía encountered certain difficulties in keeping the city clean. Part of the problem was financial. In 1696, for example, the corregidor of Mexico City complained that

[3] *Ordenanzas que se han de observar y guardar en la muy nobilíssima y leal ciudad de México, del reyno de Nueva España, aprobadas, y confirmadas por el señor rey D. Phelipe Quinto . . . por su real cédula de qüatro de Noviembre de mil setecientos y veinte y ocho años*, p. 31v. An earlier edition of the *Ordenanzas* was printed in Mexico City in 1683, and the edition of 1728 was reprinted in 1755. See also *Memoria administrativa y económica que la Junta Directiva del Desagüe y Saneamiento de la ciudad de México presenta a la Secretaría de Gobernación (1896–1903)*, pp. 169–170.

[4] As late as 1900 they had still not been formally repealed: "The ancient municipal ordinances, and certain other earlier laws and regulations, serve as the model for the works of the Corporation [Ayuntamiento]. [However], it must be said that the municipal ordinances are now of almost no effect." See D[omingo] Orvañanos, "De la organización del ayuntamiento de México considerado desde el punto de vista de la salubridad pública," *Gaceta médica de México*, XXXVII (March 15, 1900), 113.

[5] There is no precise English equivalent for the Spanish word *corregidor*. This official was a royal commissioner who assumed wide administrative tasks and undertook financial and judicial functions at the local level. Within his own local district the corregidor enjoyed substantial power and influence. Frequently he was regarded with suspicion—indeed hatred—by the residents of his district. Since the word "*corregidor*" carries its own special meaning, it has not been translated into what would be at best only a rough English equivalent.

[6] *Ordenanzas . . . de México* [of 1728], p. 29. See also p. 20v.

[7] Mariano de Zúñiga y Ontiveros (ed.), *Calendario manual y guía de forasteros en México para el año de 1797*, pp. 104–105.

many essential public works in the capital were in need of immediate repairs but that the city did not even have enough money to clean its streets. He said that many of the bridges lay in ruins, while others could hardly be used. Furthermore, the numerous canals were nearly all clogged, and their stagnant waters were blamed in part for "the epidemic which is attacking the city."[8] As a means of alleviating this general problem, he suggested that if cobblestones paved the streets it would make them much easier to clean. But once again financial obstacles could not be overcome, although in this instance it was not the impoverishment of the city treasury but the miserliness of certain property owners that aggravated the problem. The corregidor had proposed that those persons whose properties fronted along the major streets should pay the cost of cobblestoning. Most of these properties belonged to "convents of monks and nuns or to other ecclesiastics," and the corregidor soon discovered that these institutions preferred to spend their money for purposes other than cobblestones.[9] In 1721 the superintendent of the drainage project, Joseph Alphonso de Valladolid, eager to improve the totally inadequate interior-drainage system of the city, revived the proposal of cobblestones. But he was no more successful in this endeavor than had been the corregidor.[10]

Much of the city refuse was disposed of by simply dumping it into one of the many canals which crisscrossed the capital. By 1637 there were seven major canals plus innumerable smaller ones, all of which ultimately carried their burdens to the city cesspool—Lake Texcoco —where more things floated than just the gardens. As mentioned, several of the canals were heavily traveled by Indians in canoes to bring provisions to the heart of the city. Efforts were made from time to time to clean out the canals, since they were considered to be "the most favorable focus of endemic and epidemic sicknesses."[11] Gangs of chained workmen, some tributary Indians, some prisoners from the two jails, Cárcel de Corte and the Acordada, worked annually in the springtime to shovel the miscellaneous contents of the canals to

[8] Ex-Ayun., "Policía, Salubridad," Vol. 3668 (P. 245), Tome I, Exp. 1, fol. 1v.
[9] *Ibid.*, fols. 1v–2.
[10] AGN, "Desagüe," Vol. X, no Exp. number or title, fol. 73.
[11] *Memoria administrativa y económica*, p. 178.

the banks alongside. Here the refuse was allowed to dry out in the sun before being carted off to the outskirts of the city.[12] Some viceroys tried to close the filth-choked canals altogether, but none was successful.

In 1728 the revised ordinances for Mexico City laid down the following rules, among others, for keeping the city clean:

No person shall dare to throw rubbish or human waste in the streets, plazas, canals, nor fountain[s] of this city, under penalty of two pesos for each time that he might throw it; and if it cannot be determined who has done it, then the citizen who is closest to the spot where the said rubbish might be found shall be ordered to remove it within three hours, and if he does not remove it, he shall pay a peso, and the place shall be cleaned at his cost. . . . No person shall throw clean or dirty water through the windows or doors into the streets by day, or until curfew has sounded, under penalty of one peso for each time that he might do it. . . . Because of the scant care that is taken to remove dead animals, and because of the bad odor that results from leaving them in the streets and plazas, and since they are a cause of sickness in the republic [city], it is ordered that no person shall throw into the streets, plazas, or canals, dogs nor horses, nor other dead animals, under penalty of ten pesos for each time that he might do it; and if it cannot be determined who has done it, then the citizen who is closest to the site of the dead animal shall be ordered to remove it within three hours, and if he does not remove it, he shall pay two pesos, and it shall be carried to a rubbish pile at his expense.[13]

The ordinances do not specify whose job it would ultimately be to perform such onerous chores, but, as mentioned, convict labor was frequently so used. Furthermore, in 1771 José de Gálvez suggested that the Indians from the two wards (*barrios*) of San Juan and Santiago Tlatelolco should be made to clean out the canals of the city. Until 1737 a portion of the Indians' annual tribute had been earmarked to help defray the costs of cleaning the canals. In that year, however, as a consequence of the outbreak of a severe epidemic, that money which had been earmarked for cleaning was diverted to some other purpose. Gálvez argued, somewhat unreasonably, that since none of the Indians' tribute was then being used in the capital for

[12] *Ibid.*, pp. 180, 195.
[13] *Ordenanzas . . . de México* [of 1728], p. 30.

purposes of cleaning, they should be forced to contribute their labor in its stead to get the job done.[14]

In 1776 Pedro Josef Cortez wrote that despite the various official proclamations and municipal ordinances which had been issued through the years by the viceroys and ayuntamiento, no effective program of street cleaning had ever been implemented in Mexico City. Cortez submitted a proposal to the city council which called for the construction of outbuildings on each street of the city where the citizens would be asked to deposit trash and body waste. As the prospective contractor, he would agree to arrange for carts to transport all such materials to the outskirts of the city. Expenses could be met by imposing a weekly tax of one *real* on each household. Cortez foresaw four benefits which would accrue to the city with the adoption of his plan: the waters would flow freely through their appointed channels, as the sewers and canals; the tiles and cobblestones of the city streets would have a longer life; the "general convenience and brightness" of the city would be enhanced; and the people would be protected from those sicknesses which result from the decay of fetid materials, and such sicknesses, said Cortez, were known to be very common in the city.[15]

Cortez' proposal was not adopted by the Ayuntamiento, which agreed that it was sound but contended that since the city ordinances already prohibited the throwing of trash and dead animals into the streets no further action was needed than for the law to be obeyed. Unfortunately it was not obeyed, and the problem continued. Villarroel wrote in 1787: "Many have been the edicts and measures which have been published regarding the cleaning and paving of the streets, but none has been observed."[16] He said that property owners, if they took any action at all, simply had the refuse from their places swept into the nearest canals or open ditches. These, being constantly clogged, gave off "a pestilential stench, harmful to health."[17]

[14] [*Despacho de*] *Don Joseph de Gálvez, del consejo y cámara de su Magestad. . . . Hago saber al señor ministro Juez Superintendente, Cavallero Corregidor, Capitulares. . .* , p. 18, par. 53. This *despacho* has no title, and the above is taken from its first sentence.

[15] AGN, "Ayuntamientos," Vol. CVII, Exp. 1, fols. 1, 5–6.

[16] [Villarroel], *México por dentro y fuera*, p. 97.

[17] *Ibid.*

The Ayuntamiento specified as a matter of policy that those persons with whom it entered into contract, and whose type of business might contribute to the general sanitary problem, must themselves assume part, or all, of the cleaning burden. For example, in 1801, the Ayuntamiento canceled its contract with two butchers who had been supplying meat to the city because of their nonobservance of this requirement. They had agreed "to clean annually the ditches which serve as a fence around the marshes of La Piedad and San Antonio where they pasture their cattle, and also to maintain the causeways of La Piedad and San Antonio, repairing the mudholes which they make, and replacing the trees which they trample down."[18] But for three successive years the butchers had ignored their obligations, and therefore the city let their contract to another butcher. In a second example, the Ayuntamiento required that all persons licensed to milk cows or sell produce in the city must agree to keep the grounds which they used as clean as they had found them. Failure to do so could lead to cancellation of their contract.[19]

Viceroy Miguel José de Azanza (1798–1800) wrote that the city had traditionally had two contractors who assumed responsibility for the cleaning of the streets and plazas. Azanza considered this joint arrangement inefficient, and in 1799 he gave sole reponsibility for this work to a single contractor.[20] The first man named was José del Mazo, an architect, who was said to have performed his duties satisfactorily. Unfortunately del Mazo failed to establish a precedent for efficiency, and by 1813 the Ayuntamiento reported that its current contractor was so inattentive to his duties that he had been fired. The city was forced to go to court to break his contract, and for the time being the aldermen had to assume direct responsibility for the hiring of workers to clean the streets.[21] On the eve of independence from Spain the problem was far from being solved. The Ayuntamiento reported in 1821 that "the principal reason for the increase of fevers among the inhabi-

[18] Ex-Ayun., "Actas de cabildo (1796–1802)," Vol. 380, p. 17, session of January 16, 1801.

[19] *Ibid.*, "Ordeñas de vacas," Vol. 3392, Exp. 2, fol. 2.

[20] Ernesto de la Torre (ed.), *Instrucción reservada que dió el virrey don Miguel José de Azanza a su sucesor don Félix Berenguer de Marquina*, p. 61, par. 66.

[21] AGN, "Epidemias," Vol. VIII, Exp. 7, fols. 39–41.

tants of this city is the lack of cleaning and sweeping of its streets, since one sees so much dirt and refuse that there are even places where the sacred viaticum may not be carried without obvious desecration and indecency."[22]

Despite the obvious defects in its program of municipal sanitation it is probable that the record achieved by Mexico City in these years would bear comparison with most contemporary cities of similar size. The fact remains, however, that the ayuntamiento never fully or permanently resolved its outstanding problems in the field of sanitation, and that such deficiencies were clearly related to the spread of disease and epidemics.

Water Supply: The ayuntamiento was primarily responsible for providing and maintaining a potable water supply. Two aldermen took direct cognizance of this area—the judge of the aqueducts (*juez de arquerías*), and the judge of the conduits, or water pipelines (*juez de cañerías*). The former was responsible for the means of bringing water into the city, the latter for its internal or local distribution. The two aldermen were frequently at odds with each other, and Viceroy Azanza considered their quarrels as responsible in part for the numerous problems related to the city water supply. Consequently he recommended to his successor, Félix Berenguer de Marquina (1800–1803), that he combine their functions into a single office.[23] Shortly thereafter the position of judge of waters (*juez de aguas*), was established.

In colonial times the drinking water for the capital was drawn neither from the semisaline and contaminated lakes nor from the small streams of the valley, but from natural springs or from wells, whose sources were some distance from the heart of the city.[24] Since

[22] Ex-Ayun., "Policía, Salubridad," Vol. 3668 (P. 245), Tome I, Exp. 13, fols. 1–1v.

[23] Torre, *Instrucción . . . de Azanza*, pp. 58–59, pars. 57, 59.

[24] Blanco M., "El abastecimiento de agua a la ciudad de México: Su relación con los recursos naturales renovables," *Boletín de la Sociedad mexicana de geografía y estadística*, LXV (March–June, 1948), 202. To supplement the waters from the natural springs, various wells were sunk in and about the city, but in time these became contaminated and could not be used for drinking water: "Although the well water in Mexico City is not potable, it serves for domestic uses. The poor people use it almost exclusively to wash their household

early in the seventeenth century two huge aqueducts had brought this spring water to the capital. The first aqueduct, finished in 1620, was supported by nearly 1,000 imposing stone and masonry arches and brought the water to a point near the central plaza (*zócalo*). By 1654 it was already in a poor state of repair, as more than 40 of its arches were damaged. The second aqueduct, borne by 904 arches, was not completed until 1779. It terminated at the fountain of Salto del Agua, a few blocks southwest of the central plaza. It brought water from the natural springs in the forest of Chapultepec, and over the same route which the Aztecs had once used to build an aqueduct to service Tenochtitlan.[25]

Once the aqueducts had brought water to the center of the city, it was redistributed to various public and private fountains. By 1806 there were 505 private fountains but only 28 public ones. Certain types of businesses which dealt in vital services, such as bakeries, pharmacies, and butcher shops, were authorized by the city ordinances to have a private fountain, but most fountains were distributed among "the nobles, the convents, the rich bourgeoisie, the rich merchants, the public officials, and the public baths."[26] The great majority of people obtained their water from one of the 28 public fountains. The water carrier (*aguador*) earned his living by carrying jugs of water from these fountains.

The municipal ordinances on water were adopted in 1710 and were approved by Viceroy Francisco de la Cueva Enríquez, Duke of Albuquerque (1702–1710). They were in force during the remainder of the colonial period. The need for a high degree of cleanliness in the

---

goods, it is generally drunk by horses, and it serves for sprinkling, scrubbing, etc." The foregoing was written in 1866, but the conclusion is inescapable that the contamination of the ground water must have started many years earlier. See José M[aría] Reyes, "Higiene pública: Limpia," *Gaceta médica de México*, II, [Pt. II], (April 15, 1866), 115.

[25] Manuel Romero de Terreros, "Los acueductos de México," *Anales del museo nacional de arqueología, historia, y etnografía*, 4th Ser., III (April–June, 1925), 132–133.

[26] Manuel Carrera Stampa, "Planos de la ciudad de México (desde 1521 hasta nuestros días)," *Boletín de la Sociedad mexicana de geografía y estadística*, LXVII (March–June, 1949), 288.

water supply was clearly stated in the ordinances, which called for periodic cleaning of the springs and culverts, and a prohibition against laundering in the public conduits and fountains.[27] But the letter of the law notwithstanding, "the conditions for health under which the water ran and was supplied to the people were practically nil. It was in vain that measures were dictated for the periodic cleanings of springs, culverts, and fountains so that mud, dirt, branches, and other refuse might be removed."[28]

Beginning in 1682, lead pipes were placed within one of the city aqueducts,[29] and lead pipes were also used throughout the city for the local distribution of water. Once installed, many citizens blamed them for causing "gastrointestinal sicknesses."[30] In 1698 Father Agustín Vetancourt blamed "the water which comes through lead pipes," along with the dampness of the soil, for the frequent outbreaks of dysentery and diarrhea in Mexico City, which in turn had caused numerous deaths.[31] The Protomedicato recommended that the lead pipes be replaced with pipes made of clay. This change was initiated in 1731, but unfortunately the clay pipes were of small diameter and carelessly laid. Consequently they frequently broke, particularly as a result of the common earth tremors, and occasional earthquakes, in the city. On many occasions water from the ruptured clay pipes, which was presumed to be potable, became contaminated by mixing

[27] *Memoria económica de la municipalidad de México formada de orden del Exmô. Ayuntamiento, por una comisión de su seno en 1830*, pp. 109–110. Printed on these pages of the *Memoria* is an abstract, made in 1829, of the water ordinances of 1710.

[28] Carrera Stampa, "Planos de la ciudad de México," *Boletín de la Sociedad mexicana de geografía y estadística*, LXVII (March–June, 1949), 289.

[29] Romero de Terreros, "Los acueductos de México," *Anales del museo nacional de arqueología, historia, y etnografía*, 4th Ser., III (April–June, 1925), 132.

[30] M[anuel] S. Soriano, "Origen de las cañerías de barro para la distribución de las aguas potables en la ciudad de México," *Gaceta médica de México*, 2d Ser., V (September 15, 1905), 233.

[31] Agustín de Vetancourt, *Tratado de la ciudad de México, y las grandezas que la ilustran después que la fundaron Españoles*, Pt. IV, paginated separately, of *Teatro Mexicano: Descripción breve de los sucessos exemplares, históricos, políticos, militares, y religiosos del nuevo mundo occidental de las Indias*, p. 5, par. 19.

with the contents of the drainage culverts. As would be expected, this produced the "most serious consequences for health."[32]

Cemeteries: The location and maintenance of cemeteries were primarily the responsibility of the Church, but the ayuntamiento was nonetheless sometimes involved. When it did intervene regarding cemeteries, it was usually because of some condition considered a threat to the public health. Throughout colonial times most burials in Mexico City were effected within the city confines, usually in cemeteries which were close to, and operated by, various churches, convents, or hospitals. It was also a common practice in those times to entomb certain corpses in the interior of churches, especially those persons who had led unusually distinguished or meritorious lives. But given the limitations of space inside churches, and even in their cemeteries, it was necessary from time to time to remove the older corpses for reinterment or disposal elsewhere to make room for the new arrivals.

In 1802, for example, the Ayuntamiento learned that the priests of the Sagrario, the parish church adjacent to the metropolitan cathedral, at the heart of the city, had ordered the removal of bodies from the parish cemetery. The soil which was being removed from the cemetery was seen, or known, to contain numerous human fragments, and the townspeople feared that this was the cause "of the sicknesses and even the deaths that have been reported these past few days."[33] Furthermore, the prevailing winds were carrying "putrid exhalations" throughout the city. The Ayuntamiento appealed to Viceroy Berenguer de Marquina to order the priests to halt the removal of "unripe" bodies. His first order was ignored, but a second one, sent by the Viceroy to the dean and chapter house (*cabildo*) of the metropolitan cathedral, had the desired effect. The ecclesiastics agreed to wait a while longer in order "to avoid that contamination of the air [which] might introduce an epidemic of the most tragic consequences."[34]

---

[32] Soriano, "Origen de las cañerías de barro para la distribución de las aguas potables en al ciudad de México," *Gaceta médica de México*, 2d Ser., V (September 15, 1905), 233.

[33] AGN, "Ayuntamientos," Vol. I, Exp. 1, fol. 4v.

[34] *Ibid.*

It was generally agreed that from the viewpoint of the public health it would be desirable to effect all burials in isolated cemeteries safely beyond the confines of the city. In December, 1820, José María Casasola, an alderman of the Ayuntamiento, prepared a detailed résumé of the history of cemeteries in Mexico City. He wrote that many efforts had been made through the years to have cemeteries placed "away from the populated areas and in ventilated places."[35] But all such efforts had failed, including those made repeatedly on behalf of this cause by Archbishop Alonso Núñez de Haro y Peralta (1713–1800), who until the time of his death had been the most outspoken advocate of such locations. Núñez de Haro made various representations to the court in Madrid, and on one occasion he had offered to spend 12,000 pesos for construction costs.[36]

In 1807, in an action of which Casasola said "to tell the truth, [it] cannot be understood," the Ayuntamiento opposed the construction of a well-ventilated public cemetery outside the city. The councilmen believed that its cost would be excessive, particularly in view of the substantial number of cemeteries already in operation, albeit within the city. Casasola wrote that because of the Ayuntamiento's failure to act in 1807, "there was lost without doubt the most opportune occasion, since in that year New Spain enjoyed complete tranquillity, and the greatest abundance. It would have been very easy to have begun, and perhaps to have completed, the work with the use of all those resources which today would be most difficult [to obtain]."[37]

Casasola recorded that during a severe epidemic in Mexico City in 1813, the burial of corpses in churches was prohibited for the duration of the crisis. But as soon as the epidemic had run its course the people reverted to their previous practice, "and Mexico City remained in a worse state than ever."[38] In 1819, in a royal edict, King Ferdinand VII issued a comprehensive statement on burial policy. He condemned the practice of placing "six, eight, and even ten [bodies] in a single grave without division by sexes . . . and mixing the bodies and

---

[35] *Ibid.*, Vol. II, Exp. 10, fol. 111.
[36] *Ibid.*, fol. 111v.
[37] *Ibid.*, fols. 113v–114.
[38] *Ibid.*, fol. 114v.

worthy ashes of the anointed of the Lord with the others, contrary to what is ordered and disposed in the sacred rites."[39] Restrictions were placed on burials inside churches, but the practice was not forbidden. Certain sepulchres of "distinction" could be maintained for those persons who enjoyed a valid proprietary claim to such a privilege, or who in the future might make a "payment of fair price to the Church." Furthermore, persons of "virtue or saintliness" might still be entombed inside a church once the priests had prepared a list of their "virtues or miracles."[40]

Casasola argued that despite the costs, and the lack of resources in the municipal treasury, Mexico City could ill afford any further delay in the construction of public cemeteries beyond the city. Much of the burden of his argument rested on the unfavorable location and wretched upkeep of some then in use in the capital:

On all sides, and in the path of all winds, there are cemeteries. Most of them are located in the most humid and muddy places, which do not permit the regular depth [of burial] because of the excessive water. . . . [Consequently] the bodies are placed almost at the level of the ground; and furthermore bodies are buried in all the churches which we have in the midst of our city. . . . Each of these is a focus from which there continually emanate foul exhalations which are concentrated in the center of the city, and which oblige us to breathe continually a poisonous and nearly fatal atmosphere. This is saying nothing about the many other abuses and excesses which are committed in these same cemeteries. Because of their unfortunate location and lack of depth, it customarily happens that in order to bury one body another is removed which is in a state of imperfect decomposition! What great harm such a practice must bring to the public health . . . and if one also considers the decadent state in which one finds the general cleanliness [of the city], one must confess that either the temperament of Mexico City is in some manner fortunate, or else the inhabitants of this place live miraculously, surrounded as they are by such causes that conspire against life.[41]

---

[39] *Ibid.*, Exp. 11, fol. 145. The decree makes specific reference to the abuses in Cartagena, Nueva Granada, but it applies to all the Spanish colonies.

[40] *Ibid.*, fols. 145v–146.

[41] *Ibid.*, Exp. 10, fols. 114v–115.

Casasola proposed a site for a new cemetery which he assured the Ayuntamiento would admirably serve the desired purpose. It was some distance from the city near the sanctuary of Nuestra Señora de Los Angeles. At this place one could probe to a depth of more than ten feet without encountering water. He suggested that a special commission, to be composed of four city councilmen, three prominent citizens, and the attorney of the metropolitan cathedral, be established to study the feasibility of a cemetery at this location. The commission's first responsibility, said Casasola, should be to avoid "business dealings and written replies" since experience had shown that such transactions merely "delay, complicate, and confuse" the business at hand. As a means of raising revenue for the construction of the cemetery, Casasola suggested increasing the costs of burial services. There might be added "four pesos to the parish fee for luxurious burials, two for those of medium luxury, one for the regular [service], and four *reales* for those which cost seven pesos."[42]

Casasola's report was submitted to the syndic (*síndico*) of the Ayuntamiento, who forwarded it to the Viceroy with the recommendation that it be adopted. The syndic said that Casasola's suggestions were in accordance with both civil and ecclesiastical law. By the end of the following summer of 1821, however, no action had been taken, and it was then that the Ayuntamiento commissioned José Paz, an architect, to make a personal inspection of existing burial sites in Mexico City. He was accompanied by Juan Francisco Azcárate, a lawyer who was a member of the Ayuntamiento:

The first place that was inspected was the so-called holy ground of San Lázaro. Expressions are lacking to express the astonishment that is caused at seeing its state of abandonment. It is a small piece of ground protected on the west and north by a fence, of which the greater part has been destroyed. . . . It is so extremely muddy that one finds water on at least three-fourths of the site; consequently the corpses are covered with only a very thin layer [of soil]. . . . That which Your Excellency has been told, that from time to time cattle and other animals enter this cemetery, would not be strange [since there are many places of entry]. . . . Neither is it strange that on occasions the dogs have carried off parts of the bodies. . . . Is it not

[42] *Ibid.*, fols. 115v–116v.

likely that this [cemetery] is one of the principal causes of the malignant fevers which have been experienced, and which have afflicted this city for more than six years without being extinguished?[43]

Paz and Azcárate continued their inspection of the cemeteries of Mexico City by visiting the one called Cavallete, which had deteriorated more, if possible, than had San Lázaro: "This is the place where the hogs of the butcher, José Yniesta, have been found, who places them there to fatten them, an extremely grave offense . . . for which he has never been punished as he deserves."[44] Paz concluded the report with the observation that perhaps the long neglect of cemeteries might have contributed to "the twenty epidemics of fevers which have afflicted the kingdom since the year 1525 until the present."[45]

The Protomedicato

The Tribunal of the Protomedicato, established in New Spain by a royal decree of 1646, was the agency charged with maintaining high professional standards among members of the medical and allied professions. The principal members of this board were the three examiners (*protomédicos*), who were selected from the faculty of medicine of the University of Mexico. In addition to these three physicians, there were several assistants attached to the board: a lawyer, a notary, and three assistant examiners (*alcaldes examinadores*), who aided the protomédicos in administering the professional examinations for candidates seeking licenses to practice in medicine, surgery, and pharmacy.[46] By 1788 a fourth assistant examiner, a botanist, had been added to the staff of the Protomedicato.[47]

The primary purpose of the Protomedicato was to conduct the professional examinations for prospective physicians, surgeons, pharmacists, and phlebotomists so that only those candidates who possessed

[43] *Ibid.*, Exp. 13, fols. 177–178.

[44] *Ibid.*, fols. 183v–184.

[45] *Ibid.*, fol. 184.

[46] *Ibid.*, "Protomedicato," Vol. I, Exp. 1, fol. 7.

[47] Archivo Histórico de la Escuela de Medicina [de la Universidad Nacional Autónoma de México], "Protomedicato," Leg. 2, Exp. 17, fol. 2. It is possible that the examiner for botany was authorized before 1788.

the requisite background and training would be licensed to practice. The experience of Ignacio Esquivel indicates the rigidness and scope of the conditions imposed. In 1768 he asked permission of the Tribunal to be examined for a license to practice surgery. He was required to produce a copy of his certificate of baptism, and a notarized statement that he had served, as required by law, as an apprentice of surgery for five years under the personal supervision of a licensed surgeon. He also had to produce documentary evidence that his parents had been legally married, that he was of legitimate issue, and that his parents were Spanish Christians who had no admixture of Moorish, Jewish, Chinese (Philippine?), or Negro blood, and that they had never been punished by the Inquisition.[48] The prudent Protomedicato even took the precaution of placing an exact physical description of Esquivel in his file.

Esquivel, having satisfied all the preliminary requirements, was finally admitted to examination. He was asked various questions about the "theory" of surgery. Then he was subjected to a "practical" examination, whereby he visited four patients at Hospital de Jesús Nazareno. In the presence of the examiners he was asked to diagnose the nature and cause of the ailments of the four patients, and to prescribe a proper course of treatment. Having passed this hurdle, Esquivel had only to pay a fee, and to swear "to defend the mystery of the immaculate conception of Our Lady the Virgin Mary, to observe the royal orders of this Royal Tribunal, and to treat the needy-poor without charge" in order to receive his license.[49] This gave the recipient permission to practice surgery "in all the cities, towns, mining camps, ports, villages, and settlements where he might live or reside."[50]

The second major duty of the Protomedicato was to inspect phar-

---

[48] *Ibid.*, Leg. 1, Exp. 3, fols. 3v–4.

[49] *Ibid.*, fol. 6.

[50] *Ibid.* For a detailed description of the manner of conducting the examinations for the physicians and pharmacists, as well as for further details on surgeons, see Manuel S. Soriano, "Algunos apuntes sobre el Protomedicato," *Gaceta médica de México*, XXXVI (October 15, 1899), 563–585. Pages 567–579 of this article contain a document titled "De los protomédicos," written by Dr. Manuel de Jesús Febles. Soriano gives no date, but it was probably written between 1813 and 1830. The item by Febles is a very valuable source for the study of the Protomedicato.

macies every two years to make certain that the various pharmacists had been licensed to practice their profession and that their stocks of drugs were fresh and effective. For example, in 1812 the Protomedicato inspected the pharmacy of Vizente Zamora of Mexico City. It was found that many of the medicines in his place were spoiled, and these were destroyed by the simple expedient of dumping them into the nearest ditch. Zamora's shop was closed, and the keys confiscated, until such time as he could prove that his medicines were properly in order. He was warned that he would be sent to jail if he tried to reopen his pharmacy without permission.[51]

The authority of the Protomedicato technically extended throughout New Spain, as the Tribunal at Mexico City was the only one of its kind in the colony. Occasionally the Tribunal sent inspectors (*visitadores*) to some of the larger provincial cities, especially Puebla, Guadalajara, and Vera Cruz. In 1778 Miguel Díaz Chacón was named by the Tribunal to inspect the pharmacies of Querétaro. He was instructed to make certain that the pharmacies of that city employed only "examined and approved masters, and that the medicines, simples, and compounds were prepared in accordance with the pharmaceutical art. . . . At the same time he will devote himself to the correction of the frequent abuses and excesses which are committed by various healers (*curanderos*)."[52] He was authorized to fine any unlicensed person who was working as a pharmacist, and to destroy all corrupted medicine that he might encounter.

Díaz Chacón was also instructed by the Protomedicato to be on the alert for any new and valuable sources of drugs and medicines:

If in any place within the said city [Querétaro] and its jurisdiction there might be any plant, fruit, flower, stone, soil, animal, or anything else that might have a particular virtue, and specific faculty against any ailment, you are to investigate it, and send it, together with a clear description of

[51] Archivo Histórico del Museo Nacional de Antropología, "Legajos de expedientes relativos a exámenes en la facultad de medicina, 1812," Exp. (unnumbered), "Expediente de oficio con motivo a la vicita bienal que dió Don Vizente Zamora," fols. 205–212, esp. fols. 208–208v.

[52] AGN, "Protomedicato," Vol. II, Exp. 5, fol. 11.

whether it is a tree, herb, plant, in what region it can be found, and for which sickness it might serve, and the manner of using it.[53]

In addition to its primary functions of licensing physicians, surgeons, pharmacists, and phlebotomists, and of inspecting pharmacies, the Protomedicato was frequently consulted by the viceroy in other matters relating to medicine and public health. Various examples of the consultive role of the Tribunal are included in Part II, the section on epidemics.

The Viceroy

The viceroy frequently used his immense power to intervene in the area of public health and sanitation. Generally his pronouncements were intended to affect the entire colony, but on occasion he intervened to handle specific grievances on the local level. This was particularly true of Mexico City, the capital of New Spain, and the usual place of residence of the viceroys. The viceroy's role in public health derived from his authority as the governor of the colony, acting in the king's name. But concurrently he was competent in various other areas since he was also the captain general and vice-patron of the colony, posts which involved him, respectively, in military and ecclesiastical affairs from time to time. But as the governor of New Spain he issued directives in such areas as public works, including roads, aqueducts, and canals; the control of hospitals; municipal sanitation; and the maintenance of ample supplies of grain, meat, and water.

The viceroy's usual prerogative in the area of public health was to lay down certain guidelines of policy, but the implementation of these policies rested upon a host of lesser officials, who, because they enjoyed the most diverse motivations and capacities, often chose to frustrate or flout viceregal pronouncements. In a time of crisis—and epidemics constituted a recurrent and outstanding type—the viceroy could less afford to tolerate the failings of his underlings, so he generally assumed direct personal control of the situation. An increase in efficiency was usually a concomitant of viceregal intervention.

In the ordinary course of events, however, the viceroy's attitude to-

[53] *Ibid.*, fol. 17.

ward enforcement of his edicts was flexible and lenient. In 1769, for example, Viceroy Carlos Francisco de Croix (1776–1771), one of the more competent viceroys of New Spain, issued a comprehensive edict which addressed itself in great detail to the "extremely important object of the general cleanliness" of Mexico City.[54] It stated that pests and other sicknesses would continue there so long as the citizenry tolerated, or persisted in the practice of, the dumping of all manner of refuse in the streets, plazas, and canals. Croix also recited a long list of other offenses and omissions which substantiated his contention. The edict had been meant to strengthen the Ordenanzas de Policía which Croix reported had been largely of no effect, but it conferred the powers of enforcement, as did the Ordenanzas, on the overworked and undermotivated Junta de Policía. That the decree of 1769 was ignored when it was not forgotten would be inferred from a remark of Hipólito Villarroel in 1787: "The true elements of a well-directed program of cleanliness . . . are unfortunately unknown in this capital; or, if they exist, that happy moment when they are to be placed in execution has not yet arrived."[55]

Villarroel was harshly critical of the local administrators, who were ultimately responsible for the health and well-being of the people of Mexico City. He wrote that the leading official of the Ayuntamiento [*Juez Superintendente*], the corregidor, and the aldermen, both proprietary and honorary, constituted "a heavy burden on the people."[56] He described as merely "apparent" the efforts of the aldermen to regulate the price, quantity, and manner of sale of essential foodstuffs, whereas, in fact, this realm had been reduced to a state of almost "total abandonment."[57] In Villarroel's view, "the only recourse that remains to the inhabitants of this populous city is the hope of [the adoption of] the measures of the most excellent Lord

[54] Eusebio Ventura Beleña (comp.), *Recopilación sumaria de todos los autos acordados de la Real audiencia y sala de crimen de esta Nueva España, y providencias de su superior gobierno; de varias reales cédulas y órdenes que después de publicada la Recopilación de Indias han podido recogerse asi de las dirigidas a la misma Audiencia o Gobierno, como de algunas otras que por sus notables decisiones convendrá no ignorar*, Vol. II, No. 62, pp. 338–346, esp. pp. 339–340.
[55] [Villarroel], *México por dentro y fuera*, p. 69.
[56] *Ibid.*, p. 71.
[57] *Ibid.*, p. 72.

Viceroys upon these subjects. . . . [The Viceroys should involve themselves more frequently] with the state of the supplies, their prices, scarcity or abundance, the cleaning of the streets, the lighting . . . [etc.]."[58] He complained that the granary was not serving its purpose, that cattle brought to Mexico City died from lack of local pasture before they could be slaughtered, and that the city's contracts with the butcher were not approved until gratuities of 2,000 pesos were given to the viceroy, 1,500 to his secretary, and 400 to each of the aldermen.[59] Although he included the viceroy in his recital of grafting officials, Villarroel believed that only the king's chief representative had sufficient authority to stop certain flagrant abuses which so adversely affected the public health and welfare.

Events quickly made a prophet of Hipólito Villarroel. When the Conde de Revilla Gigedo was appointed viceroy of New Spain in 1789, a new day dawned on the streets, canals, markets, outhouses, and butcher shops of Mexico City. C. H. Haring writes:

Before his time, in spite of the efforts of his predecessors, Mexico City was filthy beyond description. The great central plaza was given over to vendors of *tamales* and fruits, most of the streets were unpaved, unlighted at night, and infested with thieves. Under Revilla Gigedo the city began to wear the aspect of a modern metropolis, the central streets were paved and lighted, and the policing improved. The plaza was cleared and new markets were established in several quarters of the city.[60]

It is certain that in large measure Revilla Gigedo's formidable reputation rests upon the innovations that he effected in the area of public health and sanitation. The problems which confronted him, as well as the methods he used to try to solve them, are cogently set forth in his remarkable *Instrucción*—a lengthy memorandum which he wrote for his successor, the Marqués de Branciforte. It describes in great detail numerous administrative problems from the area of public health and medicine, such as hospitals, granaries, public baths, cemeteries, fumigation, lazarettos, sanitation, clothing (and the lack of it), floods, fires, potable water, public fountains, and epidemics.[61]

---

[58] *Ibid.*, p. 81.
[59] *Ibid.*, p. 90.
[60] C. H. Haring, *The Spanish Empire in America*, p. 129.
[61] [Conde de Revilla Gigedo], *Instrucción reservada*, passim.

Revilla Gigedo held that the failings of previous administrations were in part responsible for the recurrence of epidemics in New Spain: "If in the government of New Spain there might have always been proper attention given to the matter of public health, then the frequent epidemics, to which are justly attributed in large part the depopulated state which characterizes the provinces of the kingdom, would not have occurred."[62] As specific causes of epidemics he mentioned the failure to locate cemeteries safely beyond populated areas, the reuse of clothing that had been taken from the sick and the dead, the failure to use lazarettos opportunely, the unrestrained wanderings of cows, hogs, and other animals through the streets of the city, the practice of the poor of going about naked, or nearly so, and the scant respect for hygiene both in public places and in private homes.[63]

Revilla Gigedo addressed himself with remarkable energy and persistence to the improvement of such conditions. His success was such that it clearly indicates that the authority of the viceroy, as Villarroel had said, offered the best hope for a systematic attack on the social and administrative abuses which threatened the public health. Yet much of Revilla Gigedo's success was ephemeral, and he failed, through no fault of his own, to set a lasting precedent for similar actions on the part of his successors. He was, in fact, brought to trial at the close of his term of office in 1794 because of charges leveled by the Ayuntamiento, which resented his free-wheeling innovations and reforms. Although completely exonerated in due course, he was charged at the time with such "offenses" as having improperly ordered and arranged the city markets, naming the streets and numbering the houses, and of establishing various new public fountains.[64] In the latter area —to cite a further example of executive frustration—Revilla Gigedo, as a means of keeping the fountains reasonably free of floating impurities, had ordered them enclosed so that water could be drawn from them only through a spigot. But forty years later this law had never been implemented, and an official of the Ayuntamiento wrote that "it

[62] *Ibid.*, p. 55, par. 237.

[63] *Ibid.*, pars. 208, 227–229, 233, 246–248, 251, 303.

[64] *Memoria de los principales ramos de la policía urbana y de los fondos de la ciudad de México presentada a la serenísima regencia del imperio . . . por el prefecto municipal*, p. [109].

remains without effect, as always remain such laws which lack justice, public convenience, and the means of enforcement."[65] Herein lies the epitaph for most of the pronouncements of the viceroys of New Spain in the area of public health, even though some of these men, notably Revilla Gigedo, made valiant efforts to improve the general state of affairs.

The Audiencia

Except on those infrequent occasions when the audiencia substituted for the viceroy ad interim, as during his absence or following his death, it was rarely involved in matters of public health, and never as a formulator of policy. Traditionally one of its judges served as judge of hospitals (*juez de hospitales*), but otherwise the role of the court, as it related to public health, was that of arbiter in those occasional suits which came before it, and which might happen to be related to this area. For instance, as of the eighteenth century, the audiencia was authorized to hear appeals against the judgment of the Tribunal of the Protomedicato.[66]

The fact that one of its members served as the judge of hospitals gave the court its only routine, but rather tangential, connection with health and medicine. It would appear that the authority of the judge applied only to a single hospital—Hospital Real de Indios, which was reserved exclusively for Indians, and which was supported, in part, by royal funds. Every two years one of the senior judges of the audiencia was appointed, or reappointed, to this position.[67] After 1776, when the post of regent was created, this official, who was the leading member of the audiencia, and who ranked next below the viceroy, was supposed to be so named. However, this rule was not invariably followed, for on at least one occasion after this time—in 1805—the dean (*decano*), who ranked next below the regent, was named.[68] In any event it is clear that any legal question which involved Hospital Real de Indios could be brought directly before one of the ranking judges

[65] *Ibid.*, pp. 60–61.
[66] Haring, *The Spanish Empire*, p. 130.
[67] AGN, "Hospitales," Vol. LIII, Exp. 6, fol. 1.
[68] *Ibid.*, "Ayuntamientos," Vol. I, Exp. 5, fol. 76. The dean who served as judge was Ciriaco González Carbajal.

of the audiencia, an arrangement which gave this hospital a unique
and valuable privilege.

In 1729 Juan Picado Pacheco was the judge. It came to his attention that the pharmacist of Hospital Real de Indios, Francisco del
Rosal y Ríos, was said to be altering his prescriptions. Picado ordered
an immediate and secret investigation, which produced sworn statements from various members of the hospital staff that the accusations
were indeed true, and that substantial harm had resulted to the patients.[69] In 1769, in another case, when Joseph Rodríguez del Toro
was the judge, it was again reported that the pharmacy of that same
hospital was not stocked with helpful and well-prepared medicines; on
the contrary it contained many which were useless or harmful.[70] Another investigation was ordered, of which the final results—as in the
case of 1729—are unknown.

In 1806 Ciriaco González Carbajal was the judge. In that year he
ordered the chaplain of Hospital Real de Indios, Francisco Reyes, to
initiate the practice of burying all patients who died at that hospital
in the cemetery of San Andrés, beyond the city limits, rather than in
the one attached to the hospital itself, which was near the center of
town. González wrote: "Experience has clearly shown that it is a certain and unchanging principle that cemeteries which are located within the great capitals are very . . . harmful to the public health, even
more so when they are adjacent to hospitals, where the congregation
of the sick makes the atmosphere which surrounds these [hospitals]
almost pestilential."[71] Reyes, who stood to lose the lucrative burial
fees if the bodies were buried outside his parish, argued vociferously
for preserving the *status quo.* He could see no valid reason why burials
should not continue to take place in the hospital's own cemetery since
its soil, he claimed, was replaced every four months. Furthermore,
the true cause of epidemics was not exhalations from cemeteries but
"public filth," and since Mexico City had been cleaning its streets and
plazas for fifteen years, during which time there had been no "pest or
contagion," the chaplain failed to understand why bodies should not

[69] *Ibid.,* "Hospitales," Vol. LVI, Exp. 7, fols. 1–4v.
[70] *Ibid.,* "Audiencia," Vol. XIV, no Exp. number or title, fol. 331.
[71] *Ibid.,* "Ayuntamientos," Vol. I, Exp. 5, fol. 76.

be buried in the center of town.[72] (He also failed to mention the terrible smallpox epidemic of 1797, which was certainly contagious, and which took the lives of more than 7,000 people in Mexico City alone.) Reyes suggested "continuing as before," which seems to be what happened, the order of the judge notwithstanding.

The various questions of law which related to public health, and which came before the audiencia from time to time, were highly diversified in character. The following examples suggest the variety. In 1766 the two guilds (*gremios*) of bakers and grocers were involved in a lawsuit over the practice of bakers selling bread in their own shops, a practice forbidden by the city ordinances. The law required that bread be retailed by the grocers, and only in certain places formally designated for the purpose. While the suit was pending before the court, the corregidor and his associates on the Tribunal of the Fiel Ejecutoría[73] had temporarily halted their periodic inspections of bakeries. The Audiencia reminded the members of the Tribunal that the lawsuit did not constitute proper grounds for neglecting their duties, and that they must proceed at once to observe the city ordinances requiring them periodically to inspect the city's bread both as to quality and honest weight "so that the public [interest] will not be prejudiced."[74]

In 1768 the doctor, surgeon, and pharmacist who were employed by the Audiencia to attend prisoners in the royal jail brought suit before the court to force it to pay their back wages, which they claimed had not been paid for two years. The claimants told the court that collectively it owed them 1,500 pesos in back wages; the court answered that it had no money. The pharmacist announced that he would supply no more medicine to the sick prisoners, and ultimately he was given the amount of 519 pesos, or about two years' wages, since his annual salary was 250 pesos.[75] The record makes no mention of any settlement made with the doctor and surgeon.

[72] *Ibid.*, fols. 77–78.

[73] This Tribunal was responsible for inspecting weights and measures, and also was charged with the supply of foodstuffs and the adjustment of market prices.

[74] *Ibid.*, "Audiencia," Vol. XII, no Exp. number or title, fols. 325–327v.

[75] *Ibid.*, Vol. XIV, no Exp. number or title, fols. 183, 187.

In 1775 José Antonio Alzate, the editor and scientist, was given a
license by the Audiencia "to manufacture and sell the new coconut-oil
soap," which, if marketed, might be thought to have some connection
with the public health.[76] The license was granted despite the counter-
suit brought against it by the baconsellers of the city, who manufac-
tured a more traditional product and may have feared the competition
of a soap which was in fact new and improved. In 1787 the judge of
the Audiencia, Eusebio Ventura Beleña, received a petition from the
abbot of the shrine of Nuestra Señora de Guadalupe charging that the
meat supplier was giving short weight. The ecclesiastics contended
that if the contractor did not give the same weight for the same price
which he gave in the capital, the small village of Guadalupe would be
retarded in its growth, a prospect which the King would surely regard
with disfavor.[77] Again, in 1769 the Audiencia informed Viceroy
Croix that the court, in accordance with its usual practice, was assigning various criminals to the cleaning brigade of the city.[78] Thus, in
various and miscellaneous ways, the audiencia occasionally took cognizance of matters which were related to the public health.

The Church

The most significant involvement of the Church in the affairs of
public health derived from its traditional control of hospitals and
cemeteries. All the hospitals of Mexico City of the colonial period
were at least staffed by clerics, although, as already mentioned, the
administration and financing of one of them—Hospital Real de Indios
—was in the first instance a function of the Crown and not of the
Church. From time to time, as will be seen in later chapters, the Ayuntamiento did sponsor temporary hospital facilities, but always in the
spirit of supplementing, rather than contravening, the undisputed
primacy of the Church in this area. The involvement of noneclesias-
tics with regard to cemeteries was even more tangential than it was for
hospitals. Since both burial grounds and hospitals are discussed elsewhere in broad detail, it has not been thought necessary to elaborate
at this point on either of them. Historians may turn with confidence to

[76] *Ibid.*, Vol. XX, no Exp. number or title, fol. 79.
[77] *Ibid.*, Vol. XXXI, no Exp. number or title, fols. 21–21v.
[78] *Ibid.*, Vol. XIV, no Exp. number or title, fol. 413.

the two-volume study of the hospitals of New Spain by Josefina Muriel,[79] and cemeteries are discussed as an integral part of each of the five chapters on epidemics which follow.

The Church's role vis-à-vis cemeteries and hospitals was primarily a function of its temporal authority, but in the spiritual realm its involvement in the related areas of sickness, suffering, and death was both direct and obvious. Francisco Xavier Clavigero, an eighteenth-century Jesuit of New Spain, wrote that "the most important duty of the priest, and the Mexican's principal religious ceremony, consisted in making offerings and sacrifices on certain occasions to obtain a favour from heaven or in thanks for favours received."[80] On behalf of the supplicants, Clavigero and his fellow priests directed their prayers and appeals to various of the hierarchy of saints, some of whom were reputed to be especially helpful when approached about certain specified medical problems. For example, the Jesuit Juan de Esteyneffer (1664–1716), who, although not a physician, published in 1712 a popular medical handbook,[81] informs us that San Marcial, San Francisco Xavier, and Santa Rosalía were all attentive to sufferers of measles and smallpox; San Vicente was thought likely to hear appeals from persons with broken bones; and Santa Dorotea was the

---

[79] Josefina Muriel [de González Mariscal], *Hospitales de la Nueva España,* Vol. I, *Fundaciones del siglo XVI* (México, [D.F.], 1956), Vol. II, *Fundaciones de los siglos XVII y XVIII* (México, [D.F.], 1960).

[80] Roberto Montenegro, *Retablos de Mexico(Ex-votos): Mexican Votive Painting,* p. 11. The text of this dual-language publication is printed in Spanish and English.

[81] *Florilegio medicinal de todas las enfermedades sacado de varios clásicos autores para bien de los pobres y de los que tienen falta de médicos, en particular para las provincias remotas, en donde administran los reverendos padres misioneros de la Compañía de Jesús, reducido a tres libros: el primero de Medicina, el segundo de Cirujía, con un apéndice, que pertenece al modo de sangrar, abrir y curar fuentes, aplicar ventosas y sanguijuelas. El tercero contiene un catálogo de los medicamentos usuales, que se hacen en la botica, con el modo de componerlos* (Mexico City, 1712). Esteyneffer, or Steyneffer, as the name properly should be written, was a Jesuit from Silesia who served as "a missionary to the provinces of Sinaloa, Sonora, Tarahumara, and [Lower] California." I have not seen a copy of any of the various editions of this work, some of which were printed in Madrid, and my information on the book and its author has come from Samuel Fastlicht, *Bibliografía odontológica mexicana* (México, D.F., 1954), pp. 34, 36. Fastlicht's bibliography is a work of outstanding merit, even though confined to the very specialized area of the dental history of Mexico.

saint thought most likely to intercede on behalf of victims of dislo-
cated knee joints.[82]

If the supplicant recovered from his affliction, this happy state was
attributed to the intercession on his behalf of that saint to whom the
appeal had been directed. Such miraculous favor could not pass un-
acknowledged, and it was often requited through the act of commis-
sioning a votive painting, which would serve the purpose of repro-
ducing "an actual incident—an accident or an illness—culminating in
a cure by means of prayers made to some member of the Catholic
hierarchy."[83] The painting could then be hung in some appropriate
place, preferably in a church, where it would make known to all the
favor bestowed and the debt repaid. A great many of these votive
paintings make reference to some specific ailment, and the explana-
tory caption at the bottom of the canvas often contains scraps of information of a medical nature. But the chief significance of these
paintings in the area of medical history is the forcefulness with which
they illustrate the fact that in earlier days a patient's recovery from
disease was customarily attributed to the miraculous intervention of
some supernatural authority.

Although divine intercession was frequently solicited as an aid to
recovery, it is also true that the Church was prepared to offer a more
mundane type of assistance, and frequently this form of help seems
to have been thought more expeditious. Certainly the archbishop had
the authority to act promptly in the temporal realm if he so desired.
Activity seems to have been a state of being for one of the greatest
archbishops of New Spain, Alonso Núñez de Haro y Peralta, who held
that exalted position from 1771 to 1800. Much will be said of this
energetic cleric in later chapters; here a few random examples of his
work suffice to illustrate the role of the Archbishop as it related to
matters of health.

In the second year of his incumbency as head of the archdiocese of
Mexico, Núñez de Haro advised the various priests of the Church in
New Spain that on the occasion of the death of a pregnant mother,

---

[82] Juan de Esteynef[f]er, *Abogados para toda clase de enfermedades del
florilegio medicinal por el hermano Juan de Esteynef[f]er. Impreso en México
el año de 1712*, Biblioteca Aportación Histórica, unpaginated, pars. 79, 124, 133.
[83] Montenegro, *Retablos de México*, p. 12.

and in the absence of a surgeon, the local priest was charged with the responsibility of removing the fetus from its mother's womb by means of a Caesarian section.[84] Such an operation offered the only means of saving the soul, and perhaps the life, of the unborn child. Consequently all parish priests were ordered to secure a copy of a booklet on this operation which had been translated from the Italian by the Reverend Father Josef Manuel Rodríguez, a Franciscan.[85] It contained instructions which, if carefully followed, made the performance of a Caesarian operation "convenient and easy."[86] As a means of reinforcing the authority of the Archbishop in this matter, Viceroy Antonio María Bucareli y Ursúa (1771–1779), himself a priest, issued a directive on November 21, 1772, which advised "parents, husbands, and relatives of the deceased" that they incurred criminal liabilities if they sought to interfere in the prompt performance of a Caesarian operation on the bodies of deceased pregnant women.[87]

There were also occasions relating to the common welfare when the viceroy requested that the archbishop use his authority to reinforce his own. For example, in 1797 Viceroy Branciforte asked that Núñez de Haro post throughout the parishes of the city some sixty copies of a viceregal decree on the prevention of fires, so that there "might be avoided the disorders which such misfortunes commonly produce."[88] In 1801 the successor of Núñez de Haro, Francisco Ignacio Gómez Rodríguez de Pedraso, announced a plan whereby the bells of the churches of Mexico City would be sounded according to a prearranged plan so that the location and seriousness of fires might immediately be made known.[89]

When matters of policy relating to the Church's control of cemeteries and hospitals had to be decided, such a decision lay customarily

---

[84] Nicolás León, *La obstetricia en México: notas bibliográficas, étnicas, históricas, documentarias, y críticas de los orígenes históricos hasta el año de 1910,* pp. 204–206.

[85] *La caridad del sacerdote para con los niños encerrados en el vientre de sus madres difuntas, y documentos de la utilidad, y necesidad de su práctica. Traducidos del idioma Italiano al Castellano por el R. P. Fr. Josef Manuel Rodríguez* (Mexico City, 1773). See León, *La obstetricia,* pp. 204, 207.

[86] *Ibid.,* p. 205.

[87] *Ibid.,* p. 204.

[88] AGN, "Bienes Nacionales," Leg. 873, Exp. 119, fol. 1.

[89] *Ibid.,* Leg. 550, Exp. 46, fols. 1–2.

within the province of the archbishop. Núñez de Haro was so attentive to detail that he personally approved the hiring and firing of medical personnel in the various hospitals and convents. In 1797 he approved the appointment of Dr. Joseph Anastacio Pardo to serve as the surgeon of the Convent of Jesús María,[90] and in 1789 he fired Dr. Joaquín Pío de Eguía y Muro from the staff of Hospital de San Andrés, which was under the personal control of the Archbishop.[91] Dr. Pío de Eguía later redeemed his reputation with his appointment, in 1795, to the Tribunal of the Protomedicato, but on the occasion of his being fired he was accused of squandering the "patrimony of the poor" through expenditures in his ward of more than 500 pesos per month on drugs. The Archbishop contended that such extravagance contributed in part to the exorbitant general expenditure for drugs throughout the hospital of some 40,000 pesos in just nineteen months.[92] Pío de Eguía told Núñez de Haro that he would not resign his position since there was no precedent for the Archbishop's action but that he would "leave the job" after his successor had been named.

The archbishop also used his diverse authority to supervise the activities of the various confraternities (*cofradías*), associations of laymen who joined together under the auspices of a particular church for some common devotional, charitable, or social purpose. All these groups could be said to have had at least some slight connection with the public health in that they provided for their members "medicines in case of sickness, and when they died, 'coffin and candles' and assistance in meeting certain other expenses," as, for example, masses for the souls of the dead.[93] In this aspect of their work the organizations comprised a rudimentary type of insurance company, in that their members in good standing could at least count on a decent burial of their body, and a minimum suffrage for their soul, through the guaranteed payment to the priests of sufficient funds for the celebra-

[90] *Ibid.*, Leg. 873, Exp. 155, fol. 1.

[91] *Ibid.*, Leg. 575, Exp. 35, fols. 1–3. For more information on Pío de Eguía, who was a prominent physician, see *ibid.*, "Hospitales" Vol. 62, Exp. 15, "El doctor don Joaquín Pío Muro sobre que se le nombre protomédico de merced por ascenso del doctor y maestro don José García Jove," fols. 1–6.

[92] *Ibid.*, "Bienes Nacionales," Leg. 575, Exp. 35, fol. 3.

[93] Gonzalo Obregón, Jr., *El Real Colegio de San Ignacio de México (Las Vizcaínas)*, p. 14.

tion of certain appropriate masses. A closer connection between such groups and health arose from the fact that they often supported, and sometimes managed, a hospital.[94] In Mexico City, for instance, the *archicofradía* of La Santísima Trinidad, which was made up of various component cofradías, all of which met at that church, helped finance the small hospital for priests which was known as San Pedro.

One cofradía had a quite specific connection with health and medicine in that its membership was restricted to "masters of the art of phlebotomy, surgery, and pharmacy."[95] It was known as Cofradía del Santo Christo de la Salud, and was founded at the church of La Santísima Trinidad in 1652.[96] In the early years of the eighteenth century this organization was vigorous and affluent. Its total membership is not known, but in the years 1714–1715 and 1717 it paid for the burial services and masses for some twenty of its deceased members each year; this figure would seem to indicate a substantial total membership.[97] In 1720 this group had a total income of 1,530 pesos, and a surplus at the end of the year of exactly 400 pesos.[98] Little is known of its activities during the middle years of the eighteenth century, but in 1783 it spent 508 pesos to help defray the costs of handsome new clothes for the images of the two saints San Cosme and San Damián.[99] The two images were honored with stately green robes adorned with gold, as were also their new capes and tasseled caps.[100] For reasons which are unknown Santo Christo de la Salud had markedly declined in membership and wealth by the last decade of the eighteenth century. In 1792–1793 it recorded only four deaths of members for each of those two years, and by the end of 1793 its treasury showed a deficit of 1,713 pesos.[101] In general, the role of the cofradías in colonial society is badly in need of clarification,[102] but available evidence indi-

[94] Haring, *The Spanish Empire*, p. 195.
[95] AGN, "Bienes Nacionales," Leg. 197, Exp. 1, fol. 12.
[96] *Ibid.*
[97] *Ibid.*, Exp. 16, fols. 59v–60v, 78–78v; *ibid.*, Exp. 17, fol. 2.
[98] *Ibid.*, Exp. 13, fol. 12v.
[99] *Ibid.*, Exp. 9, fol. 4.
[100] *Ibid.*
[101] *Ibid.*, Exp. 18, fols. 2v–3v.
[102] For a list of hitherto unused source materials on cofradías, and also on Hospital de San Pedro, see Donald B. Cooper, "A Selective List of the Colonial

cates certain important connections with hospitals, burials, and medical personnel.

Much will be said in later chapters of the important role of the Church in fighting epidemics. It is already clear, however, that even in more ordinary times the legal and customary authority of the Church, in both the temporal and spiritual realms, was noteworthy in its connections with health and medicine.

In summary, we have seen that responsibility for policy matters in the field of public health and sanitation was dispersed among various separate and competing authorities, including the ayuntamiento, the Protomedicato, the viceroy, the courts, and the Church. There was no central authority—not even the viceroy—clearly in charge. The result was duplication, indecision, and confusion in an area intimately related to the general welfare. Venerable abuses persisted for years after they had been condemned by competent authorities, as in the case of the failure of Archbishop Núñez de Haro to convince lesser church leaders of the dangers of interment inside churches, and the frustration of leaders like Viceroy Revilla Gigedo in their efforts to ensure a pure water supply for the city. The ayuntamiento was frequently characterized by a dog-in-the-manger attitude. It was unwilling or unable to guarantee high standards in municipal sanitation, but resented and at times zealously opposed the efforts of certain viceroys, such as Revilla Gigedo, to correct the abuses. The Protomedicato busied itself within the narrow confines of examining and licensing professional medical personnel—a valuable service, to be sure—but it seems ordinarily to have eschewed avoidable controversy, and to have shunned any larger role as the "gadfly" demanding comprehensive attention at all administrative levels to general problems of public health and sanitation. It is true, as we shall see, that in a time of crisis, such as an epidemic, the various health authorities could usually close ranks in the face of common danger, but on a day-to-day basis they tended to go their own way, at their own speed, and on their own terms.

Manuscripts (1564–1800) in the Archives of the Department of Health and Welfare, Mexico City: A Newly Discovered Source for Religious and Architectural History," *Hispanic American Historical Review*, XLII (August, 1962), 385–414, esp. 388–389.

PART II

THE FIVE EPIDEMICS

chapter three

Typhus and Smallpox: Partners in Death
(1761–1762)

THE EPIDEMIC of 1761–1762 is an important milestone in the history of Mexican epidemiology. It was the last major appearance in the eighteenth century of the venerable scourge of New Spain, the terrible *matlazahuatl*. This disease, usually identified as typhus, had repeatedly swept over the colony. The worst outbreak of all time was apparently that which lasted from 1576 to 1581. Only a few Spaniards were affected, but nearly all the Indians were and thousands of them died. Records of the occurrence of this disease are sparse for the seventeenth century, but in 1737–1739 the matlazahuatl, in a fury reminiscent of the calamitous epidemic of 1576, broke forth again. It was widely believed in 1737 that these two epidemics were caused by the same disease.[1] José Antonio Alzate estimated that more than a third of the inhabitants of the colony died in what was the worst epidemic of the century.[2] An anonymous writer of 1813 estimated that 60,000 persons died during the epidemic of 1737–1739 in Mexico City alone, and that about 200,000 died throughout the colony.[3] The epidemic of 1761–1762, to which this chapter is devoted, while severe, was not a catastrophe of the magnitude of that of 1737–1739.

[1] Charles Gibson, *The Aztecs Under Spanish Rule*, Appendix IV, "Epidemics," pp. 448–451.
[2] Francisco de las Barras y Aragón, "Viaje del astrónomo francés [Jean] Chappe a California en 1769, y noticias de J. A. Alzate sobre la historia natural de Nueva España," *Anuario de estudios americanos*, I (1944), 767.
[3] *Diario de México*, 2d Ser., I (May 18, 1813), 600 (cited hereinafter as *Diario*).

Both typhus and smallpox contributed to the twin epidemic of 1761–1762, although typhus struck first and seems to have been the chief offender. It started late in the summer of 1761, and in time it attacked not only the capital city but many provincial areas as well. Alzate wrote that it "caused great destruction and depopulated the kingdom."[4] In Mexico City the first victim of the epidemic was buried on September 1, 1761. Eventually so many persons were stricken that the city's hospitals, even when extra beds were placed in the corridors, could not accommodate the sick. At Hospital Real de Indios a temporary wooden annex was erected to provide for the overflow; ominously, but not without a certain grim logic, it was built in the cemetery[5]. Altogether more than 9,000 patients were treated in all units of the hospital. Of this number, according to Alzate, only about 2,000 survived. He attributed this extremely high mortality rate in part to what he considered two improper procedures on the part of physicians —the excessive practice of bleeding and use of purgatives. He wrote: "I have observed that the purgatives and the bleedings were very harmful, so much so that the persons who were bled or purged for other illnesses were immediately attacked by matlazahuatl."[6]

At least three other temporary hospitals are known to have been established for the duration of the emergency. One was operated by the Jesuit Agustín Márquez, who was affiliated with the Casa Profesa, a

[4] Josefina Muriel writes: "In 1761–62 all the country suffered a severe epidemic of smallpox improperly called *matlazahuatl*." See Muriel, *Hospitales de la Nueva España*, II 248. At least four contemporary reports, however, specifically mention that both diseases were present concurrently. Francisco Martínez Falcón, in a letter written July 12, 1762, refers to "the two epidemics of smallpox and *matlazahuatl*." See AGN, "Epidemias," Vol. XIII, Exp. 2, fol. 1v. The Bishop of Puebla, in a letter to Viceroy Cruillas, June 18, 1763, writes that of the mortality reports submitted to him by the parish priests of Puebla, "some . . . are of the epidemic of smallpox, others of the *matlazahuatl*." See *ibid.*, Vol. XIII, Exp. 3, fols. 20–20v. See also the quotation from Juan Joseph de Farazua, documented in note 13 of this chapter. J. A. Alzate also mentions both diseases. See Barras de Aragón, "Viaje del astrónomo francés [Jean] Chappe a California," *Anuario de estudios americanos*, I (1944), 767.

[5] Luis González Obregón, *Epoca colonial: México viejo; noticias históricas, tradiciones, leyendas y costumbres*, p. 80.

[6] Barras de Aragón, "Viaje del astrónomo francés [Jean] Chappe a California," *Anuario de estudios americanos*, I (1944) 768.

seminary belonging to the order.[7] Another was Hospital de Manzanares, sponsored by the Ayuntamiento "for the proper treatment and convalescence of the unfortunate Indians, poor Spaniards, and mulattoes in the present epidemic."[8] It was established upon the recommendation of Viceroy Joaquín de Monserrat, the Marqués de Cruillas (1760–1766). At this hospital there was performed, on March 22, 1762, an interesting autopsy on a victim of the epidemic. Dr. Manuel García, professor of surgery, dissected the body of a mulatto. He ran certain tests in an effort to discover a more effective treatment for the victims of the epidemic, proceeding, in part, as follows:

Having separated into four distinct parts the bile contained in the [gall] bladder, to one [part] I mixed spirits of nitric acid; to the second, sal ammoniac [soluble ammonium chloride]; to the third, lemon juice; to the fourth, pulque. . . . The reflections which may be deduced from the experiments made with the bile are sufficiently obvious and instructive, and thus we say, regarding pulque, that this liquor, taken medicinally, and in the proper proportion, can be very helpful in this disease.[9]

The Professor's conclusions may have been singular, but he did proceed empirically in performing the autopsy, collecting and observing samples and recording his findings for future study.

Another temporary hospital, which opened its doors on March 7, 1762, was established in the royal jail. Obviously the prisoners could not be treated conveniently in the regular clinics of the city, but it would appear that they were well attended in the prison hospital.[10] Each man received his own sleeping mat, blanket, pillow, and chamber pot. He was also given each day a generous dose of a bittersweet tonic made from vinegar, honey, and lemons. This homemade preparation was no doubt highly regarded as a useful remedy for some of the discomforting symptoms of the disease. As an added precaution

[7] Cayetano Alcázar Molina, *Los virreinatos en el siglo XVIII*, p. 54.

[8] Ex-Ayun., "Asistencias," Vol. 386, Tome I, Exp. 1, fol. 56.

[9] Rómulo Velasco Ceballos (ed.), *La cirugía mexicana en el siglo XVIII*, "El Protomedicato describe una disección practicada en un cadáver durante la epidemia de 1762," pp. 411–413. A second autopsy was performed that same day at Hospital Real de Indios. See *ibid.*, p. [415].

[10] AGN, "Audiencia," Vol. II, Exp. 2, fols. 193–197.

against the pest, an unidentified powder was burned each day to fumigate the jail; on inspection days double the regular amount was
burned. Assuming that adequate portions were given, the food was
quite suitable for a sick or convalescing patient. A typical purchase
order is that of April 5, 1762, which lists expenditures for beef, bread,
chicken, ham, peas, chocolate, rice, sugar, wine, lard, and pulque. A
corn-meal gruel (*atole*) was usually available. Some of the choicer
items may have been reserved for the staff, as, for example, butter,
listed on the order with the notation "For assistants only." The best
indication of the adequate treatment of patients at the royal jail was
the very low mortality rate. Altogether 134 patients were admitted for
treatment; of this number only 6 died.[11] On June 5, 1762, the prison
hospital in the royal jail ceased operation.[12] Apparently the epidemic
within the restricted confines of the jail was over, but that it continued
for some months to afflict the rest of the city is established by the following statement, made in July, 1762, by Juan Joseph de Farazua, a
scribe of the Audiencia:

I certify . . . that this capital and most of the villages and towns, both near
and far, find themselves distressed by the struggle against the general
contagion of pestilential fevers, and that many of their inhabitants of
both sexes, and of all ages and conditions, have died. At the same time
there has broken out another [epidemic] of equal mortality, smallpox.
For the present neither one has been mitigated by the assistance . . .
offered by the Most Illustrious Archbishop, the Ayuntamiento, and other
persons of means, both ecclesiastics and laymen, in both the spiritual
[realm] with prayers, and in the temporal with alms, food, medicine, and
the increase of hospitals for the poor people, of which a growing number
abound in this capital.[13]

———

[11] *Ibid.*, fol. 193v. Curiously enough, in one sense a prisoner in this jail was
worth more dead than alive. To bring a prisoner to jail required a payment of
one *real* to the attendant, but to carry the prisoner's corpse to the cemetery cost
three *reales*, since two attendants were needed, and a cheap shroud was provided which also cost one *real*. (A *real* was worth one-eighth of a peso, or twelve
and one-half centavos.)

[12] Another prison hospital was operated concurrently in the jail of the Tribunal of the Acordada. Less is known about this hospital, but 159 of its prisoners had died (mainly of typhus) by July 8, 1762. See AGN, "Epidemias," Vol.
XIII, Exp. 2, fol. 5v.

[13] Ex-Ayun., "Asistencias," Vol. 386, Tome I, Exp. 1, fol. 58.

The intensity of the morbid fears frequently provoked among the public by the spread of communicable sickness is suggested by the extremely harsh penalties which could be assessed legally against doctors who failed to report cases of contagious disease. For the first offense the negligent doctor was to be sentenced to thirty days in the local jail; a second offense brought four-year banishment to a remote presidio on the frontier. The law also required that clothing and furniture which had been in contact with victims of contagious diseases be burned, and even that the bricks from the floor of their sickroom be removed and destroyed.[14]

Early in the summer of 1762 the Ayuntamiento cooperated with the Archbishop, various lesser clergymen, the Audiencia, and some of the Tribunals of the city in holding a novena—a special nine-day religious ceremony to invoke divine assistance in fighting the epidemic. The novena began with the sacred image of the Most Holy Virgin Mary of Loreto, one of the revered images of the capital, being borne through the streets on the shoulders of the faithful. According to local tradition an appeal to the Virgin of Loreto had been instrumental in halting an epidemic of measles in 1727, and once again, in a time of crisis, when neither temporal nor spiritual measures had availed, her divine intercession was besought.[15] Such religious processions were commonly held during severe epidemics, as they were in other times of great public emergency.

The mortality exacted by the epidemic of 1761–1762 in Mexico City is unknown, although two estimates exist. The figures are widely divergent, but since one report was compiled before the epidemic had run its course, they are seemingly reconcilable. The first estimate is 14,600 deaths through July 8, 1762.[16] This figure is based upon the

[14] *Ibid.*, "Cedularios," Vol. 451, Tome II, "Cédulas pasta pergamino," no Exp. number or title, fol. 173v. This *cedulario* contains copies, which appear to be paraphrased, of municipal ordinances. The one cited is dated February 23, 1763, or at a time when the epidemic was apparently over. An earlier, and similar, ordinance of June 23, 1752, is mentioned. There is no known instance of these severe penalties having been in fact imposed against doctors who had failed to report cases of contagious diseases.

[15] *Ibid.*, "Asistencias," Vol. 386, Tome I, Exp. 1, fols. 46, 58, 71. For further information on appeals made to the Virgin of Loreto during the epidemic of 1762, see *ibid.*, "Hospital de Naturales," Vol. 2309, Tome I, Exp. 1, fols. 1–10.

[16] AGN, "Epidemias," Vol. XIII, Exp. 2, fol. 17.

official reports of burials in the parish cemeteries, which were submitted by the parish priests to the Archbishop. The second figure, which is given by Alzate, an on-the-scene observer, is of "at least 25,000" deaths in the capital.[17] Since the epidemic apparently continued throughout 1762, and certainly was not over by July 8, there is no obvious reason to rule out the approximate accuracy of Alzate's estimate.

Nearly half of the deaths reported by the priests were concentrated in the heavily populated parish of the Sagrario, at the heart of the city. As of July 8, Father Francisco Martínez Falcón reported 6,815 burials in the two cemeteries of his parish. The number of victims had been so overwhelming that the second cemetery had in fact been dedicated on December 9, 1761, expressly to meet the needs of the emergency. Martínez Falcón reported that the identity of 4,382 of the victims, or nearly two-thirds of the total number, was unknown. Ordinarily the name of a person who died was recorded, along with the date of death and the location of the burial site, in a parish register kept by the priests. But it seems that the victims of the epidemic, some of whom were found in the cemeteries, on the steps of the hospitals, or in the streets, were routinely buried without delay. Often there was no time to try to establish identification, for the public health demanded immediate interment. Young children accounted for a high percentage of the victims. In the parish of Santa Cruz y Soledad, which reported 514 burials as of July 8, more than 60 per cent (329) were *párvulos*, or, as defined by the priest who made the report, persons who had not reached the age of puberty.[18]

It is not known precisely when the epidemic of 1761–1762 finally released its deadly grip on the stricken capital of New Spain. It appears to have continued throughout the year of 1762, since in April, 1763, the Ayuntamiento recorded that the capital had been afflicted "by a grave epidemic of fevers throughout the year just passed."[19] It had caused great suffering and loss of life, and the only consolation would seem to have been that the disease did not return again in force

[17] Barras de Aragón, "Viaje del astrónomo francés [Jean] Chappe a California," *Anuario de estudios americanos*, I (1944), 767.

[18] AGN, "Epidemias," Vol. XIII, Exp. 2, fols. l–lv.

[19] Ex-Ayun., "Asistencias," Vol. 386, Tome I, Exp. 1, fol. 71.

for more than half a century, or until 1813, thus sparing one generation, at least, from the horrors of a major typhus outbreak. Feelings of intense relief always followed the passing of another epidemic, but the people, especially the elders, realized that, phoenix-like, the next outbreak might spring from the ashes of the last. The fear of further struggle against epidemic disease—that ancient and unconquerable enemy—blighted the joyful celebration of another battle ended.

chapter four

Inoculation: Rejected Lifesaver
(1779–1780)

MEXICO CITY's respite of nearly two decades from the ravages of a major epidemic ended when several cases of smallpox were reported in August, 1779. For several weeks the outbreak was mild, few persons were affected, and there seemed to be no cause for general alarm.[1] But the cautious optimism of late summer had given way by early fall to ominous forebodings, and on September 20 the presence of an epidemic was officially established.[2] Once in motion, it proliferated rapidly throughout the city. Thousands of children and young adults, born since the last major outbreak of 1761, had not previously been exposed to the disease, and hence had never acquired any immunity. Dr. Esteban Morel wrote that the *virus varioloso*, or the virus of smallpox, attacked "all the houses" of the city.[3]

The reality of a general epidemic was vividly made known to Viceroy Martín de Mayoraga (1779–1783) on October 13, when Father Joaquín Izquierdo, prior of the Hospital de San Juan de Dios, advised Mayoraga that because of the growing number of sick-poor seeking medical aid his hospital required immediate assistance. Izquierdo asked that the viceroy use his superior authority and influence to procure such help from the Ayuntamiento. Specifically he requested that the city authorities, using municipal rent moneys, be directed to supply the hospital with a hundred wooden beds, mattresses, and

---

[1] AGN, "Correspondencia de los Virreyes," Vol. CXXIV, Letter 151, fol. 18.
[2] Ex-Ayun., "Policía, Salubridad, Epidemia Viruela," Vol. 3678 (P. 255), Tome I, Exp. 3, fol. 5.
[3] *Ibid.*, fol. 1v.

blankets and four hundred sheets. Such a request, in spite of its urgent nature, could not be sent directly to the Viceroy. In accordance with the usual policy observed in such matters, Izquierdo's proposal was given a thorough preliminary screening by a viceregal adviser, in this case the *Fiscal de lo civil*, a legal specialist. However, the fiscal acted promptly, and recommended that the Viceroy endorse the request. Furthermore, he recommended that the hospital be given a supplementary allowance of 100 pesos per day for food and medicine, and that letters be sent "to the well-to-do citizens in order that they might help with their alms." Mayoraga approved the suggestions of the fiscal, and he promptly informed the Ayuntamiento of his official endorsement of Izquierdo's request. Reacting to the stimulus of viceregal pressure, the municipal council on October 18 approved the request, and three days later the beds and other supplies were delivered.[4] Ultimately nearly 12,000 pesos was spent by the city for enlarging and equipping Hospital de San Juan de Dios, and another 11,000 was spent for the same purpose at Hospital de Nuestra Señora de Belén.[5]

The growing numbers of sick and needy persons prompted other officials to take immediate action. Archbishop Núñez de Haro (always in the forefront of charitable activities) endeavored to expand still further the hospital facilities of the capital, specifically to open a provisional hospital at the College of San Andrés.[6] This building was still referred to popularly as a "college," although it had not been used as such for some years. It had once belonged to the Jesuits, but this religious order had been expelled from the entire Spanish empire in 1767 after incurring the powerful enmity of King Charles III of Spain. Since the time of expulsion all former Jesuit properties had been administered by an agency of the state. The College of San Andrés, once the property of the best-trained teachers in the colony, had passed into the hands of the Army for use as a barracks. The Archbishop wanted the soldiers turned out to make room for the provisional hospital. When Mayoraga approved the plan, it became the

---

[4] AGN, "Epidemias," Vol. XVI, Exp. 2, fols. 1–1v.

[5] Ex-Ayun., "Policía, Salubridad, Epidemia Viruela," Vol. 3678 (P. 255), Tome I, Exp. 3, fol. 32v.

[6] AGN, "Hospitales," Vol. XI, Exp. 6, fol. 1.

turn of an agency of the state to be evicted, and the former Jesuit property passed once again into the hands of the Church.[7]

The Archbishop, full of plans for renovating the building, ordering supplies, and selecting a staff, set out at once to inspect his new property. He was so shocked at its deteriorated state that he wrote at once to the Viceroy:

Yesterday afternoon I went to inspect the hospital, and I can assure Your Excellency that it filled me with discomfort and sadness to find it so dirty, run down, and neglected. This building, which the soldiers have used, is like a stable, and there is even a blacksmith's shop in the cemetery. The water pipes are clogged, and the lower parts of the college are under water. . . . The upstairs rooms are full of leaks, and since some of the windows have been left open there is even grass growing in several of them. . . . In a word, I've never seen any habitation so filthy and forsaken.[8]

But the need was great and Núñez de Haro, a resourceful man, was determined to meet that need as quickly as he could. His appeal to Mayoraga set off a flurry of activity, as the Viceroy ordered that the college be cleaned, repaired, and made habitable without any further delay. Once the renovation was accomplished, three hundred beds were installed, and the Archbishop named Francisco Chacón y Torres as director of the new Hospital de San Andrés. Soon he and his staff were working around the clock to do what they could to aid the victims of the epidemic.

The Ayuntamiento, as a part of its contribution to the general effort against the epidemic, announced that it would publish at its own expense a pamphlet on the nature and treatment of smallpox. The author of *An Instruction Which Can Serve to Cure the Sufferers of Epidemic Smallpox* was Dr. José Ignacio Bartolache (1739–1790).[9] The work

---

[7] Hospital de San Andrés remained in control of the archbishop of Mexico until 1861, when it came under the control of the ayuntamiento of Mexico City. The building was demolished in 1905 to make way for the present Secretariat of Communications and Public Works. See Juan de Viera, *Compendiosa narración de la ciudad de México*, prologue and notes by Gonzalo Obregón, [Jr.] (México [D.F.], 1952), p. 118, n. 89. (The *Compendiosa narración*, one of the outstanding contemporary descriptions of eighteenth-century Mexico City, was written in 1777, but no copy was found until 1948. See *ibid.*, p. [7].)

[8] AGN, "Hospitales," Vol. XI, Exp. 6, fols. 6–7.

[9] *Instrucción que puede servir para que se cure a los enfermos de las viruelas*

is divided into three sections. The first discusses Bartolache's ideas on the nature of smallpox; it contains nothing new or original. The second contains his prescriptions for treating the disease, which were so well received that they remained popular for many years.[10] The third is a frank condemnation of certain popular medical remedies concocted from a bewildering variety of strange ingredients, often with unfortunate results to the patient.

Although advanced in his views on pharmacology, Bartolache was not equally enlightened in all other aspects of medical practices. In a separate communication to the Ayuntamiento, he proposed certain additional and rather quixotic measures for curbing the spread of smallpox. He suggested two ways of preventing or at least reducing "infection of the air," a supposed atmospheric condition which at the time was thought to contribute to the spread of contagious disease. First, great bonfires should be started in the streets; second, cannons should be fired to purge the atmosphere of impurities. It was recognized that such positive measures might alarm the people. Bartolache recommended therefore that church bells be rung at night to gladden and reassure the public. Not to ignore those persons who were actually suffering from the disease, Bartolache, a precursor of Muzak,

---

epidémicas, que ahora se padecen en México, desde fines del Estío, en el año corriente de 1779, extendida y presentada a la Nobilísima Ciudad por el Dr. D. José Ignacio Bartolache, Profesor que ha sido de Medicina y Matemáticas en esta Real Universidad, y ahora Apartador general del Oro y Plata de todo el Reyno [Mexico City, 1779]. There is a microfilm copy (negative) of this rare item at Brown University.

[10] The pamphlet by Bartolache was reprinted, in revised form, in 1797. Referring to this fact a colonist wrote: "The simples [of Bartolache] have proven good even to the present, and because of small cost his method has been generally adopted." See AGN, "Epidemias," Vol. III, Exp. 17, fols. 211–211v. Dr. Francisco Fernández del Castillo, [Jr.], professor of the history of medicine at the National Autonomous University of Mexico, has also commended Bartolache's treatment of 1779: "Although in order to explain the pathology of the sickness he adopted the beliefs of his contemporaries, based on the ancient humoral theory, the practical measures which he recommended are a model of simple therapy in those times of complete polypharmacy, abundant bleedings, and other aggressive measures which the majority of his contemporaries employed." See Fernández del Castillo, [Jr.], "La inquieta vida del Doctor Bartolache," *El Médico*, Vol. VII (April, 1957), Pt. II, p. 62. "Polypharmacy" may be defined as the preparation of remedies containing various ingredients; also, the excessive use of such remedies.

suggested that organ music would soothe the nerves of patients who were being fed or given medicines.[11] Obviously Dr. Bartolache was concerned about the mental as well as physical well-being of the community.

The epidemic worsened despite the concerted efforts of Bartolache and various other officials. On October 31, the Ayuntamiento announced that a sudden upturn had been noted in both its intensity and virulence. Once again, as during the fearful outbreak of 1761, the hospitals were unbearably overcrowded, and elsewhere in the capital there existed a multitude of sick-poor who clamored for food and medicine. The first step taken to meet this crisis was to prepare enrollments which endeavored to list the names of all the destitute persons in the city.[12] Social lines were drawn, as the compilers of the lists were asked to take note of the personal circumstances and social standing of the people, as well as of the seriousness of their ailment. The city was divided into special districts, and a commissioner was named for each. These officials were charged with making periodic inspections of their districts to continue the search for indigent sick, who were to be provided with "food, clothes, medicine, and other aids which common sense dictates."[13] A manifesto was issued which informed the public of the need and estimated costs of the emergency program of public relief.

The money needed for this program was not provided in the main by the Ayuntamiento, but by private citizens. On October 24, the city officials sent out printed forms to many well-to-do residents asking them to assume temporary financial responsibility for the destitute sick-poor from their own districts. These benefactors were aided and advised by parish priests, whom the Archbishop designated as their

[11] My discussion of Bartolache's pamphlet of 1779 is based in part on Muriel, *Hospitales de la Nueva España*, II, 248–249. See also AGN, "Epidemias," Vol. XVI, Exp. 2, fols. 2–2v.

[12] [Ayuntamiento of Mexico City], *Noticia de las providencias tomadas por esta N[obilísima] C[iudad] acerca de la asistencia de los enfermos, y precaución del contagio, para su más puntual execución* (Mexico City, 1779). I have used a microfilm copy of the *Noticia* from the California State Library, Sutro branch.

[13] *Ibid.*, p. 2.

assistants. The corregidor also offered his counsel; in particular, he coordinated arrangements for aiding those districts which had few or no well-to-do residents and perforce relied upon outside help.[14]

The Ayuntamiento, though soliciting financial assistance from private sources, in no way minimized the concurrent responsibilities of the public administration. The manifesto prudently explained that the need was so great that all possible sources of aid—private and public —would have to be tapped:

> The necessity is so obvious that nobody could dispute it who would consider the conspicuous difference between this capital and any one of Europe. Here one sees innumerable people who, in perfect health, unfortunately have no shirt to put on, nor bed in which to rest; and all of them, when they find themselves sick, must consider themselves as the most wretched of persons—destitute of all those aids which are esteemed and reputed to be indispensable and necessary, not only for recovery and comfort, but for human subsistence; to demonstrate this it is not necessary to go to the suburbs of this great capital, where the misery of its inhabitants is most visible and common; but in its very center considerable nudity is seen, and in each outlying area one also sees this unfortunate spectacle. Considering the growing number of unfortunates . . . the measure that has been announced is indispensable. . . . In this manner one can guard against the contagion, which might inflict itself on the great number of needy persons, who compose more than two-thirds parts of Mexico City.[15]

The manifesto stated that nobody would be forced to contribute to the relief program, but since its sole purpose was "to succor and cure the sick, and to avoid contaminating the others," it was felt that most persons would, as a matter of course, wish to give as much as they could.[16] In general, the response to the solicitations for funds was generous. Two of the leading Tribunals of the city—Consulado and Minería—each gave 10,000 pesos, and Viceroy Mayoraga donated 1,000 pesos from viceregal funds. Ultimately the substantial sum of

[14] Ex-Ayun., "Policía, Salubridad, Epidemia Viruela," Vol. 3678 (P. 255), Tome I, Exp. 1, fols. 2–3.
[15] *Noticia de las providencias*, pp. 1–2, 8–9.
[16] *Ibid.*, pp. 13–14.

147,263 pesos was collected, of which two-thirds (99,304) came as gifts from private sources and one-third (47,958) from the municipal treasury and other official sources.[17]

Among the measures adopted by the Ayuntamiento was one to provide a special cemetery outside the city for victims of the epidemic. Altogether, 5,468 pesos was spent in the preparation of the cemetery and for burials.[18] Furthermore, bonfires, fed in part with branches of aromatic herbs, were started in various key locations to sweeten and purify the air.[19] On October 29 the Ayuntamiento also initiated "an extraordinary general cleaning of the streets of the city." On that date 355 peons, bossed by 5 foremen, set about collecting and carting off all manner of trash. For the performance of this public service, the peons were paid 2 *reales* (one-fourth of a peso, or 25 centavos) per day, while the foremen received 3 *reales* per day.[20] On the second day of work only 82 of the peons reported for duty. Perhaps they decided, after getting downwind of their new duties, that it just wasn't worth it to work for 2 *reales* a day, and at labor so degrading it was sometimes performed by convicts.[21] Despite the fluctuating labor force, which finally averaged out at 173 peons per day, the city expended in six weeks 1,760 pesos on street cleaning—a sum considered enormous.[22] Many years earlier, for example, in 1696, the city had spent only 25 pesos a week on cleaning the streets, although the corregidor complained at the time that this paltry expenditure meant that the streets were generally dirty, and that the health of the public was in jeopardy.[23]

[17] Ex-Ayun., "Policía, Salubridad, Epidemia Viruela," Vol. 3678 (P. 255), Tome I, Exp. 3, fols. 23*bis*, 32v–33.

[18] *Ibid.*, fol. 32v.

[19] *Noticia de las providencias*, pp. 12–13.

[20] Ex-Ayun., "Policía, Salubridad, Epidemia Viruela," Vol. 3678 (P. 255), Tome I, Exp. 3, fols. 11–11v. Such remuneration was standard in these years in Mexico City for unskilled labor.

[21] AGN, "Audiencia," Vol. XIV, no Exp. number or title, fol. 413. Prisoners awaiting transportation to presidios were among those assigned to the "cleaning brigade."

[22] Ex-Ayun., "Policía, Salubridad, Epidemia Viruela," Vol. 3678 (P. 255), Tome I, Exp. 3, fols. 11v, 32v.

[23] *Ibid.*, "Policía, Salubridad," Vol. 3668 (P. 245), Tome I, Exp. 1, fols. 1v–2.

With the Ayuntamiento coordinating the fund-raising activities, Viceroy Mayoraga undertook to enlist the assistance of the local physicians and priests. In a letter to the Archbishop, he reminded the clergy of their sacred obligation to aid the sick and the dying, and a second viceregal letter, directed to the Protomedicato, called upon physicians, surgeons, and phlebotomists to be mindful of their special responsibilities.[24] All the medical personnel had taken an oath (when their licenses to practice had been granted by the Protomedicato) to aid, as needed, and without charge, the truly indigent sick.[25] Dr. Esteban Morel reported that various physicians from time to time held medical conferences in the chambers of the Ayuntamiento to discuss matters related to the epidemic.[26]

In a personal letter the Viceroy set forth the magnitude of the tragedy which had befallen the capital city of New Spain: "There is nothing but corpses seen in the streets, and throughout the city one hears only outcries and laments. [The people] frequently make novenas to the holy images, upon whom they bestow the deepest veneration and affection. Lastly, all these things have produced an incalculable distress."[27]

At the time, a useful preventive for smallpox was known, which, if it had been widely used in the city, would have substantially reduced the mortality from this disease. Inoculation, or variolation, had been practiced in some parts of the world for centuries.[28] It was a crude, and potentially dangerous, forerunner of vaccination:

[24] AGN, "Epidemias," Vol. XVI, Exp. 2, fols. 2–2v.

[25] Archivo Histórico de la Escuela de Medicina de México [de la Universidad Nacional Autónoma de México], "Protomedicato," Leg. 1, Exp. 3, fol. 6.

[26] Ex-Ayun., "Policía, Salubridad, Epidemia Viruela," Vol. 3678 (P. 255), Tome I, Exp. 3, fol. 6v.

[27] AGN, "Correspondencia de los Virreyes," Vol. CXXV, Letter 278, fol. 68v.

[28] The first known reference to inoculation is from a verse of the tenth or eleventh century: " 'In order that variola [smallpox] may not produce death among tender babes, put into their veins a favorable variola.' " See Arnold C. Klebs, "The Historic Evolution of Variolation," *Bulletin of The Johns Hopkins Hospital,* XXIV (March, 1913), 70, n. 7. Inoculation was introduced into England from Constantinople in 1718, and into New England in 1721. In the latter region, "this important discovery was opposed and neglected for some years," although Cotton Mather was among its champions. See John T. Barrett, "The Inoculation Controversy in Puritan New England," *Bulletin of the History of*

The technique consisted of transplanting pus from the pustules of a small-pox victim into an incision or puncture in the skin of a healthy person. The resultant infection was usually mild and chances for survival far greater than in cases of infection through ordinary contact. Since the normal fatality rate ranged anywhere from ten to fifty per cent and the ubiquitous nature of the smallpox virus made infection almost certain during epidemics, thousands of persons resorted to variolation as the lesser of two evils.[29]

Inoculation was a relatively safe procedure in the early stages of an epidemic, but only relatively, and "the individual inoculated was capable of infecting nonimmune contacts with a loathsome and deadly disease."[30] Yet considering the extraordinary dangers inherent in a smallpox epidemic, it is clear that inoculation—imperfect as it was—was capable of saving great numbers of human lives.

A minority of physicians in Mexico City in 1779 opposed the use of inoculation on the grounds that it was a dangerous and unproven innovation. Dr. Domingo Rusi, for example, a surgeon, condemned the operation before the Ayuntamiento,[31] but most of his contemporaries seemed to believe that the benefits were well worth the risk. Viceroy Mayoraga, probably unaware that he was setting another milestone along the trail of Mexican medical history, issued a cautious approval of inoculation in 1779. He ordered that "in the [Hospital de] San Hipólito there shall be set aside, or constructed, one or more rooms so that all may be inoculated who might want voluntarily to submit themselves to this operation, after the Royal Tribunal of the Protomedicato

---

Medicine, XII (July, 1942), 169–171. Francisco Guerra, though giving no date and citing no authority, attributes the introduction of inoculation into New Spain to Dr. José Ignacio Bartolache. See Guerra, *Historiografía de la medicina colonial hispanomericana*, pp. 119–120. No mention is made, however, of Bartolache's part in introducing inoculation in Francisco Fernández del Castillo, [Jr.], "La inquieta vida del Doctor Bartolache," *El Médico*, Pt. I, Vol. VI (March, 1957), pp. 54–62. It would appear (see n. 35 of this chapter) that Dr. Esteban Morel has a much stronger claim than does Bartolache to have been the first to introduce inoculation to New Spain.

[29] John Duffy, *Epidemics in Colonial America*, p. 24.

[30] Personal communication, John Duffy to Donald B. Cooper, December 10, 1964.

[31] AGN, "Epidemias," Vol. XVI, Exp. 2, fol. 2v.

has determined whether or not its use in a time of epidemic would be of value."[32]

The approval of the physicians was forthcoming, and the city issued a handbill both warmly praising inoculation and advising the public on the manner of obtaining it. Because of this handbill's great rarity, unusual interest, and short length it appears here in its entirety:

> The admirable effects which the inoculation against smallpox has produced in many countries of Asia, Africa, Europe, and some of America, and even in this city [are such] that it is not only suitable for, but has been carried out on, the Sovereign Persons of the Kings, who have caused hospitals to be constructed so that it might be administered to their subjects: This Most Noble City, with due regard to the good results which have been attributed to this operation, and wishing to aid the public however possible, with the prior approval of the Most Excellent Lord Viceroy, and on the advisement of the physicians, has resolved to open a hospital for [the administration of] inoculation in the Convent of San Hipólito, for the individuals of both sexes of more than three years, who might wish to avail themselves of this benefit. It will be in operation on the first day of November, [and] those who go there will be treated and attended with all possible charity and painstaking devotion by Dr. Esteban Morel, who is experienced and skillful in this matter.[33]

Founding a hospital for inoculation was a major innovation which had not been approved without careful study. At the first sign of the epidemic, Dr. Morel had advised the Ayuntamiento that the contagion could not be cut short except by means of early and widespread inoculation. The city council expressed interest in the efficacy of the measure, and commissioned Morel to write a brief dissertation on the usefulness of inoculation, which the council promised to publish.[34]

---

[32] *Ibid.*, "Correspondencia de los Virreyes," Vol. CXXIV, Letter 151, fol. 19.

[33] Ex-Ayun., "Policía, Salubridad, Epidemia Viruela," Vol. 3678 (P. 255), Tome I, Exp. 1, fol. 1.

[34] *Ibid.*, Exp. 3, fol. 1. The dissertation is titled: "Disertación sobre la utilidad de la ynoculación escrita de encargo de la Nobilísima Ciudad de México por el Doctor Dn. Esteban Enrique Morel de las Universidades de Aix en Provenza, y de Montpellier: Médico por el Rey que fue en la isla de Guadeloupe, etc." It is found in *ibid.*, Exp. 2, "Disertación presentada al Ayuntamiento . . . sobre la inoculación de la vacuna," fols. 1–63. It is accompanied by a letter from

The task would be completed with uncommon speed, and when finished the author would claim that his work embodied all the justifications for inoculation that could be collected, and that he had especially related them to the peculiar climate of Mexico City.

Morel was no mere theorist. Within one week after being commissioned by the city to write the dissertation, he set up, at his own expense, a small clinic in his own home. Therein was performed, in October of 1779, the first definitely authenticated operation of inoculation in New Spain. Seven persons were inoculated, and a member of the Ayuntamiento testified to the complete recovery of each of these unsung medical pioneers.[35] His arguments capped with this important success, Morel hastened to complete the dissertation and to await the approval of the Viceroy and the physicians, which, as we have seen, was quickly forthcoming. No sooner was this obtained than Morel set about to dispose and make ready the wards at the hospital. Nearly 2,000 pesos was spent for this purpose.[36] Abandoning the author's pen for the physician's scalpel, Morel waited expectantly for the lines to form at the hospital. Had he not proved that inoculation would save lives? Each day he went to San Hipólito to administer the serum to whoever might come. But nobody ever came.[37] He could save the people, but the people would not be saved. He sat alone with his revelation, a prophet unhonored in his own land, and, worse still, an author without a publisher, for the Ayuntamiento reneged on its promise to publish his volume.

In a pathetic letter to the Ayuntamiento, Morel philosophized upon his failure to actuate the people:

Everything was prepared and made ready, but the innate repugnance of those who were naturally healthy to voluntarily contract a sickness by artificial means, as well as their hopeful expectations that they might

---

José Ignacio Bartolache to Mayoraga, June 19, 1780, recommending that it be published. *Ibid.*, fols. 64–65v.

[35] *Ibid.*, Exp. 3, fols. 2, 5v, 9. Morel also inoculated several persons in their own homes. *Ibid.*, Exp. 2, fol. 4v.

[36] *Ibid.*, Exp. 3, fol. 32v. The exact amount was 1,951 pesos.

[37] "The hospital remained empty. . . . The only person who came to the hospital was attacked by the variolar fever on that same day." *Ibid.*, Exp. 2, fol. 4v.

avoid being among those who would be infected, all of this served to persuade the people that they need not be inoculated: and the new hospital served no other purpose than as an authentic testimony to the dedication and charity of Your Excellencies.[38]

After such a disappointment, Morel was willing to settle for lesser triumphs. To look ahead momentarily, the city council declared that it owed him nothing for writing the dissertation nor any reimbursement for his expenses in setting up his own clinic. It maintained that the fact that these efforts had failed to culminate in a general program of public inoculation at San Hipólito invalidated its agreement with Morel. The doctor, beginning to have some doubts about the "dedication and charity" of the Ayuntamiento, got a lawyer. His counsel advised him to demand a payment of 500 pesos for his literary efforts, and an additional 200 pesos for his expenses in providing food, medicine, and blankets for the seven persons who had been inoculated, and had convalesced, in his home. In his claim against the city Morel pointed out that "in the sugar mills and plantations on the islands [Guadeloupe] where they inoculate the Negroes, eight pesos are charged for attendance upon each of them." Morel apparently believed that since he had inoculated seven vassals of the Crown, and not seven Negro slaves, the fee per patient should reflect the distinction. Finally, on December 20, 1782, Morel was paid the 700 pesos, but, seeking at this point the glory and not the gold, he still complained that his dissertation had not been published.[39]

Despite the failure of inoculation to be accepted, the Viceroy by late December was able to report both the decline of the epidemic and some preliminary estimates of the grim toll it had claimed. Through December 27, there had been reported in the city 44,286 cases of smallpox. Of this number only 7,566 persons had had the pri-

[38] *Ibid.*, Exp. 3, fol. 6.
[39] *Ibid.*, fols. 9–9v, 10–10v. I have inferred that by "the islands" Morel meant Guadeloupe since he considers the fact that he once served there to be of such importance that he mentions it in the title of his dissertation. Furthermore, Guadeloupe was a major producer of sugar in the eighteenth century; it was also a French possession, and Morel, judging by his last name and the source of his university training (Aix and Montpellier), was probably of French descent. See note 34 of this chapter.

vate resources to care for themselves. The vast majority—36,720—
had relied entirely or in part on aid provided by charity. There was
reported a total of 8,821 deaths, but the final death count was somewhat higher, since in December the epidemic was merely declining,
and had not been extinguished.[40] Nearly twenty years later Cosme de
Mier y Trespalacios, the senior judge of the Audiencia, reported that
"in the year of 1779, according to a careful estimate, there died [from
smallpox] in Mexico City alone more than 18,000."[41] Dr. José Flores
of Guatemala, a contemporary of Mier's, wrote in 1803 that smallpox
had killed 22,000 persons in Mexico City in 1779.[42] However, Alexander von Humboldt gives a much lower estimate. He wrote that the
mortality from smallpox in Mexico City in 1779 was "more than
9,000 persons. Every evening tumbrels passed through the streets to
receive the corpses, as at Philadelphia [in 1793] during the yellow
fever."[43] Mier's figure would appear to be the most accurate of the four
since at the time of recording his estimate of 18,000 deaths he had the
records of the epidemic of 1779 in his personal possession. Nevertheless the point remains in doubt because of the considerable discrep-
ancy in the various estimates.

Despite the decline of the smallpox the Viceroy found little reason
for celebration: "My cares must continue, not only because the contagion has spread to other cities and towns of the kingdom, but because the war [with Great Britain] goes on."[44] One town to which the
contagion had spread was nearby Toluca, which as late as February 3,
1780, was afflicted with smallpox. The corregidor of Toluca reported
that the town was "infected [and] completely without assistance."[45]
Mayoraga asked the Archbishop to do whatever he could to send aid
to the beleaguered curate of Toluca. Some incidence of smallpox prob-

[40] *Ibid.*, "Correspondencia de los Virreyes," Vol. CXXV, Letter 278, fol. 68.
[41] *Ibid.*, "Epidemias," Vol. XVI, Exp. 6, fols. 79–79v.
[42] Gonzalo Díaz de Yraola, *La vuelta al mundo de la expedición de la vacuna*,
p. 108.
[43] Alexander von Humboldt, *Political Essay on the Kingdom of New Spain*, I,
111–112. Humboldt cites no authority for his estimate; it is probably based on
Mayoraga's letter of December 27, 1779, written before the end of the epidemic.
[44] AGN, "Correspondencia de los Virreyes," Vol. CXXV, Letter 278, fol. 70.
[45] *Ibid.*, "Arzobispos y Obispos," Vol. XVIII, no Exp. number or title, fol. 1.

ably continued in Mexico City through the early months of 1780, for not until August 28, 1780, did the Viceroy send the customary expressions of gratitude to the Ayuntamiento and various other citizens for their support during the emergency.[46] This action indicates the final extinction of the terrible smallpox epidemic of 1779–1780, significant as a time when in the midst of death the people of Mexico City spurned a preventive measure that might well have saved a great many of their lives.

[46] AGN, "Epidemias," Vol. XVI, Exp. 2, fol. 3.

chapter five

Sickness in a Time of Famine
(1784–1787)

THROUGHOUT the years from 1784 to 1787, central and southern New Spain suffered a prolonged and probably continuous visitation of communicable disease. The outbreak fluctuated in intensity, at times reaching epidemic proportions. Concurrently the region suffered "a series of natural calamities which completely destroyed the grain crop and reduced large sections of the population to a state of extreme poverty and famine. That winter [of 1785] and the spring of 1786 saw thousands of desperate farmers and workmen roaming the countryside, swarming into the towns in search of food, and dying of starvation and disease."[1] Alexander von Humboldt, writing about twenty years after these events, said that the great famine which began in 1784 [sic] gave rise to asthenic diseases, and that ultimately 300,000 persons died of famine and disease throughout the colony.[2]

It is clear that Mexico City suffered a serious visitation of epidemic disease early in 1784, or before the beginning of crop failure and famine. The harvest of 1784 was light but not critically so, but that of 1785 was so small it reduced portions of central New Spain to a state of near starvation.[3] In January, 1784, or some months before the crop failure, the *Gazeta de México* reported that much of the city had been attacked by pneumonia. Novenas were held to honor the Virgin of Los

---

[1] S[herburne] F. Cook, "The Hunger Hospital in Guadalajara, an Experiment in Medical Relief," *Bulletin of the History of Medicine*, VIII (April, 1940), 533.

[2] Humboldt, *Political Essay*, I, 121. There is no doubt that Humboldt meant 1785 rather than 1784.

[3] Cook, "The Hunger Hospital in Guadalajara," *Bulletin of the History of Medicine*, VIII (April, 1940), 534, esp. n. 2.

Remedios, San Nicolás Tolentino, and particularly San Paulino, Obispo de Nola, reputed to be the special protector of sufferers of pneumonia.[4]

A writer in the *Gazeta* attempted to offer a "rational" explanation of the rising incidence of disease in the capital. He blamed unseasonably wet weather, "evil winds," and the unfavorable positions of the sun and the moon:

The autumn of the previous year of 1783 was much wetter than those of the five previous [years]. . . . Since December 7, the winds from the south and southeast have blown with greater frequency;[5] [furthermore], by this date the sun had moved . . . more than forty degrees farther south, and the moon was nearly full. At the same time, there began to appear the sicknesses which are called pneumonia (*pulmonías*) ; pleurisy (*dolores de costado*) ; apoplexy (*insuitos*) ; angina (*esquinencias*), inflammation of the throat; and finally, other [ailments] which, although customary during this season of the year, began to be felt with greater frequency, and virulence.[6]

By the early spring of 1784, pneumonia had attacked not only Mexico City but Guadalajara, Pachuca, Puebla, and other cities of central and southern New Spain.[7] So many deaths had occurred in the capital that it was difficult to find suitable burial space, particularly in those cases where it was preferred that the body be laid to rest within a crypt of a church. Bartolomé Joaquín de Sandoval, curate of the

---

[4] *Gazeta de México*, I (January 14, 1784), 2; (January 28, 1784), 12 (cited hereinafter as *Gazeta*).

[5] For centuries the people of the Valley of Mexico had considered the south winds as "evil" and as the harbinger of epidemics: "The winds from the south . . . blow in the months of March, April, and May. . . . The ancient Aztecs called them the winds of death. . . . The chroniclers of the period refer to them as the precursors of the matlazahuatl and other epidemics, and in the celebrated one of 1737 the south winds blew like hurricanes from March until December of 1736." See José M[aría] Reyes, "Panteones," *Gaceta médica de México*, VIII (October 1, 1873), 157. See also Humboldt, *Political Essay*, I, 176.

[6] *Gazeta*, I (March 10, 1784), 46–47. John Duffy has informed the author that "the angina or *esquinencias* in all probability was diphtheria, or a virulent form of scarlet fever." Personal communication, John Duffy to Donald B. Cooper, December 10, 1964.

[7] *Acontecimientos acaecidos en los años de 1784 á 1788*, p. 11; *Gazeta*, I (February 25, 1784), 25.

parish of San Miguel, had no room for additional burials within his parish church without ordering the premature removal of some bodies that were only partially decomposed. Sandoval sought permission from Juan de Dios Segura, prior of the Convent of San Agustín, to make use of, for the duration of the epidemic, certain vacant crypts within the convent.[8] Segura's refusal was firm and abrupt: under no circumstances would he allow the burial of bodies from another parish within the confines of his own church. "The epidemic," he explained, "is very contagious . . . [and] I have given an order to the sacristan that he shall not admit any body for burial that might have died of the epidemic, since above all I esteem the health of the nuns."[9] Segura was determined to assume no unnecessary risk of contaminating the convent, and he believed that risk might well be incurred if bodies from another parish were buried there, since less would be known of the cause of their death. In fact, his determination was so fixed that he told Sandoval he had already rejected offers of 50 and 100 pesos, respectively, for the privilege of burying bodies from another parish within the convent.

Sandoval, faced with a difficult problem of his own, was undaunted by Segura's refusal. He now appealed to Archbishop Núñez de Haro, who promptly wrote to Segura:

The curate of the parish of San Miguel of Mexico City has informed me that because of the growing number of parishioners who daily die from the present epidemic, he finds himself without sepulchres for burying the corpses; and that if he were to open some containing bodies not fully disintegrated it is feared that he would expose the public to a greater infection than that which attacks it. To help him cope with such a serious and urgent necessity, he has asked that I pass an official letter to . . . [you] so that bodies from the named parish might be buried in the church of the convent [of San Agustín] during the course of the said epidemic.[10]

Núñez de Haro said that such a course of action had been followed in the previous epidemic (of 1779), and he requested that it be done again. Segura's response is unknown; presumably he would not defy the Archbishop, particularly since other ecclesiastics were offering

---

[8] AGN, "Bienes Nacionales," Leg. 266, Exp. 74, fols. 1–1v.
[9] *Ibid.*
[10] *Ibid.*, fol. 2.

their full cooperation in solving the problems posed by the shortage of sepulchres.

The prior of the Convent of Santo Domingo, Antonio García, informed the Archbishop that his convent stood ready to do whatever it could to assist him in the present emergency. The priests of the parish of the Sagrario, for example, "might send [to my church] all the bodies they want to, and each will be placed in a sepulchre. . . . [I ask only] that the said *señores* priests consider sending the burial fees along with the bodies."[11] The prior of the Convent of Carmelite Nuns, Joseph de la Natividad, said that his church would receive for burial any bodies from the parish of Santa Catarina.[12]

As the epidemic continued, various treatments and remedies, some of them bizarre, were printed in the *Gazeta*. One writer suggested that the best way to prevent the pest and other contagious sicknesses was to fumigate with sulphur. In particular, bedsheets should be boiled in a solution of one-half ordinary water and one-half sulphur. This helpful household hint was said to be equally effective in the prevention of smallpox and measles. Another writer, who may have followed the better part of wisdom in not signing his name, suggested the following:

In the present epidemic of pleuritic pains which currently attacks this city, not a single patient has died who has been treated with the following method. At the first instant of pain . . . [apply] a poultice prepared from a cup of bran, a small amount of horse manure, half a handful of camomile tops (*cabezuelos*), a pinch of salt, and a pitcher of white wine (if not available one can use vinegar, or human urine), all stirred, well mixed, and boiled until it reaches the proper consistency to be placed between two thin linen rags. The painful area should be rubbed before placing [the poultice] over it, and the poultice should be left in place until it cools, or brings discomfort; this treatment should be repeated three or four times a day, or at the moments of greatest pain.[13]

This splendid example of polypharmacy was only one half of a double-barreled remedy which, according to its formulator, had restored the health of many sick people. His complementary, and sim-

[11] *Ibid.*, fol. 4.
[12] *Ibid.*, fol. 5.
[13] *Gazeta*, I (March 24, 1784), 54; (April 7, 1784), 61.

pler, remedy reads as follows: "From the first moments of pain give the patient a cup of warm water which has been boiled with a small piece of the heart, or core, of the little pumpkins called *guatecomates* which are sold in the markets, and which are sweetened with virgin honey. This same liquid, or potion, should be repeated three times a day."[14]

There are no documented references to support the probability that the epidemic in Mexico City continued during 1785, although several exist for other places in south central New Spain, as, for example, Guanajuato, Valladolid, and Guadalajara.[15] Several also exist for the crop failures and famines of 1785, which seem to have contributed in large part to the epidemic in that general region.[16] But early in 1786 the record of an epidemic in Mexico City suddenly reappears. Three pieces of evidence from 1786 suggest the unbroken existence of the epidemic since 1784, although the absence of data for 1785 might appear to belie this view. On April 12, 1786, Dr. José Ignacio García Jove, a prominent member of the Protomedicato, called a meeting of the city's most competent physicians to discuss the prevention and treatment of an outbreak of pneumonia then active in the city. The doctors concurred that an epidemic was inevitable, and that there were no defenses or precautions which could prevent it or even modify its effects. It seems unlikely that the physicians would have unanimously agreed on such a gloomy prognosis unless prolonged experience had shown the futility of conventional treatments.[17] On another occasion, on May 19, 1786, García Jove referred to the fact that the pneumonia epidemic had started in "that sad time in the

---

[14] *Ibid.*, pp. 61–62.

[15] *Ibid.*, pp. 226, 297–300; Cook, "The Hunger Hospital in Guadalajara," *Bulletin of the History of Medicine*, VIII (April, 1940), *passim*.

[16] See the important order of Viceroy Bernardo de Gálvez, October 11, 1785, as printed in Eusebio Ventura Beleña (comp.), *Recopilación sumaria de todos los autos acordados de la Real audiencia*, Vol. II, No. 1, pp. 1–5; *Gazeta*, I (1785), 411–416, 443–444, 459. Cook writes that documents relating to the *año de hambre* "are numerous but scattered widely throughout many archives," but he cites no references for any place other than Guadalajara. See Cook, "The Hunger Hospital in Guadalajara," *Bulletin of the History of Medicine*, VIII (April, 1940), 533.

[17] Ex-Ayun., "Policía, Salubridad, Epidemias," Vol. 3674 (P. 251), Tome I, Exp. 4, fol. 1.

year of 1784."[18] Lastly, and most to the point, several hundred deaths from the epidemic were later reported by Hospital de San Andrés as having occurred during 1785.[19]

The absence of data for the epidemic in Mexico City during 1785 is strange; even the *Gazeta* contributes nothing. It may be that although the sickness was widespread in 1785 the mortality rate was low, and that consequently few records were kept. In fact, García Jove stated in 1786 that the number of deaths had been "notable" but lower than most people believed.[20] It would thus appear that although disease was widespread in the capital in 1784, and continued throughout 1785 (when the miseries which it caused were compounded by famine), it was not until 1786 that it reached epidemic proportions. The Junta de Policía reported on April 15, 1786, that the considerable amount of sickness in the city, and the increasing number of deaths, indicated the presence of a condition which could truly be described as "epidemical."[21]

The Protomedicato believed that unseasonably cold weather was the root cause of the outbreak, but it also placed great blame on the reluctance of the common people to repair in time to the hospitals for proper treatment. To the detriment of the general welfare, said the Tribunal, the lower-class people, who were chiefly affected, persisted in spending the crucial early days of their sickness at home in their shacks, where they received either very inadequate treatment or none at all. When finally they were brought to the hospital it was simply "to die with the sympathy of the doctors who saw them," or, as in some cases, they were already dead and were merely brought there for burial. Though castigating the negligence of the poor and wringing its hands in despair, the Protomedicato's sole recommendation at that time for treatment of the malady was to advise the public to abstain from the use of "chilled and sour [drinks of] orange and lemon." Above all, no use should be made of ice or snow,[22] which was fairly easily available the year around from the summits of the nearby snow-

---

[18] *Ibid.*, fol. 22.
[19] *Ibid.*, fol. 16. This item dated May 2, 1786.
[20] *Ibid.*, fol. 21.
[21] *Ibid.*, fol. 3.
[22] *Ibid.*, fols. 1–1v.

capped mountains, Popocatépetl and Ixtaccíhuatl. Meanwhile, the Tribunal reported that studies were proceeding satisfactorily on the bodies of the dead: "Anatomical dissections are being performed and will be continued: the results will be given to the physicians for their enlightenment, and, if necessary, to the public."[23]

Certainly the Protomedicato had been most vague in its recommendations for stopping the epidemic. Viceroy Bernardo de Gálvez (1785–1786) took action in the one area where it appeared that his authority could effectively reinforce that of the Tribunal. He ordered that "the destitute poor be taken to the hospitals as soon as they are attacked by the present sickness."[24] Furthermore, when a death occurred at a hospital as a result of the epidemic the victim should be given a deep and immediate burial. Having done what he could to implement the Protomedicato's scanty recommendations, Gálvez asked the doctors to prepare "a clear and appropriate formula for treatment which could serve as a guide in the ordinary cases."[25]

Gálvez sent letters to the various hospitals of the city requesting their strict cooperation in the matter of prompt burial of fever victims. Antonio de Arroyo, of Hospital Real de Indios, reported that bodies of fever victims were never allowed to remain in that hospital's morgue for longer than twenty-four hours. But even so he promised to notify all members of the hospital staff of the Viceroy's instruction, particularly the chaplains who celebrated the burial services. José de Quintanilla, of Hospital de San Andrés, said that his institution also effected the burial of fever victims within twenty-four hours.[26] Manuel de Moncada y Zaragoza, of the Convent and Hospital de San Juan de Dios, told Gálvez that few deaths had occurred at his establishment as a result of the epidemic. The daily average was only three or four, he said, indicating that this was a very small number in comparison to the numbers being reported elsewhere.[27]

No estimate exists for the total number of deaths in Mexico City resulting from the epidemic of 1784–1787, but the considerable at-

[23] *Ibid.*, fol. 2.
[24] *Ibid.*, fol. 3. (Marginal note.)
[25] *Ibid.*, fol. 3v. (Marginal note.)
[26] *Ibid.*, fols. 6v, 12.
[27] *Ibid.*, fols. 11–11v.

tention which was given to burial procedures and sites is a strong indication that the number must have been high. Early in 1786, a new cemetery was opened to receive the dead from Hospital de San Andrés. "There was blessed with the greatest pomp and ceremony by the Most Illustrious Archbishop the chapel of El Salvador, constructed in the place they call Santa Paula, in the center of the cemetery which belongs to Hospital de San Andrés. The purchase of the site and the construction of the chapel cost His Excellency [the Archbishop] 15,000 pesos. The cemetery is 260 varas in length, 141 wide, and 36,660 squared."[28]

Archbishop Núñez de Haro issued a set of rules and procedures to be observed at the cemetery:

We order: . . . First: that the bodies shall be brought after the evening prayers and in the cart which is now ready for use, [and be] covered with a shroud of black canvas (*lienzo encerado*). Second: as soon as the bodies have arrived at the cemetery the gravedigger shall summon . . . the vicar of the parish of Santa María . . . who shall perform the ceremony of burial and the last obsequies; and we allow him seventy-five pesos annually for this work. Third: the said vicar shall bless the graves, and begin with the antiphony *in paradisum* until he has concluded that sacred ceremony, so that . . . the souls of the faithful dead will receive the most suffrage, and the living will properly esteem these holy ceremonies, and so lose the terror which they have of cemeteries. Fourth: that the vicar shall neither receive nor demand anything [for the performance of the ceremony] even though it be called an alms . . . [although] we do not prohibit . . . that he may say masses in the chapel . . . providing he does not ask a greater payment than that permitted in this diocese. Fifth: that the gravediggers shall take care to dig the graves five or six feet deep, and place them alongside of one another.[29]

Several hundred patients had died of the epidemic at San Andrés during 1785 and early 1786. Núñez de Haro told Gálvez that in the period from December 1, 1784, until November 30, 1785, a total of 6,518 patients had entered the hospital; of this number only 337 had died, a mortality of 5 per cent. From December 1, 1785, through

[28] *Acontecimientos*, p. 23.
[29] Ex-Ayun., "Policía, Salubridad, Epidemias," Vol. 3674 (P. 251), Tome I, Exp. 4, fols. 13–13v.

April 30, 1786, a total of 3,105 patients had entered the hospital; of these, 374 had died. This mortality rate of 12 per cent would indicate a period of much greater intensity for the epidemic during this five-month period. Núñez de Haro offered several extenuating factors to account for the sudden rise in the mortality at San Andrés: "It is worth mentioning that in the time of the recent epidemic there were more than 500 ambulatory patients and that many of the sick were admitted in such a deplorable state they died soon after their arrival, and that others were dead on arrival. . . . Finally, I point out that on the day on which there occurred the greatest number of deaths from the epidemic there died [only] 16 patients [at San Andrés], despite the fact it has been said that more than 30 have died each day."[30]

As mentioned earlier, Viceroy Gálvez had requested that the Proto-medicato prepare a clear and simple formula for treating the ordinary cases of sickness in the epidemic. In compliance with this superior request, the Protomedicato, and several other prominent physicians, met together on May 2. Those in attendance included Ignacio Segura, Juan Vicuña, José Francisco Rada, José Gracida y Vernal, Joaquín Pío de Eguía y Muro, and the three members of the Tribunal—José Giral, Juan Josef Matías de la Peña y Brizuela, and José Ignacio García Jove. The report submitted by these physicians to Gálvez is interesting and important as a reflection of contemporary views on the causes of disease.

The doctors stated that the most common cause of disease was the contamination or infection of the air, a condition said to result from the presence of certain harmful "corpuscles," or strange particles. When these entered the human body through the normal processes of breathing, a person inhaling them became susceptible to disease. The possibility of the air's becoming contaminated was always greater during periods of change in the weather, especially abrupt or unseasonable changes. In August of 1785, the report points out, there had occurred early and damaging frosts. The unseasonably cold weather had persisted throughout the following autumn, winter, and early spring, a situation which tended to produce an unhealthful atmosphere. No major outbreak had developed during these colder months, but on

[30] *Ibid.*, fol. 16.

March 29, 1786—at the time of the new moon—the warm weather suddenly returned, and the population, already predisposed to sickness because of the previous unseasonable weather, immediately found itself in the midst of an epidemic. The doctors reported that in that short interval between the appearance of the new moon and the full moon there was scarcely a person in the capital who had not taken sick.[31]

Although the basic cause of this and other outbreaks of disease was the infection of the air, "we must also suppose that [in times of] constant coolness of the atmosphere the air will bear down more heavily on the bodies of living creatures, impeding perspiration, or sweating, oppressing the lungs, thickening the blood, and making it incapable of circulating, at least through the smaller vessels of the body, [and] this is the cause of inflammations in the larger sense."[32] In treating the symptoms of this condition, the problem of the physician was to reduce the body's sluggishness resulting from the cooler atmosphere. This could be accomplished either through warm clothing or through medicines which would induce sweating.[33] In some cases, but not in all, bloodletting would dilute the thickened blood and hence relieve the inflammation.

The doctors held that most of the deaths which occurred during the epidemic had resulted more from the personal excesses and failings of the victims than from the working of the disease itself. They cited the fact that it was mainly the poor people who had been affected, and that this class was generally licentious or delinquent. It was conceded by the physicians that the general poverty and misery of the poor made them more susceptible to disease, but still they were culpable for their own sickness, because "in health they do not submit themselves to the shelter of a Poor House, or to a hospital when they are sick." It was true, they said, that the poor lacked clothing warm enough to induce sweating—an indispensable adjunct to treating the infection—and that lacking this advantage they tended to incur in-

[31] *Ibid.*, fols. 18–18v, 19–20.

[32] *Ibid.*, fol. 20.

[33] The belief in the efficacy of sweating explains the advice of the Protomedicato (see n. 22 of this chapter) that victims of the epidemic should abstain from cold drinks and the use of ice and snow.

flammations, and frequently death ensued. Nevertheless, in spite of their disabilities, the poor must be blamed for their refusal to repair to hospitals until their condition had already become terminal. In sum:

> Here you see, Your Excellency, the cause of ruin among the poor people: their vices in eating and [in their use of] intoxicating beverages; their nudity during unseasonable and intemperate weather; their use of popular medicines which some curandero prescribes, praises, and claims to be necessary for such occasions (for example, in that sad time in 1784 when pneumonia broke out, they took strong drink [*aguardiente*], and during this [present outbreak] pulque with orange [juice], etc.). In large part the epidemics which are propagated in this capital result . . . [from such abuses].[34]

After thus describing in some detail the causes of disease and epidemics as it understood them, the Protomedicato was ready to consider the Viceroy's request that it prepare a clear and simple formula for treating the current invasion of epidemic disease. It reported that after conferring with various physicians it was the consensus that it would be unwise to comply with the Viceroy's request. To suggest a "universal" formula, even for "ordinary" cases, would be impracticable, indeed harmful. To serve the Viceroy in this instance would be to render a disservice to the people. The doctors pointed out that such a formula could be intended for use only in those places which had no physician, and that if these were so remote as to have no doctor, neither would they be likely to have a pharmacy, so, in the absence of the essential ingredients, the formula would be worthless. Furthermore, an amateur "doctor" could not possibly make sound decisions regarding certain technical procedures, such as, for example, the proper occasion for the practice of bloodletting. Even in the capital physicians often disagreed on the value of this procedure in any given case. Could such a decision be entrusted to some provincial amateur who had no guide except the Protomedicato's formula? Lastly, how could such an untrained person make an intelligent decision on the use of purgatives, which were potentially more dangerous to the

---

[34] Ex-Ayun., "Policía, Salubridad, Epidemias," Vol. 3674 (P. 251), Tome I, Exp. 4, fols. 21–22.

patient than was bloodletting? Several popular medical guides had already been published, including Gregorio López' (1542–1596) work, *Tesoro de medicinas*,[35] published posthumously in 1672, and Juan de Esteyneffer's work of 1712, *Florilegio medicinal de todas las enfermedades*.[36] These works were well written and carefully arranged, according to the Protomedicato, but even so the pseudo-doctors who had tried to use them had made mistakes at every turn.[37] The Tribunal could have no part in preparing and endorsing another aid to quacks and meddlers.

The Protomedicato terminated its report to Gálvez by recounting briefly some of the general causes of disease in the capital and the provinces:

We will speak first of Mexico City. Here, in addition to the common causes that could give rise to epidemics, there are others that could set them in motion, or foment them. We will not say anything about the lakes, or canals, which regularly are likened to evil stepmothers of this city, because much has been said on this point, and each day official measures are being taken to help ensure that their waters will circulate and stay clean. Neither will we talk about the privies since so few houses have them, or about their lack of ventilation and cleanliness; nor about those places where [the inhabitants of] the community houses (*casas de vecindad*) deposit filth in the streets, where it . . . offends the senses of smell and sight of those who pass by, and is very harmful to health. We will not consider for now the fact that even in the principal streets in the mornings the people void their water, which may, or may not, run off through the gutters—these being the depository for all manner of filth, and they contaminate with their foul odor the houses, inhabitants, and the passers-by. We shall not discuss the old clothing which is sold in the second-hand

---

[35] *Tesoro de Medicinas para todas enfermedades. Compuesto por el Venerable Varón Gregorio López. Reconocido e ilustrado con algunas notas, por el doctor Matías de Salcedo Mariaca, médico del excelentísimo señor Marqués de Mancera, Virrey, Gobernador y Capitán General de esta Nueva España y Presidente de su Real Cancillería. Con licencia. Impreso en México por Francisco Rodríguez Lupercio, mercader de libros en la puente de Palacio. Año de 1672.* For more information on *Tesoro de Medicinas* and its author, see Fastlicht, *Bibliografía odontológica mexicana*, pp. 32–33.

[36] See Chap. Two, n. 81.

[37] Ex-Ayun., "Policía, Salubridad, Epidemias," Vol. 3674 (P. 251), Tome I, Exp. 4, fols. 23–23v, 26–27v.

store (*baratillo*), and pawned in the grocery stores (*pulperías*), from which [traffic] there results in large part the sicknesses in this city, because one does not know whether what he buys there came from a person who had been healthy, sick, dying, or dead; and another thing is that the items of the sick are mixed with those of the healthy, so that the latter, when he redeems his own item, carries away in it the seed of the contagion. We have said nothing about the mixing of clothes by the launderers, in which there is an equal risk . . . [or about] the mixing [reuse] of the sleeping mats which have served as a pallet for the sick. . . . There is little attention [given] . . . to the dead animals in the street, whose corruption infects the air and those who breathe it.[38]

The Protomedicato's reason for not dwelling upon these various causes of disease and epidemics was that in a previous communication to the Junta de Policía it had discussed them in some detail.[39] The doctors hinted that they were well informed about still other causes of disease, "but we will not discuss them because of their complexity or familiarity, and because of the wilfulness of those same [lower-class] people they would be irremediable, and our counsel, even when reinforced with the authority of Your Excellency, would be of no effect."[40]

In January, 1787, the Ayuntamiento asked that the Protomedicato inform it "of the status of the sickness of fevers which has been attacking Mexico City." García Jove replied that there were a great number of sick persons both inside, and removed from, the hospitals. The fevers were very similar to matlazahuatl, but less deadly than that dread disease. Still the malady was spreading, especially among the women, and since it was contagious, precautions should be taken to see that it did not become a major epidemic. Such a possibility was feared because there were some homes in the city where six or eight persons were afflicted with the fevers. García Jove suggested that the time was opportune to seek divine assistance by means of a novena to

---

[38] *Ibid.*, fols. 29–30v.

[39] The communication to the Junta de Policía was an official letter (*oficio*) dated April 12, 1786. No copy is known to exist. *Ibid.*, fol. 30v.

[40] *Ibid.*, fol. 31.

the Virgin of Guadalupe, and several days later arrangements for such a celebration were under way. The Ayuntamiento appropriated 350 pesos, deemed a sufficient amount to discharge the financial obligations associated with the first and last (or ninth) days of the novena. The city at that time was faced not only with general sickness but also with the "scarcity and high cost of foodstuffs of prime necessity." Therefore the Virgin was asked to intercede that the epidemic might cease and not return, that the crops might be successful, and that a remedy might be found for "all necessities and calamities."[41]

The last contemporary reference to the epidemic of 1784–1787 came on June 19, 1787, when the fiscal briefly mentioned, in a letter to Viceroy Gálvez, that "most of the causes of epidemics are related to the proper policing and sanitation of the city's streets."[42] He had reached this judgment after studying the records relating to the recent epidemic. Three years later a physician, Dr. Manuel Moreno, also referred to the epidemic in a treatise which he submitted to the Proto-medicato. It set forth his thesis that some form of liver ailment had been responsible for the siege of sickness which began in 1784. Moreno stated that during the epidemic he personally had treated more than 500 sick persons, and that cattle as well as human beings had contracted the disease. He wrote a most interesting explanation of the origin of the epidemic:

Since the year 1784 the variations in the atmosphere have been more frequent than in previous years, the frosts very early, the rains scarce, the exhalations of the land very copious, the heat intense, the feed grasses scarce and poor, and the harvests of the principal seeds inferior. By taking into account all these circumstances one can easily deduce, first, that the mortality of livestock, insects, and other animals which feed on grasses and seeds has necessarily increased in relation to this same scarcity. . . . Second, that the common people, reduced to fewer foods—and those of inferior quality because of their high price—have contracted a degenerative disposition in their humors. . . . Third, that the surface of the dry and arid land placed less of an obstacle to the emanation of the mineral

---

[41] *Ibid.*, Exp. 5, fols. 1–1v, 3, 4.
[42] *Ibid.*, Exp. 4, fol. 35.

exhalations. . . . Fourth, that the stagnant waters of the lakes, less abundant and more corrupt, caused vapors of the same quality.[43]

Dr. Moreno's theory was that the various unhealthful exhalations and miasmas, as "explained" above, had caused a general infection of the air which, after entering the bloodstream of human beings and animals, had in turn caused various diseases, especially a disease of the liver.[44] His theory that liver disease was the chief offender in 1784–1787 was supported by Dr. Joaquín Pío de Eguía y Muro, who also reported that many autopsies had been performed on victims of the epidemic.[45]

Sherburne F. Cook, who has studied this epidemic with particular regard to its social consequences in the city of Guadalajara, writes as follows:

It is probable that no clear-cut epidemic occurred in the sense of a single specific disease caused by a definite micro-organism. It is more likely that several maladies which were already present in the region became intensified due to the bad sanitation, increased crowding, and extreme malnutrition with consequent lowered resistance. Evidence for this is of various types. In the first place, there are no data whatever in the contemporary documents indicating the presence, *by name*, of any particular widespread sickness. . . . Secondly, only the poorer social group seems to have been affected. . . . In the third place, many diseases were already active when the food shortage arose. . . . In the fourth place, there are references to different diseases. . . .

It appears that both gastro-intestinal and respiratory infections were involved. Indeed if health conditions in modern Mexico are a valid criterion it is quite likely that the epidemic complex of 1786 included at least typhoid, dysentery, pneumonia, and influenza. The mortality in 1785–6

---

[43] [Joseph Giral, Joseph Francisco Rada, and Joseph Ignacio García Jove], *Públicas demostraciones de celebridad y júbilo que este real tribunal del protomedicato de N[ueva] E[spaña] hace en la gloriosa proclamación y exaltación al trono supremo de las Españas, de los señores Don Carlos Qüarto y Doña María Luisa de Borbón, su muy digna esposa, a quienes Dios Guarde Muchos Años* (Mexico City, 1791), "Disertación sobre las obstrucciones inflamatorias del hígado, que el Lic. Don Manuel Moreno presenta al Real Tribunal del Protomedicato," pp. 3–4. Moreno's dissertation was published as a part of the *Públicas demostraciones*, but it was paginated separately.

[44] *Ibid.*, "Disertación sobre las obstrucciones," pp. 4–6.

[45] *Ibid.*, *Públicas demostraciones*, p. 11.

must have been considerable, although no detailed figures seem to be available.[46]

In spite of the fragmentary evidence it is clear that hunger and disease stalked the south central regions of New Spain in 1784–1787, and that these terrible calamities brought great unrest, suffering, and mortality to the hapless people of the lower classes of the colony.

[46] Cook, "The Hunger Hospital in Guadalajara," *Bulletin of the History of Medicine*, VIII (April, 1940), 537–538. With regard to identifying the liver ailment, John Duffy has written that "one can only guess on the basis of limited information, but liver abscesses were a common sequela of amoebic dysentery." Personal communication, John Duffy to Donald B. Cooper, December 10, 1964.

chapter six

Smallpox: Word of Terror
(1797–1798)

THROUGHOUT the world in the eighteenth century recurrent epidemics of smallpox cut short many thousands of lives. It is estimated that 60 per cent of mankind were attacked and 10 per cent died of this disease during that century. Smallpox was probably brought to New Spain in 1520, and by the eighteenth century it had become semi-endemic. Since the disease was not indigenous in the New World the Indians were acutely vulnerable to its effects, as they had had no opportunity, prior to the Conquest, to acquire any immunity to the disease. They, in particular, died in great numbers from smallpox. In 1797 a colonial official wrote: "Twenty consecutive years do not pass without it assaulting [North] America with force and cruelty," and he saw this as a major cause of depopulation.[1]

The epidemic of 1797, which was the last great outbreak of smallpox in New Spain before the introduction of vaccination there in 1803, was not the most destructive of the several which attacked Mexico City and other parts of the colony in the eighteenth century. Considerably more people died in the outbreaks of 1737, 1761, and 1779.[2] However, because of the fortuitous survival of records, it is possible to learn much more about the outbreak of 1797 than about its predecessors. Contemporary records are extremely fragmentary

---

[1] AGN, "Epidemias," Vol. III, Exp. 2, fol. 131v. Letter from Juan Felipe Velázquez de León to Viceroy Branciforte, September 1, 1797. Velázquez was the subdelegate at Cuautla, a town of central Morelos.

[2] See preceding chapters for mortality estimates for the epidemics during these years.

for the epidemics in Mexico City prior to 1797, but for the outbreak which occurred in that year almost the entire correspondence is extant. The record is so complete, in fact, that it is possible to reconstruct in considerable detail the administrative, social, and medical problems posed by this epidemic, an undertaking not always possible in every respect for the four other epidemics examined.

Early Reports of Smallpox

Although in Mexico City the epidemic centered about the year 1797, earlier and milder outbreaks of smallpox had occurred in other parts of the colony since 1790. Several isolated cases were also reported in Mexico City in that year.[3] In 1791 the intendant at Mexico City, Bernardo Bonavia, reported the discovery of a case of smallpox at Hospital Real de Indios. The patient was a young provincial male, described as a "wild Indian" (*meco*). The physicians' efforts to learn his place of origin were frustrated, since he could neither speak nor understand Spanish. Fortunately his case was benign, even though it was said to be complicated with scurvy.[4] In 1793 smallpox was reported in several provincial places—Puebla, Vera Cruz, Tabasco, and Campeche.[5] Little is known about these pre-1797 outbreaks, but the mere fact of their occurrence tends to undermine, if not refute, the contemporary explanation of the origin of the epidemic of 1797. Viceroy Branciforte, and others, too, believed at the time that this epidemic had spread as a result of infection brought in by sea from South America in 1796, a theory discussed later in this chapter. It is clear, however, that various pockets of smallpox were already active in several places in the colony, and that the residium from any one of these could have given birth to the fearful outbreak of 1797.

In 1793 an outbreak of *viruelas* in Mexico City and in its vicinity caused general alarm for a time.[6] The word *"viruelas"* is usually translated into English as "smallpox," but more specifically it refers to

[3] S[herburne] F. Cook, "The Smallpox Epidemic of 1797 in Mexico," *Bulletin of the History of Medicine*, VII (October, 1939), 941; AGN, "Epidemias," Vol. XVI, Exp. 2, fols. 3–4.

[4] AGN, "Epidemias," Vol. III, Exp. 3, fols. 96–97.

[5] Cook, "The Smallpox Epidemic of 1797," *Bulletin of the History of Medicine*, VII (October, 1939), 941–942.

[6] AGN, "Epidemias," Vol. VII, Exp. 6, fols. 1–29.

pustules on the skin, thus the term could refer to a relatively harmless disease, such as chicken pox. The outbreak of 1793 was, in fact, chicken pox, but this was not immediately known; in the meantime, public-health authorities prepared for an outbreak of virulent small-pox. The precautionary measures which they employed are of some interest because they anticipate measures which were used four years later, in 1797.

The first report of viruelas in Mexico City in 1793 came on May 31. A young Indian girl was afflicted. A physician quickly reported that her case was benign, but on personal orders from Intendant Bonavia, who wished to run no unnecessary risk, the child was quarantined in Hospital Real de Indios. Several days later the Protomedicato informed Viceroy Revilla Gigedo that it had reason to suspect the existence of other, and potentially more dangerous, cases: "This Tribunal presumes that in Mexico City there is a fair number of sufferers from smallpox [*virolentos*], because one observes certain children in the streets who are already recovered, but pockmarked; from which defacement it cannot be doubted that they have suffered from the said disease."[7]

The Protomedicato foresaw serious consequences if the threat of smallpox was ignored. In early summer there was no immediate general danger, the physicians explained. But experience had taught that in Mexico City the greatest incidence of infectious disease usually coincided with the cooler months of autumn; thus, by October, if indicated precautions were flouted, the city might face "great and lamentable ruin." Of all the precautions to be observed, the most important one was to isolate all virolentos the instant their condition became known. If not already in existence, special lazarettos, or provisional hospitals, should be established for this purpose at a safe distance from settled areas. The Protomedicato was aware that few virolentos would report voluntarily for confinement; however, without exception they were a menace to the public health, and should, if necessary, be forcibly isolated. But gentler measures should not be forsaken; since many virolentos and their families felt that no treatment at all was better than confinement in a lazaretto, the Viceroy

---

[7] *Ibid.*, fols. 1, 4, 7.

should urge the populace "to give warning [of new cases], to seek assistance, and not to expose their sick to bodily and spiritual ruin for fear of separation."[8]

In view of the potentially disastrous consequences of a smallpox epidemic, the viceroy was routinely informed of the occurrence of new cases. Ordinarily he took no direct action until an emergency, clearly foreseen, was deemed too serious, or too costly, to be dealt with by lesser officials. In evaluating the merits of a given situation, he relied heavily on the opinions of his advisers and assistants. On this occasion the fiscal[9] (a legal specialist who was frequently consulted) was asked by Viceroy Revilla Gigedo to evaluate the gloomy report of the Protomedicato on the threat of smallpox.

The fiscal probed the doctors' report in search of specific evidence to confirm their forecast of "great and lamentable ruin" by October. He found none. His lawyer's appetite for facts was not satisfied with vague opinions about unknown persons who from a distance looked as if they might have had smallpox. Not a single name and address of those shadowy virolentos had been listed. On the basis of the scanty evidence provided by the Protomedicato, the fiscal could see no reason to share its alarm, but he did endorse the need for further investigation. He suggested that the ward chiefs discreetly canvass their districts in search of virolentos, and that all medical personnel, and even the priests, should report the names of any virolentos who came to their attention.

These suggestions were adopted by Intendant Bonavia, who added one of his own. To the list of informers he added the tribute collectors, who "because of their work go about among the people, deal with them closely, and gain admittance to their houses."[10] After an interval

---

[8] *Ibid.*, fol. 7v.

[9] The fiscal was an attorney for the Crown attached to the audiencia. By the end of the eighteenth century there were three fiscals attached to the Audiencia of Mexico City. They handled civil, criminal, and exchequer cases, respectively. "The *fiscal* was a sort of royal watchdog who defended the king's interests wherever they might appear. . . . He also tendered legal advice to the viceroy . . . in matters of administration." See Haring, *The Spanish Empire*, p. 130, n. 17. Unless otherwise stated, the term "fiscal" as used in this study means the "fiscal de lo civil."

[10] AGN, "Epidemias," Vol. VII, Exp. 6, fols. 8v–10, 13v.

of two weeks had passed, none of the investigators had made any report about smallpox, and on June 17 Bonavia concluded that there was no reason to fear an imminent outbreak in the capital.

The Protomedicato tried in its own way to continue the investigation. It sought to identify some of the pockmarked children who had been seen in the streets. Unfortunately it discovered the perils of acting outside one's special area of competence. Sighting the young virolentos was actually rather easy, but attempts to bring them to bay were invariably frustrated. Somewhat sourly the doctors advised the Viceroy: "It is not easy to take a child from the street without this causing a violent appeal to its father or mother, who direct it to resist, to cry out, and to make other demonstrations which stir up the onlookers."[11] Admitting defeat by insubordinate youth, the Protomedicato announced that henceforward it would confine its role to making recommendations; others could see to their adoption and enforcement. Meanwhile the recalcitrant children, some of whom no doubt actually were virolentos, walked undisturbed through the streets of the city.

About this same time another false crisis developed in Tlalnepantla —a small Indian town just north of the capital. On April 29, the parish priest of Tlalnepantla, Father Julián Crisóstomo Quintana, alerted Archbishop Núñez de Haro to the possibility of smallpox in his village. In making his report the priest was complying with standing regulations which had been issued on May 28, 1788, by Viceroy Manuel Antonio Flores (1787–1789), and which required that all curates and vicars of the colony notify higher authorities at the first sign of smallpox. Because of the proximity of Tlalnepantla to Mexico City, the Archbishop fully realized the potential threat to the health of the capital. At once he informed Intendant Bonavia of the priest's report.

The Intendant's reaction was to order the subdelegate with authority for Tlalnepantla, Luis Miqués, to go without delay to that village and prepare an exact résumé of the virolentos, showing their number, age, and personal circumstances. If Tlalnepantla lacked a

[11] *Ibid.*, fol. 29.

doctor, or necessary pharmaceutical supplies, Miqués was to arrange to provide these as quickly as possible. Furthermore, he was told to find some practical means of isolating the virolentos from the rest of the community, "since quarantine is the only method of avoiding the propagation of the contagion."[12] Obviously Bonavia assumed that the viruelas in Tlalnepantla was actually smallpox, although the first report of the sickness had been sent not by a doctor but by a priest.

Miqués, aided by Father Crisóstomo, began his assignment by endeavoring to win the cooperation of the various members of the town council of the village. This sensible approach was not sufficient to convince the Indians of the necessity of isolating their sick in some makeshift community house away from family and friends. Father Crisóstomo explained that most of his villagers were uncultured, simple people, and at the mere suspicion of confinement to a lazaretto both the sick and the well would flee. They would hide themselves in secret places in the countryside where, fearful of discovery, and not understanding the reasons for isolation in their village, they might well die without benefit of doctor or priest.

Seeking to dispel the fears of the Indians, Miqués proposed a compromise on the matter of quarantine. He suggested that instead of sheltering the virolentos in a single community house set apart from the settled area, as was the usual practice, the Indians of Tlalnepantla should build small individual grass huts at some far corner on each family's plot of ground. Supplies for the construction of such huts were abundant in the area, and without cost. Only the labor of one man for two days would be required.[13] The small family huts proposed by Miqués constituted, of course, almost a complete flouting of the principle of quarantine; however, under the circumstances, it seemed the best he could do. In such huts the virolentos could be attended by their families, who would bring them food, drink, medicine, and solace.

The favorite local treatment for smallpox was simply a tea brewed from two common herbs, borrage and poppy, "which is [the remedy] the natives are used to, and with it they treat themselves without ne-

[12] *Ibid.*, Vol. VII, Exp. 7, fols. 1, 5–5v.
[13] *Ibid.*, fols. 8–8v.

cessity of a physician or a pharmacy."[14] Father Crisóstomo explained to Miqués that the Indians had little confidence in Spanish medicine. In their view, it would be a matter of scant importance if they were never visited by Spanish doctors or treated with Spanish drugs. The priest said: "All those who have had experience with the Indians (as I have had, since in my sixty years of age I have managed them for thirty-five) will relate how they are opposed to treating themselves with Spanish medicine, and how they go through life convinced that these [the Spaniards] deceive them."[15]

Fortunately it was not necessary to attempt to impose a strict quarantine on the virolentos of Tlalnepantla, and thus the threat of a mass flight from the village was avoided. Upon receiving Miqués' disturbing report, Bonavia sent Dr. Esteban Morel, who had introduced inoculation to New Spain in 1779, to make another inspection, and to offer his professional services as needed. Morel discovered that the virolentos of Tlalnepantla, happily few in number, were not even suffering the dread disease of smallpox, but rather the superficially similar, but unrelated and relatively harmless, disease of chicken pox. Naturally the Indians were delighted with Dr. Morel and his diagnosis, while he, in turn, was incensed that they should have been needlessly upset by false reports of smallpox. All talk of lazarettos ceased, and even the small family huts which Miqués had suggested were judged useless by Morel. The doctor thought it best not to molest the simple villagers with new and strange measures. They would ignore them anyway, and this would only have the unfortunate result of furthering their disregard for the laws of the land.[16]

The only restrictive measure which Morel did seek to impose was to try to confine all the virolentos to their village for forty days. Father Crisóstomo stated that even this relatively liberal quarantine could not be enforced: "All these villagers support themselves by no other means than by preparing, and transporting to Mexico City, firewood,

[14] *Ibid.*, fols. 8v–9. Borrage (*borraja*) is credited with possessing diuretic and sudorific properties, and is often utilized in the form of a tea of 4 per cent strength. Poppy (*amapola*) has narcotic properties, especially the seeds, from which a tea is also prepared. See Jean Parker, *Mil plantas medicinales*, pp. 33, 61.

[15] AGN, "Epidemias," Vol. VII, Exp. 7, fol. 30v.

[16] *Ibid.*, fol. 24.

boards, and charcoal. Considering that they are all poor, they scarcely recover [from a sickness than] they continue in their work without keeping convalescence."[17]

Dr. Morel, in his report to Bonavia, condemned the often too hasty equation of viruelas with smallpox. The Indians of Tlalnepantla had been unduly alarmed "by the terrible sound of the name of smallpox," when in fact they were suffering from only a relatively mild ailment. Morel addressed himself rhetorically to any future investigator who might come to the village, but obviously he felt that the point he was making had universal application: "I earnestly request from whoever might come [to Tlalnepantla] that in the name of humanity and justice, he not form an opinion, nor take a sudden fear, after hearing the vague word 'viruelas,' even on those occasions in which the doctors, and even the protomédicos of this court use it, since with [the use of the term] they confuse two entirely distinct illnesses, in spite of the clarity with which I have related to them . . . and to the Superior Government, their serious and frequent errors in this matter."[18]

The outbreaks of 1793 in Mexico City and nearby Tlalnepantla had been "false alarms." It would not be considered strange, therefore, if public officials, lulled into a sense of security after their easy victory, showed little interest in pushing ahead with new plans to prevent any future spread of smallpox. Actually no victory had been won, of course, since the enemy had failed to appear, and events elsewhere indicated that Mexico City had merely won a reprieve—not a pardon —in her centuries-long fight against smallpox. In the provinces of Tabasco and Campeche this disease was sweeping across the land with epidemic intensity; smaller pockets of infection were also reported in the cities of Puebla and Vera Cruz.[19]

Since 1790 various persons in the capital had suggested that adequate arrangements should be made for a municipal lazaretto before the outbreak of another epidemic. At the time, smallpox patients were being confined at Hospital de San Antonio Abad. Since this place was

[17] *Ibid.*, fol. 31.
[18] *Ibid.*, fol. 24.
[19] Cook, "The Smallpox Epidemic of 1797," *Bulletin of the History of Medicine*, VII (October, 1939), 941; AGN, "Epidemias," Vol. VII, Exp. 8, fols. 5–10.

a leper asylum, the confinement of virolentos there meant that both groups of patients—lepers and virolentos—were exposed to an additional disease. In 1791 nine children, reportedly suffering from smallpox, were moved from the city Foundling Home to San Antonio Abad. By February 17, 1793, all nine of them had died of a horrible unknown sickness, which was apparently neither smallpox nor leprosy.[20] But in any event, a leper asylum was manifestly unsuitable as a house of quarantine.

In 1793 the city attorney for the Ayuntamiento (*síndico personero*) proposed the establishment of a separate lazaretto for virolentos. No action was taken during that year, nor the next, although the attorney's second proposal, in 1794, contains a clear assessment of the city's current resources for handling a smallpox crisis:

There is constantly observed during the time of a smallpox epidemic the most serious lack of means to assist the patients, and to effect their healing. From this fault there spring innumerable deaths, which would not occur if the more unfortunate people had [a place] to be sheltered and treated. The hospitals of this city are not capable of receiving all the sick in such critical moments, and even the setting up of provisional [ones] does not suffice.[21]

The attorney's plea that the Ayuntamiento sponsor a new lazaretto was unavailing. On August 11, 1796 (one year before the mass outbreak of smallpox in the capital), he again raised the issue, and told the city officials that he personally had determined a suitable place for a lazaretto. It was a substantial house near the College of San Pablo on the outskirts of the city. One of the Ayuntamiento's architects, José del Mazo, inspected the place and found the building and grounds adequate for sick wards, offices, a kitchen, a dispensary, and a granary. The attorney believed that the Viceroy would agree to earmark the receipts from the next bullfight for such a worthy enterprise.[22] However, the Ayuntamiento, still pleading the timeworn excuse of insufficient funds, took no action, except to refer the matter to the Protomedicato for further and fruitless study. No separate lazaretto was

---

[20] AGN, "Epidemias," Vol. XVI, Exp. 2, fols. 4–4v.
[21] *Ibid.*, Exp. 1, fol. 11. The name of the author of this report is unknown.
[22] *Ibid.*, fols. 11v–15v.

ready when the epidemic struck; when it did strike, the number of *virolentos* would prove to be so great that no single shelter could have met their needs. Yet a model lazaretto, competently staffed, well-supplied, and designed as a treatment center, would have been of great value during a major outbreak.

While the city officials haggled over the need and cost of a municipal lazaretto, new cases of smallpox were reported from the south of New Spain. On May 29, 1796, Fiscal Francisco Xavier Borbón informed Viceroy Branciforte that an ominous message had been received from Joseph Domas y Valle, the captain general of Guatemala. Domas sent word that several passengers aboard the merchant ship *La Bentura*, which had just arrived in Guatemala, were found to have but recently recovered from smallpox. This vessel, proceeding from Callao, Peru, with a cargo of fruit had anchored on April 21 at Acajutla, on the southwestern coast of Guatemala (El Salvador). The regent of the Lima Audiencia, Ambrosio Cerdá, was one of its passengers, and three of his five daughters, who had accompanied him on the voyage, displayed recent scars from smallpox. Domas, acting on his own authority, had imposed a strict quarantine on all the passengers, crew, and cargo of *La Bentura*. No person could disembark and no fruit could be unloaded until the Viceroy gave permission; an inconvenience, certainly, but at least no one aboard the vessel who liked fruit would go hungry.

In Mexico City Borbón acted promptly to study the implications of Domas' message. He advised the Viceroy that orders should be dispatched at once to all port authorities in the southern regions and that these officials should be instructed to impose an immediate quarantine on all ships proceeding from South America. Without exception no communication should be permitted between ship and shore, which meant, in effect, that even those ships from the south with no obvious signs of smallpox on board must still await the Viceroy's pleasure. It was preferable, argued Borbón, to inconvenience a few individuals rather than expose the entire population of New Spain to the threat of smallpox.[23]

Branciforte issued the order suggested by the Fiscal, and port au-

[23] *Ibid.*, Vol. XV, Exp. 5, fols. 3–4, 7.

thorities were sternly warned to quarantine all ships proceeding from ports which lay to the south of New Spain; negligent officials would be held personally accountable for nonobservance. But it became quickly obvious that this measure was not preventing the spread of smallpox —not even in the ports. In Acapulco, where particular caution had been required, seven children had contracted the disease by July 12.[24] By autumn, therefore, after various other places had also reported smallpox, it was decided to modify the coastal quarantine. In late September the brigantine *San Francisco de Asís*, proceeding from Guayaquil with a cargo of 1,750 pounds of cacao, sailed into the harbor of Acapulco. In accordance with Branciforte's order of June 8, the brigantine anchored four and one-half leagues from the place generally used for discharging goods and passengers. The Viceroy was notified of her arrival in port, and on this occasion he reversed his previous policy and authorized immediate unloading. He also restored authority to the various port officials so that they would be free to decide for themselves whether there was any valid basis for imposing quarantine.[25]

It is curious that the Viceroy and other responsible officials should have insisted that the epidemic of 1797 was caused by infection brought in from South America. As has been shown by S. F. Cook, there is no evidence which directly links the smallpox from the Peruvian ship *La Bentura* with those outbreaks which occurred elsewhere. It is certain that smallpox already existed in various parts of New Spain long before the arrival of the ship from Peru. It is also likely that the infection brought in by sea failed to spread beyond the ship—there was no report of further cases in Acajutla—and that the elaborate coastal quarantine merely diverted attention from the real sources of the epidemic. Parts of the Intendancy of Oaxaca did experience a severe epidemic of smallpox in early 1796, or not long after the arrival of the ship. But Cook suggests that "the epidemic arose elsewhere, spread in a normal manner and happened to reach Oaxaca coincident with the arrival of the Lima ship in the spring of 1796."[26]

---

[24] *Ibid.*, Exp. 3, fol. 3.   [25] *Ibid.*, Exp. 1, fols. 8–8v, 12.
[26] Cook, "The Smallpox Epidemic of 1797," *Bulletin of the History of Medicine*, VII (October, 1939), 939–940.

In any event, the matter of origin soon became of less consequence than the disturbing possibility of an approaching epidemic. On July 14, 1796, Branciforte sent an edict to various provincial officials announcing the advent of an epidemic of smallpox. He mentioned, with exaggeration, the "hundreds of sick persons, suffering from smallpox, who have come from the ports of Peru," and he also referred to separate outbreaks in the Intendancy of Oaxaca, and the cities of Vera Cruz and Acapulco: "I have dictated various measures designed to extinguish it, especially that of avoiding its propagation by the unmatched method of the separation of the infested [infected] persons a good distance from the cities . . . in order to treat them in solitary and distant sites, while making them observe a rigorous quarantine."[27]

Less than a month later, as a further precaution, the Viceroy ordered that a volume "on the method of preserving the people from smallpox" be reprinted.[28] This was the *Dissertation on Physical Medicine*, published in 1784 by Dr. Francisco Gil, a surgeon of the Monastery of San Lorenzo in Spain.[29] Gil was a bitter enemy of the use of inoculation, which he described as "imprudent, unjust, and contrary to charity and human rights . . . [and] harmful to public health."[30] Two hundred additional copies of Gil's volume were ordered. These, together with copies of a Royal Order of April 15, 1785 (also treating of smallpox), were distributed widely in the same fashion as the edict of July 14. The Royal Order, like Gil's volume, emphasized the time-tested preventive method of quarantine, which it reported had been recently used with considerable success in Louisiana. It discreetly made no mention of inoculation. José de Gálvez, who was apparently the actual author of the Royal Order of 1785, indicated that the question of smallpox would merit the personal attention of the King.[31]

Of the forty-one replies[32] to the edict of 1796, which were sent to

[27] AGN, "Epidemias," Vol. III, Exp. 1, fol. 1.
[28] *Ibid.*, Vol. XI, Exp. 1, fol. 2.
[29] *Disertación Físico-Médica, en la qual se prescribe un método seguro para preservar a los pueblos de viruelas hasta lograr la completa extinción de ellas en todo el reyno* (Madrid, 1784).
[30] Quoted in José Joaquín Izquierdo, *Montaña y los orígenes del movimiento social y científico de México*, p. 179.
[31] AGN, "Epidemias," Vol. XI, Exp. 1, fols. 2v, 4.
[32] *Ibid.*, Vol. III, Exp. 1, fols. 1–62. On fol. 5 there is a reference to the

Branciforte by the subdelegates, only one mentioned a death from smallpox. Obviously by late summer of 1796 smallpox had not generally spread throughout the provinces of New Spain. On August 20, 1796, the single death and also one convalescent were reported from Taxco.[33] Querétaro reported on August 13: "Until now there has not been the least notice" of smallpox.[34] The Intendant of Oaxaca reported on August 5: "Until now the sickness has not struck" the city of Oaxaca.[35] (However, the disease had appeared in some of the smaller towns in the Intendancy of Oaxaca. As early as July 1, forty-eight persons had already died of smallpox in the Oaxacan village of San Miguel Chimpala.[36]) All forty-one letters contained the usual assurances of prompt compliance with the Viceroy's edict. The Intendant of Taxco reported, for example, that he had called a meeting of prominent miners and other reputable persons to discuss the implementation of the edict. A writer from the village of Chilapa stated that punctual compliance would follow "in spite of many difficulties . . . because these people will not conform . . . neither would I be able to compel them to observe it [the edict] because of the lack of supplies and assistance."[37]

In spite of the lack of reports of deaths from smallpox in the summer of 1796, the disease spread rapidly in the final months of that year. By December, the first case—quickly followed by others—was noted in the city of Oaxaca.[38] In the same month the village of Sierra

---

"forty-three copies [of the Instruction] for the subdelegates of the provinces of Mexico." Forty-one of their letters of reply are found in fols. 14–62. Most of the letters are dated July and August of 1796. Since this file of letters appears to be complete, or nearly so, it furnishes an accurate means of gauging the onset of the epidemic in the provinces.

[33] *Ibid.*, fol. 45.

[34] *Ibid.*, fol. 38.

[35] *Ibid.*, fol. 19.

[36] Cook, "The Smallpox Epidemic of 1797," *Bulletin of the History of Medicine*, VII (October, 1939), Table I, "Information concerning the spread of the epidemic in Oaxaca," 948, fourth entry.

[37] AGN, "Epidemias," Vol. III, Exp. 1, fols. 46–46v. This town is in the state of Guerrero, and is now known as Chilapa de Alvarez. In the document the name of the town is spelled "Chilapán."

[38] Cook, "The Smallpox Epidemic of 1797," *Bulletin of the History of Medicine*, VII (October, 1939), Table I, 948, next-to-the-last entry.

de Piños, in Zacatecas, reported several cases.[39] The epidemic was on the march. With new outbreaks both to the north and to the south of the capital, Branciforte feared that it might be impossible to prevent its spread to Mexico City.

Endeavoring to prevent such a fateful occurrence, Branciforte, on February 28, 1797, issued a second edict on smallpox. It sought to incorporate the best thinking of the times regarding the prevention and the treatment of this highly contagious disease. Consequently it was issued only after consultation with the Protomedicato, the fiscal of the Treasury Department, and the assessor general, who, respectively, offered medical, financial, and legal advice. Inoculation was prominently, albeit cautiously, mentioned in the edict, but the operation was recommended only on a voluntary basis. The edict stated that four precautionary measures had traditionally enjoyed general acceptance as the best defense against smallpox.[40] These were immediate isolation of the first sufferers of smallpox; the burial of victims of the disease in cemeteries far from population centers; the stoppage of all communication with affected places; and the use of inoculation, which had been practiced (mainly in recent years) on a voluntary and limited basis with some success. While still retained, and even emphasized, these four measures had proved to be inadequate in the present crisis, and various supplemental measures were thought to be necessary. Branciforte reported:

In spite of my continual vigilance, the smallpox has unfortunately spread in Oajaca [*sic*], and it will not be strange if the same thing begins to happen in other sections nearer to this capital. For this reason it has seemed to me necessary to establish new and more rigorous precautions with respect to the state of the disease in this city (Mexico), it being of the greatest importance to do this before the disease begins to appear in other towns and spreads and propagates itself.[41]

[39] AGN, "Epidemias," Vol. III, Exp. 2, fol. 106.
[40] *Ibid.*, Vol. XVI, Exp. 8, fols. 1–3v.
[41] *Ibid.*, fols. 1–1v; S. F. Cook, "Smallpox in Spanish and Mexican California: 1770–1845," *Bulletin of the History of Medicine*, VII (February, 1939), 159. In this article Cook has published, on pages 158–163, his English translation of the entire text of Branciforte's edict of February 28, 1797. For this quotation I have used his translation without change.

Besides incorporating the four traditional preventive measures, Branciforte's edict of 1797 supplemented these with additions that he and his advisers thought necessary. The edict contains thirteen sections, each of which, because of its importance, is paraphrased below.[42]

1. All towns shall provide a lazaretto of sufficient size to accommodate all virolentos of the area. The building must be situated in a remote place and face the prevailing winds. All virolentos, without any exception being made, shall be removed to the lazaretto, where they, and their nurses, shall be left in absolute separation from the town.

2. Since isolation is almost the only preventive method known, the priests, religious prelates, doctors, and subordinate judges shall immediately inform higher authorities of all virolentos who come to their attention, so that such persons may be immediately removed to the lazaretto.

3. To facilitate this method, judges shall prepare a plan for dividing their town into blocks (subdivisions), to be supervised by subordinates, city officials, or responsible citizens. The latter, by means of frequent inspections, can easily and discreetly discover any smallpox victims, and persuade them peacefully to enter a lazaretto.

4. At the first sign of a serious epidemic, all communication must be severed between affected and nonaffected areas. Guards should be posted at appropriate places and, if necessary, a *cordón* should be set up to guarantee that not the slightest means of communication are left open.

5. Communication may be had solely in conjunction with the quarantine which must be observed, without exception, by all persons who have traveled through the infected area. Freight and goods will also be subject to the same regulations.

6. If the measures described above in [Sections] four and five should become necessary, bonfires shall be placed at the entrances

---

[42] In paraphrasing this portion of Branciforte's edict I have, on occasion, followed literally Cook's excellent translation.

and exits of the towns and villages, and these shall be kept burning day and night to purify the air. Judges shall take care that no damage results to crops or real property.

7. Letters sent from infected regions shall be fumigated with sulphur, after first wrapping them in damp paper which also shall be fumigated. Messengers must wear linen clothing, which must be removed before entering any town, even if the town is not infected.

8. If the epidemic cannot be halted by the above methods, inoculation should be introduced on a voluntary basis. The lazaretto, or provisional hospital, should be enlarged to receive and to treat poor persons who have been inoculated, or who desire this operation. The Protomedicato will prepare clear and simple statements on inoculation and smallpox.

9. If the above-mentioned provisional hospital is inadequate, then charitable societies shall be organized of all persons who are able to contribute their alms to the unfortunate victims. Since the poor people ordinarily live in the suburbs, and these districts have more needy than wealthy persons, each of the poorer districts shall be made a part of a wealthier one, so that citizens of the latter may aid those of the former. The Church should use the same system with regard to assignment of parish priests. In this way all persons and classes may contribute to the relief of humanity, and cooperate for the restoration of the public health.

10. Victims of smallpox must be buried in remote places outside churches and apart from their regular cemeteries. The bishops and priests should consult with the judges concerning sites and costs.

11. Aside from measures derived from human wisdom, such as the above, nothing will do more to stop the epidemic than fervent prayers to God, His Holy Mother, and His Saints, imploring their mercy and protection by public and private supplications.

12. If all regular sources of funds have been utterly exhausted, then the judges may draw upon public funds and community property. Such withdrawals must be expended with the most rigid economy and with due process of municipal law.

13. If the magistrates, bishops, curates, justices, physicians, or other persons to whom this edict is addressed, should think of other useful methods, aside from those here described, and which would not prejudice the public funds, they should call them to my attention.

The edict of February 28, 1797, like the one of July 14, 1796, was dispatched to a great many provincial centers. Copies were sent as far from the capital as California, even to San Francisco, on the outermost rim of New Spain, although fortunately California escaped any serious visitation of smallpox at that time. The commandant at San Francisco reported that copies would be sent to all outlying missions and garrisons, and that if smallpox should appear he would set an example by having his family inoculated first.[43] Earlier, in response to the edict of 1796, the subdelegate of Otumba had stated that the Viceroy's edict would be posted, as was the custom, at the town plaza on market day. By this means inhabitants of haciendas, ranches, and villages located outside of Otumba would be informed. At the same time, the intendant at Taxco reported that the edict of 1796 was being translated into the language of the Indians.[44] It is likely that these same measures were used in Otumba, Taxco, and elsewhere to comply with the edict of 1797, as well as with all other notices worthy of public attention.

As with the earlier edict, some of the Viceroy's provincial correspondents reported in 1797 that they found it difficult to comply. For example, the subdelegate of Pachuca reported that his town had made suitable arrangements for a provisional hospital, but that the chief problem was not quarters but funds: "The major difficulty, Your Excellency . . . [is] that of providing for the nourishment and support of these people, considering that in this jurisdiction there are no community properties, nor public lands. This area is full of misfortunes and miseries since the mines are totally abandoned, with the exception of those of the Count of Regla."[45]

[43] Cook, "Smallpox in Spanish and Mexican California," *Bulletin of the History of Medicine*, VII (February, 1939), 153–154, 158, n. 7.
[44] AGN, "Epidemias," Vol. III, Exp. 1, fols. 25, 44.
[45] *Ibid.*, Exp. 2, fol. 81.

The Threat Draws Closer

The first indication, long awaited, that the epidemic might finally have reached Mexico City came early in August, 1797. On the third day of that month, José Ignacio García Jove, by then the president of the Protomedicato, reported the admission of two virolentos to Hospital de San Andrés. These patients were young soldiers who had recently been transferred with their regiment from the mountain village of Otumba, to the northeast of the city. One young man displayed virulent symptoms, and García Jove feared that the recent troop movements might have dispersed the infection over a wide area. Almost immediately additional cases of smallpox were reported in the city. García Jove personally discovered one in Hospital Real de Indios, where he was a member of the staff. He also learned that in Santiago Tlatelolco, an Indian district of the capital, many others were plagued with the same sickness.[46]

Another positive identification of smallpox was made at Hospital Real de Indios by José Francisco Rada, also a member of the Protomedicato. Although required to do so by the edict of February 28, Rada did not bother to make any official report, so the case did not immediately become known to the Viceroy. But José del Rincón, the administrator of the hospital, assured Branciforte that proper procedures had been observed; both the patient and her nurse had been isolated, and the nurse had promised in writing to observe the quarantine.[47]

The general situation worsened on August 10 with the information that smallpox had appeared in three more villages, all close to the capital. These were Texcoco to the east and Tlalnepantla and Azcapotzalco to the north.[48] Since for some months certain other areas to the south had been infected, the capital city was now surrounded on three sides by pockets of the disease. García Jove became alarmed at the thought that perhaps the hour might have passed already when the implementation of a quarantine could spare the city another epidemic. Indeed, so great was his concern that when the assessor general

[46] *Ibid.*, Vol. XVI, Exp. 6, fols. 1–3; Vol. XI, Exp. 1, fol. 5.
[47] *Ibid.*, Vol. XVI, Exp. 6, fol. 20.
[48] *Ibid.*, fol. 7v.

ordered that the two soldiers be transferred from Hospital de San Andrés to Hospital de San Lázaro (on the outskirts of the city), he refused to permit the transfer, believing that even a brief exposure of these *virolentos* in public would be an unwise risk. The assessor general, recognizing the Protomedicato's special competence in this matter, did not insist that his order be obeyed.[49]

The Audiencia also became involved in the matter of the epidemic because of the fact that the Viceroy was out of the city. Branciforte was at Orizaba, a pleasant mountain retreat, where he remained throughout the course of the epidemic. His motives for such an extended absence from the capital in a time of crisis should not be judged too hastily, for Orizaba also experienced a severe outbreak of smallpox.[50] The Viceroy sought to keep in touch with affairs in Mexico City through his frequent correspondence with the two ranking members of the Audiencia, Baltasar Ladrón y Guevara, the regent, and Cosme de Mier y Trespalacios, the senior judge (*decano*).[51] On August 10, Mier, in one of his first letters to Branciforte concerning the epidemic, reported that stricter measures were needed to prevent

---

[49] *Ibid.*, fols. 3–4, 7.

[50] Cook, "The Smallpox Epidemic of 1797," *Bulletin of the History of Medicine*, VII (October, 1939), Table II, 952. Orizaba had had 1,727 cases and 277 deaths when the epidemic was about half over. The percentage of deaths in Orizaba was slightly higher than in Mexico City.

[51] The post of regent was created in each of the various audiencias of the empire in 1776. This official ranked next below the viceroy, and in the event of the death or absence of the latter, the regent might exercise his powers ad interim. The regent was responsible for the general management of all the day-to-day details of the audiencia's organization and functions. See Haring, *The Spanish Empire*, pp. 132–133.

Mier temporarily held the title of Delegate (*Delegado*) during the Viceroy's absence. This title officially belonged to Regent Baltasar Ladrón y Guevara, who was, at the time, suffering from "afflictions" and was unable to serve. On October 9, Branciforte decided that Mier should continue in charge of "the measures related to smallpox, in spite of the fact that the *señor Regente* of the Royal Audiencia is now recovered from his afflictions." (He died in 1804.) For all other matters except smallpox, it was clearly stated that the Regent's authority was superior to that of the Chief Justice of the audiencia (*Oidor Decano*) or the City Superintendent (*Superintendente de ciudad*), both of which titles were held by Mier. Mier continued, however, to sign papers relating to smallpox as the "Delegado." See AGN, "Epidemias," Vol. I, Exp. 7, fols. 490–491v.

the further spread of the disease. Above all, he cautioned, "infection of the air" must be prevented, although he suggested no specific means for accomplishing this end.[52]

The Protomedicato acted quickly in the first stages of the epidemic to invite various prominent physicians to meet with it in joint session to discuss the general situation. It was unanimously agreed that Mexico City faced an immediate epidemic of smallpox.[53] In the doctors' view, a general program of public inoculation offered the only effective means of preventing such a calamity. This proposal was urged in spite of the feeling of some of the doctors that it seemed to run counter to the edict of February 28, which said that quarantine offered "almost the only known method" of fighting smallpox.[54] The doctors were convinced that Branciforte preferred quarantine over inoculation as the most effective preventive measure. It was true that his edict had commended inoculation, but it had also directed that its use must be completely voluntary, and that it should be generally employed only after simpler methods had first been tried. Furthermore (and this was the crux of the problem), the edict required—or so it seemed to the doctors—that all *inoculados* must be quarantined in the same strict manner as if they had acquired the disease by natural exposure. But if such a provision was to be literally enforced it would render impossible the wholesale use of inoculation. It was obviously impractical to try to force thousands of inoculados into lazarettos for many days, particularly when (in the doctors' view) their mild form of sickness rarely if ever posed any genuine threat to the public health.

The solution to the knotty problem of general inoculation hinged on Branciforte's willingness to permit the unrestricted use of the operation outside, and completely divorced from, lazarettos. The doctors were aware of the popular fear and hatred of lazarettos, and they also knew that if submitting to inoculation meant that confinement would follow, then most persons would simply refuse to be inoculated. Consequently the physicians virtually demanded that the Viceroy au-

[52] AGN, "Epidemias," Vol. XVI, Exp. 6, fol. 8.

[53] *Ibid.*, Exp. 7, fol. 8.

[54] Cook, "Smallpox in Spanish and Mexican California," *Bulletin of the History of Medicine*, VII (February, 1939), 159.

thorize unrestricted inoculation apart from lazarettos. It was their consensus that no better preventive existed; obviously they placed little reliance on quarantine.[55]

The efficacy of inoculation, particularly during an epidemic, was widely disputed in the eighteenth century. Branciforte was right when he argued that inoculation was dangerous, and that inoculados could spread the infection in the same manner as those persons who had been naturally exposed to the disease. John Duffy has written that although inoculation was a relatively safe procedure, "the individual inoculated *was* capable of infecting nonimmune contacts with a deadly and loathsome disease."[56] Furthermore, the value of the procedure varied considerably from place to place, making generalizations on its over-all value somewhat hazardous: "In England, where variolation [inoculation] was restricted to a relatively small percentage of the upper classes during the eighteenth century, the practice was of doubtful value; but in the British American colonies, where it was given a more extensive trial, it was an important factor in reducing smallpox fatalities."[57] As mentioned earlier, the records of the epidemic of 1797 have nearly all been preserved, and these leave no doubt that the most responsible members of the community in that year almost unanimously favored inoculation. Such convinced persons included the Protomedicato, private physicians, members of the Ayuntamiento, and especially the modern-minded Archbishop, Alonso Núñez de Haro y Peralta. As will be seen later in this chapter, as more of the story of inoculation has been presented, the Protomedicato claimed that the death rate for inoculados in 1797 ran less than 1 per cent.[58] At best, inoculation was the lesser of two evils, but on balance there can be little doubt that the physicians had the best of the argument in 1797, and that inoculation, in spite of the risk, was

[55] AGN, "Epidemias," Vol. XVI, Exp. 7, fols. 8–8v. As early as March 27, 1797, the Protomedicato requested that the Viceroy make arrangements for the transfer of smallpox pus from Puebla so that inoculation might be started in Mexico City. *Ibid.*, Vol. III, Exp. 2, fol. 107.

[56] Personal communication, John Duffy to Donald B. Cooper, December 10, 1964. (Italics mine.)

[57] John Duffy, *Epidemics in Colonial America*, p. 24.

[58] AGN, "Epidemias," Vol. VI, Exp. [7], fols. 204–204v.

the best weapon in the medical profession's limited arsenal against smallpox.

The Protomedicato sought to dramatize its previously expressed conviction that a general epidemic would bring disaster in its train:

This Tribunal cannot ignore the irreparable harm which comes to the bodies and souls of smallpox victims who, devoid of all assistance, suffer their ailment [alone, since] they are so afraid of being discovered that they summon neither doctors nor priests. The President of the Tribunal, for example, [learned] of such a situation today. He had been advised that on the corner of Machincuepa Street there was a sufferer from smallpox. He went immediately to visit the patient, and found him unable to be moved because of the seriousness [of his condition]. He was without spiritual assistance, which his mother wanted but did not seek, since she feared that the priest might inform on her.[59]

The doctors speculated that similar pathetic situations might be occurring frequently in Mexico City, and they feared the worst if Branciforte did not relax his orders which, in their view, had impeded the wholesale practice of public inoculations.

The doctors' report was scrutinized by Fiscal Francisco Xavier Borbón, whose lengthy evaluation for the Viceroy was compounded about equally of sycophantic praise and trenchant analysis. Borbón professed amazement that a new smallpox epidemic should threaten the city in view of the "unmatched zeal, steadfastness, and effort with which Your Excellency has proceeded to dictate incessant and continual measures to avoid the propagation and contagion of smallpox."[60] Then, preliminaries aside, Borbón shifted readily to the specifics of a dangerous situation. He advised Branciforte to demand a full report from the subdelegate of Otumba—from which place had come the infected army regiment. But he said nothing about quarantining the regiment, a measure which had been recommended by the Protomedicato.

The Fiscal rejected the doctors' arguments on the need for relaxing the stated policy on inoculation. He denied that "two or three" cases

---

[59] AGN, "Epidemias," Vol. XVI, Exp. 7, fols. 8v–9.
[60] *Ibid.*, fol. 10.

of smallpox constituted an epidemic (other sources clearly indicate that a larger, although unspecified, number of cases was actually present). From checking the records Borbón had learned of several occasions in the past when a few cases had been discovered in the city and yet no epidemic had resulted. Furthermore, why should the existence of only "two or three" cases mean that a quarantine would not be effective? If this were so, then quarantine—recognized for centuries as the best defense against smallpox—could never have been of much value. But such a conclusion was inadmissible. Borbón therefore concluded that the doctors had condemned quarantine simply to put pressure on the residents of the capital to receive inoculation.[61] Under no circumstances, therefore, would he recommend that the Viceroy modify his edict of February 28. This meant, in effect—in the Fiscal's view—that inoculados must still face the prospect of quarantine in lazarettos.

The tough-minded Fiscal also saw scant merit in the doctors' pathetic story about the virolento from Machincuepa Street, whose mother had feared to summon medical or clerical help: "Of those inconveniences which follow from the hiding of the sick, contrary to the most just and correct intentions and purposes of this Superior Government, and of Your Excellency, neither God, nor the King, nor the public is, nor can be, nor ought to be, held responsible."[62]

On the basis of the evidence, Borbón could see no valid reason why an epidemic should be considered "inevitable." This frightful sequel was unlikely to occur unless the Protomedicato knew of more cases which, because of "some private purposes or motives," had not been reported. If such cases existed they should be made known, "with the sincerity and truth which ought to be held proper in a matter of such enormous gravity and importance."[63] It seems likely that Borbón had *not* been fully informed of the true number of cases. Mier also accused the Protomedicato of submitting late and incomplete reports. This charge was hotly denied by García Jove, who said that when reports were not submitted it was because nothing had happened which

[61] *Ibid.*, fols. 11v–14v.
[62] *Ibid.*, fols. 13v–14.
[63] *Ibid.*, fol. 14.

was worth reporting.[64] As we have already seen, however, one of García Jove's colleagues, Dr. José Francisco Rada, did fail to report a case of smallpox he had discovered.

Mier wrote to the Viceroy and recommended a "wait-and-see" policy, as he too, like Borbón, deemphasized the threat of an epidemic. Hospital de San Andrés was equipped to receive many more virolentos,[65] and Mier saw no need to make any changes in the policies of prevention already in force. Branciforte concluded that perhaps the capital might yet be spared an epidemic, but he apparently had forgotten the long tradition that in Mexico City October is the month when epidemics of smallpox spring to life.

By mid-August there were valid grounds for optimism since smallpox had not appeared in force, but Branciforte, despite his initial optimism, continued to alert those persons whose cooperation might be needed. He reminded the prior of Hospital de San Juan de Dios and the administrators of Hospital de San Andrés and Hospital Real de Indios that absolute separation would be required for all virolentos: "Immediately upon entry to that hospital of any patient with smallpox you will place him in absolute separation from the others, and advise me with no loss of time, and send me each day a clear report which expresses what was done in the course of his sickness, treatment, convalescence, and quarantine."[66] The nursing staff attending the virolentos was also required to maintain quarantine.[67]

Branciforte addressed an important letter to the curates of Mexico City on August 21:

We are not, nor would God wish to see us, in the midst of a formal epidemic, but there having been found some sufferers from smallpox in Hospital de San Andrés, and in that of Naturales [Hospital Real de Indios], and fearing that among the people of the city there might also be others touched with the same sickness, who because of their fear of being removed to a lazaretto . . ., they elect to die unaided rather than seek spiritual and temporal assistance, which indeed they should have; [so we

[64] *Ibid.*, Exp. 6, fol. 90.
[65] *Ibid.*, Exp. 7, fol. 17.
[66] *Ibid.*, Exp. 6, fol. 13.
[67] *Ibid.*, Vol. XI, Exp. 1, fol. 9.

say] it is of the greatest importance that by all prudent means one should try to avoid in time the consequences of such unfortunate negligence.[68]

The curates were reminded that even in death the virolento must be segregated from persons who had died of any other cause. Furthermore, the priests must not conduct, nor permit, any funeral service inside a church or convent until it was established beyond all doubt that the deceased had not died of smallpox. The priests were also directed to cooperate with responsible citizens in the common effort to gather information on the disease. At the same time, Mier was actively engaged in developing other sources of confidential information. Druggists were ordered to report any person who purchased medicine for domestic treatment of smallpox. Confidential agents were ordered to search the city for unreported cases. Such eavesdropping, conducted mainly in the Indian neighborhoods, did disclose several new cases—most of them children. None had been seen by a doctor; their only treatment had been "borrage water, syrup of carnation, and light foods," a domestic remedy which may have done more to ease the minds of worried parents than to help the sick bodies of their children.[69]

Mier devoted himself to the problem posed by the lack of a special burial ground for virolentos. In a letter to Archbishop Núñez de Haro he suggested that grounds adjacent to the Church of San Pedro and San Pablo might be suitable.[70] But the Archbishop, in a thoughtful analysis, opposed this plan. His reasons were chiefly two. In the first place, the church was well within the limits of the city, and plentiful springs of drinking water flowed nearby. To bury the bodies of virolentos so close to a public water supply was merely to invite further contamination. In the second place, the courtyard of the church was too small for the purpose; in the dreadful epidemic of 1779 it had been entirely filled with the corpses of smallpox victims. Núñez de Haro suggested instead that the cemetery of Hospital de San Andrés would be preferable. It was safely removed from major population centers, it had spacious capacity for as many as fifteen thousand

[68] *Ibid.*, Vol. XVI, Exp. 6, fol. 22. See also *ibid.*, Vol. XI, Exp. 1, fol. 13.
[69] *Ibid.*, Vol. XVI, Exp. 6, fols. 48–48v.
[70] *Ibid.*, Vol. XI, Exp. 1, fol. 18v.

bodies, and also a very adequate chapel where the mass could be said. Furthermore, in terms of its remoteness from the paths of prevailing winds, it was one of the most healthful locations in the valley, or so the city's doctors and surgeons had declared. Núñez de Haro was fully aware that many of his coreligionists considered a "Christian" burial as synonymous with interment either in the courtyard or in the sanctuary of a church. Therefore he had taken pains to bless personally this rural burial ground at San Andrés, and also its chapel, with the "greatest solemnity, so that the people of the country might overcome the reluctance they have to bury their children, relatives, and servants in cemeteries [apart from churches]."[71] As a special concession to people of means, the Archbishop agreed that virolentos from this group might be buried in the more pretentious Convents of San Cosme and San Hipólito. These too were built in dry, well-ventilated sites in the suburbs.

The question of the need for a municipal lazaretto was again brought before the Viceroy when Mier reminded him that none had been established in the capital. All persons, Mier reported—not merely the common people—were opposed to the use of quarantine. This view was reinforced by the opinion of the Archbishop, who believed that the people "fear this measure more than the terrible effects of the epidemic." The Archbishop admitted that there was a genuine basis for the popular hatred of lazarettos, since it was public knowledge that those that had been used in Oaxaca the year before had been places of horror.[72]

During the last week of August several new cases of smallpox were reported, not only from Mexico City but from surrounding villages as well. The village of San Juánico, near Tacuba, reported one death from smallpox, and on August 26 four more virolentos were admitted to Hospital de San Andrés.[73] The curate of the parish of the Sagrario, José Alcalá, mentioned that he had learned, from the confessions of their parents, of three sick and unattended children, all of whom had smallpox. The priest suggested that "this fear [of lazarettos] is so general and so rooted in the public [mind] that no persuasion serves

[71] *Ibid.*, Vol. XVI, Exp. 6, fols. 28–29.
[72] *Ibid.*, fol. 27v.
[73] *Ibid.*, fols. 35, 40.

to dispel it."[74] That same day García Jove (he had never retracted his earlier statement that an epidemic was inevitable) advised Branciforte that "the multitude of sick persons still hidden from view indicates the spread of the contagion."[75] Inoculation, he said, should begin at once, and the fact of its delay had been wrongly attributed to motives of the Protomedicato. He sought the Viceroy's permission to begin at once a program of unrestricted inoculation in Hospital de San Andrés.

One physician, Luis José Montaña, who was one of the most distinguished Mexican doctors of his time (1755–1820), unwilling to see his young daughter "abandoned to the fortunes of the epidemic," proceeded to inoculate her without specific authorization from the Viceroy. Montaña believed that the dangerous course of the epidemic permitted no delay. "On this very day," he wrote, "there circulates reliable information that the neighboring towns, certain suburbs, and many houses of this capital find themselves infected with that epidemic." He claimed that he was proceeding in accordance with Section 8 of Branciforte's edict of February 28, overlooking that it had been addressed to certain public officials for implementation rather than to private persons. Montaña expressed complete confidence in the value of inoculation and said that its use was essential to the public welfare. The person who should ignore or disobey the Viceroy's edict on inoculation (i.e., fail to be inoculated) "would be nothing less than a traitor to the fatherland."[76] Montaña also reported that many members of the first families of Mexico City had invited him to their homes to perform the operation. A week later Branciforte took note of the fact that Montaña had proceeded without permission, but in view of the circumstances he chose to ignore the violation.

Mier, who was a man of much greater influence than was García Jove, added his voice to the growing clamor for general inoculation. He told Branciforte that the professors of the medical school were unanimous in its praises, and that the operation had been used with great success in the recent epidemic in Oaxaca. In Mexico City inoculation should begin at once, he said, since summer was waning,

[74] *Ibid.*, fol. 41.
[75] *Ibid.*, fols. 40–40v.
[76] *Ibid.*, fols. 43–44.

and the harmful chills of winter would complicate the administration of this preventive.[77] But supplemental measures would also be needed. Mier drew upon the records of the epidemic of 1779 to suggest that the capital should be divided into special districts to facilitate the relief of the poor. Funds for such assistance should be solicited from prominent corporate groups, such as the Tribunals of Minería and Consulado, and private citizens, if known to have funds, should also be enlisted.

By August 30, Pedro Jacinto Valenzuela, the Viceroy's assessor general, a leading legal advisor, had had time to evaluate all the reports submitted to Branciforte on the epidemic. On the basis of such information, as supplied by Mier, Fiscal Borbón, the Protomedicato, and others, Valenzuela concluded that the capital faced an impending crisis. Furthermore, each day brought fresh reports of smallpox from both the capital and the outlying towns. Many persons had been seen walking about the city displaying unmistakable signs of their recent recovery. The large number of such persons who had been seen in public, and the relatively small number of cases that had been officially reported, suggested to Valenzuela that perhaps the current outbreak was not especially virulent. But even so he, unlike Borbón, joined in the growing demands for inoculation. Viceregal opposition to the use of this preventive began to weaken when Valenzuela happily hit upon a formula for saving His Excellency's pride. Retreat with honor became possible. He suggested to Branciforte that if Section 8 of his edict of February 28 had been *correctly* read and understood, it would have been seen that it posed no obstacle to the free use of inoculation. Thus for more than six months, he said, the Protomedicato had already *had* the permission it was now so vigorously demanding.[78]

Using the flexible reasoning of Valenzuela as a basis, Branciforte, on August 31, sent an important letter to the Protomedicato which "reaffirmed" his endorsement of inoculation. Since it contained such a vital statement of policy, copies were also sent to various other places. The fact that a person or agency was sent a copy of the letter was a clear indication that Branciforte expected the recipient to play

[77] *Ibid.*, fols. 46–46v.
[78] *Ibid.*, fols. 49v–55, *passim.*

a major role in fighting the epidemic. Of all the officials who were sent copies of the letter, one of them, Cosme de Mier y Trespalacios (d. 1805), was emerging, even at this early stage of the epidemic, as the man who would play the leading role. As mentioned earlier, in the matter of the smallpox epidemic he was second in authority only to the Viceroy himself, and since Branciforte remained at Orizaba for the duration of the epidemic, Mier was clearly in command at Mexico City. But Mier enjoyed great power and influence aside from his close ties with the Viceroy, being also the senior judge of the Audiencia and the city's superintendent of Rents and Lands, which, because this branch of the municipal government controlled the purse strings, was the most powerful office within the complex structure of the Ayuntamiento. Concurrently, then, Mier held three key administrative positions involving viceregal service, the courts, and the city government, and it is obvious that with such great power he could get things done, for he could cooperate, coordinate, or coerce, as he thought best.

Mier's staunchest ally in fighting the epidemic was Archbishop Núñez de Haro. He was an outstanding churchman whose devotion to the spiritual and temporal well-being of his people stands forth clearly after the passing of a great many years. He seems most remarkable as an efficient administrator, one who acted quickly on various fronts to expedite the fight against the epidemic. By 1797, after twenty-six years as the archbishop, Nuñez de Haro had seen many viceroys come and go; in fact he himself served as ad interim viceroy for about a year in 1786–1787. In 1779 he had played a major role in fighting the epidemic of that same year. He knew a great deal about both viceroys and epidemics, and he cooperated superbly with the former to the diminution of the latter.

Many other persons and groups aided in the fight against the epidemic. In the ecclesiastical realm the governing body of the metropolitan cathedral of Mexico City—the dean and Cabildo—made a major contribution, as did also many of the parish priests of the capital. The Tribunal of the Protomedicato, composed of three distinguished physicians and a small staff of assistants, was the leading medical body of the colony, and played a major role in the day-to-day routine of medicine and health. But it was not equipped to handle the complex problems of a major epidemic, during which occasions its chief role was consultive. Two other tribunals of the city contributed both money and leadership in the common effort against smallpox: the Consulado, an association of merchants; and Minería, an association of miners, which enjoyed considerable independent authority in supervising the mining industry.

None of the above-mentioned groups had been expressly created for the purpose of fighting the epidemic. It was inevitable, however, that in a time of crisis they would be called upon to serve. They represented, directly or indirectly, in both the civil and ecclesiastical realms, the most powerful offices and men in the colony. All levels of government, from the King's alter ego—the Viceroy—to the ward chief who served within the framework of the Ayuntamiento, were included within the cast of those who fought the epidemic. Success or failure was their responsibility. The men who served in 1797 had inherited a long tradition of influence and power, and it was unthinkable that as the Viceroy assembled his men and resources to face the challenge of the epidemic such important men would not answer his summons. Their councils were not invariably harmonious and on occasion disagreements were pronounced. But many had seen with their own eyes, and in their own city, the horrors of a general epidemic. Duty and privilege were inherent in their stations in life, and given the terrible challenge of another epidemic, they generally brushed aside past differences and joined in the common effort. This was particularly true during the epidemic of 1797. As the contagion spread throughout the city, few of these men needed to be reminded of their obligations. Branciforte's letter of August 31, sent to all the agencies and men mentioned above, was simply the formal announcement that once again the city would go forth to fight its most dangerous foe—the terrible killer, smallpox.

Preparations for an Impending Crisis

The content of that letter of August 31 was less dramatic than its purpose. It was ostensibly nothing more than a reply from Branciforte to the Protomedicato's letter to him of August 10. This letter, which had been sent to the Viceroy following the Protomedicato's joint meeting with other prominent physicians of the city, had demanded a relaxation of his assumed opposition to inoculation. Branciforte, armed with the curious reasoning of his legal counsel Valenzuela, informed the champions of inoculation that their letter "had done nothing more than propose what I have already ordered."[79] The Tribunal was advised that *it* should delay no longer in initiating a program of free and voluntary public inoculation. Furthermore (and this was the key concession), Branciforte stated that the forced confinement of inoculados in lazarettos need not be carried out.

It would appear, however, that Branciforte had given his approval of public inoculation with mental reservations since once the program was in operation he prudently reminded the Tribunal that he expected the inoculados to observe sensible precautions and to appear in public as little as possible. He believed that it would be unwise for them to attend school or go to church. Furthermore, "It is not necessary that they breathe fresh and pure air to obtain the favorable effects of inoculation."[80] The Tribunal never became convinced that it had converted Branciforte to its own point of view regarding inoculation, and it was probably chagrined, if not startled, to read his letter of August 31 advising the doctors to expedite inoculation without further delay. "Consequently I advise Your Excellencies that you and the physicians are speedily to put into practice the aforesaid preventive method, meaning for those heads of families who truly wish to adopt it; especially after they have seen it used on the doctors' and surgeons' own children."[81] Branciforte advised the Protomedicato that he had also sought the cooperation of the parish priests of the capital in this matter. They had been instructed to make it known discreetly to their parishioners that inoculation now had viceregal approval.

Branciforte also stated that a provisional hospital would be established in the city for the purpose of performing inoculations and treating those persons who *preferred* to stay there for convalescence. If the inoculado, however, had the personal means and could buy his own medicine, he should convalesce in his own home.[82] In separate

[79] AGN, "Epidemias," Vol. XVI, Exp. 6, fol. 56.
[80] *Ibid.*, Vol. XI, Exp. 2, fol. 163.
[81] *Ibid.*, Vol. XVI, Exp. 6, fols. 56–56v.
[82] *Ibid.*, fols. 56v–57.

letters, also dated August 31, Branciforte informed Núñez de Haro, the dean and Cabildo of the Cathedral, and the priors of the Convents of San Cosme and San Hipólito that the Archbishop's recent suggestions on burial sites had been adopted.

In his fawning reply the dean of the Cathedral praised the "wise, zealous, and compassionate measures [which the Viceroy has] directed to the relief of humanity . . . and to the reestablishment of the public health."[83] He promised full obedience to the edict of February 28 and requested a copy for reference. The Archbishop, as was his custom, came directly to the point in his reply. He said that he had already arranged for placing five hundred more beds, solely for virolentos, in Hospital de San Andrés. Separate wards would be maintained for the sexes. Each would have its own laundry and service facilities completely set apart from those of the five hundred non-smallpox patients in the hospital. The Archbishop continued:

I have given the strictest orders to the curates of Mexico City, and their vicars, and I will also give them to other secular ecclesiastics, so that, in cooperation with the commissioners who may be named by the [municipal] subdivisions they may assist spiritually, temporally, and however possible the sick persons infected with smallpox who are not able to go to the hospitals. . . . I have also commanded that they transport to the [Hospital] General [de San Andrés], on the stretchers provided for this purpose, all the poor persons who may be carried there without danger.[84]

The Archbishop also promised to try to encourage the use of inoculation in the provincial parishes outside Mexico City. On October 6 he sent a circular letter to this effect to fifty-two places outside the capital, most of them in the still largely unaffected northern regions of the colony. The priests of the provinces were ordered "to exhort and persuade with the greatest zeal" so that their parishioners would consent to be inoculated.[85] Special prayers were authorized for the duration of the epidemic.

Some of the circular letters were accompanied by a copy of a small

---

[83] *Ibid.*, fol. 67.
[84] *Ibid.*, fols. 68–68v.
[85] *Ibid.*, "Bienes Nacionales," Leg. 873, Exp. 195, fol. 1.

pamphlet on inoculation, titled *A Clear, Simple, and Easy Method for Practicing the Inoculation for Smallpox*,[86] which had been written by the Protomedicato. It was intended mainly for use in rural areas where no physician was present. Unfortunately the pamphlet was not available in sufficient quantity; only ten copies were allowed for distribution to the fifty-two centers.[87] In most cases some provincial curate was charged with making a copy and then passing the original to a priest in the next town on the list. This cumbersome method so delayed distribution that some places did not receive a copy until the epidemic was over in Mexico City. The last village on the list was Santa Ana, whose copy did not arrive until April 10, 1798, six months after the circular letter had been sent by the Archbishop.[88] Once the pamphlet had finally arrived, it was copied in the Book of Dispositions, maintained by the parish curate as a register of superior orders.

The Ayuntamiento also received a copy of Branciforte's letter to the Protomedicato of August 31. After considering various ways and means of implementing the Viceroy's suggestions, it ordered that the ward chiefs undertake an exhaustive search for virolentos in the various districts (*cuarteles*) of the city. Since 1782 Mexico City had been divided, for administrative purposes, into eight major districts (*cuarteles mayores*). On September 7, for the duration of the epidemic, each of these districts was made the special responsibility of a leading member of the Ayuntamiento. Mier, "in spite of his many and grave responsibilities placed himself in charge of District No. 1, which of the eight was the most extensive."[89] Each of the eight major districts had in turn been subdivided into four minor districts (*cuar-*

[86] [José Ignacio García Jove, José Francisco Rada, and Joaquín Pío de Eguía y Muro], *Método Claro, Sencillo y Fácil que para practicar la Inoculación de viruelas presenta al Público el Real Tribunal del Protomedicato de esta N[ueva] E[spaña] por Superior orden del Exmô. Señor Marqués de Branciforte, Virrey de este Reyno* [Mexico City, 1797].

[87] The record is not clear on the number of copies. On October 6 Núñez de Haro acknowledged receipt of one hundred copies of the instruction on smallpox. Possibly the remaining ninety copies were used in the capital, even though the pamphlet was intended mainly for rural use. AGN, "Epidemias," Vol. XI, Exp. 2, fol. 151.

[88] *Ibid.*, "Bienes Nacionales," Leg. 873, Exp. 195, fol. 6v.

[89] *Ibid.*, "Epidemias," Vol. I, Exp. 7, fol. 485v.

teles menores). A ward chief (*alcalde de barrio*) served as the judge for each of these thirty-two lesser districts. In mid-August the ward chiefs, in their search of their districts, had found few virolentos. But by early September the epidemic had increased so noticeably that several dozen were discovered, most of whom had not been previously reported through the regular channels of doctors, druggists, and priests.[90]

During their search, the ward chiefs had been instructed to look also for buildings which might serve as temporary inoculation centers. As it was early in September (at which time the epidemic was fairly quiescent), the Ayuntamiento did not believe that elaborate quarters would be needed. A comfortable house would suffice; it needed only to be large enough to house one or two infected persons suffering from a mild variety of smallpox, with two beds, and a woman to assist, treat, and feed them.[91] It was also intended that these centers would be used for the distribution of relief allotments of food, clothing, and medicine. One or two virolentos housed at each center would be sufficient to provide (in their capacity as human reservoirs) the pus needed to perform the inoculations. Having once had the operation, those inoculados with ample private means would be instructed to return to their own homes, while those who needed and requested support from charity would be free to report to one of the city hospitals.

At that time the Ayuntamiento saw no need to try to provide quarters for convalescents from inoculation. But even the relatively modest amount of funds needed to rent and equip the inoculation centers was not readily at hand. It was decided that money would have to be temporarily diverted from other obligations, and that, of all possible sources, a reduction in public works would best serve the purpose. The Ayuntamiento voted to halt all expenditures for public works for the duration of the emergency except for the cleaning and lighting of streets. The money thus saved could be used to set up inoculation centers in each of the eight major districts.[92] It was thought, how-

[90] *Ibid.*, Vol. XVI, Exp. 9, fol. 2.
[91] *Ibid.*
[92] No evidence has been found to indicate that this plan was ever put into

ever, that even by economizing on expenses for public works that not
enough money could be raised for this purpose. Cautiously it was
suggested to the King's chief representative in New Spain that some
royal funds might be borrowed for temporary use during the emergency. The source under consideration was the income derived from
the royal tax on pulque, which at that time had reached the accumu-
lated total of 20,000 pesos.

In his prompt reply the Viceroy rejected the Ayuntamiento's pro-
posals. Its suggestion that royal moneys be used to fight the epidemic was apparently considered so outlandish that it was completely ignored. Nor would Branciforte permit the Ayuntamiento to
raise funds by restricting public works. He reasoned that such an
action would inevitably result in forcing many workers into the ranks
of the unemployed where, unable to support their families, they would
take to begging. They would be competing, in effect, with the needy
virolentos for the limited amount of funds which public and private
charity could provide.[93] The city council was instructed to cast about
for more suitable sources of funds.

The Viceroy realized that he was engaged in a financial sparring
match, not only with the Ayuntamiento but with other groups in the
city as well. He knew precisely which groups in the capital were
wealthy, and which ones were not. Those with ample means—reasoned the crafty Viceroy—must be persuaded to share them with the
city's numerous sick and needy poor. Christian piety and humanitarian sentiment would both be tapped in the name of public health
and public welfare. Branciforte's tactics were forceful indirection:
the open hand of praise on the right diverted attention from the closed
fist of authority on the left, at least for the time being. Public and royal
funds were not to be raided, but private sources would be asked to
give and give again.

Getting and spending such large amounts of money required an
elaborate administrative machinery which no existing agency was
equipped to supply. In his edict of February 28, Branciforte had out-

---

effect. There was an inoculation center on San Homobono Street in Mier's District No. 1, but Mier paid for its operations out of his personal funds. This center
is discussed in more detail later in this chapter.

[93] AGN, "Epidemias," Vol. XVI, Exp. 7, fol. 3v.

lined a plan for the creation of municipal charitable societies, one of which had served the city well in the epidemic of 1779. Branciforte envisioned the creation of a central Chief Council of Charity (Junta Principal de Caridad), to be headed by the Archbishop, which would coordinate the efforts of the neighborhood charitable societies. These local councils were to be organized in the various subdivisions, or blocks, throughout Mexico City. In time the Council was established, but this event did not occur until October 26;[94] meanwhile Branciforte set about to gather money for its operations as best he could.

Through the media of private letters and public pronouncements, various organizations, notably the Church and the affluent corporations, suddenly discovered that their charitable instincts were being praised to the skies. Branciforte magnanimously expressed almost unlimited confidence (expectations) in the willingness of these groups to part with their pesos—for a worthy cause, of course. He emphasized that such generosity on the part of private groups ought to provide ample funds for the public responsibilities of the Council, and its affiliated neighborhood societies. On one occasion the Viceroy wrote: "I do not doubt for a single moment the [adequacy] of the resources of the . . . charitable associations, because I see His Excellency, the Archbishop, aiding it with open hands and shedding his alms upon the poor; already he has started to spend money in this holy work."[95]

Praise was cheap and Branciforte dispensed it liberally, knowing well that, coming from the Viceroy, its recipients would neither confuse nor forget its meaning. It was obvious to Branciforte that other groups would not fail to heed the generous example of the Archbishop. One such group was that august clerical body, the dean and Cabildo of the metropolitan cathedral. It seems likely that the letter which it received from Branciforte was promptly forwarded to its treasurer. The Viceroy stated that he did not doubt the Cabildo would want to follow in the steps of the prelate, so as to make "the greatest effort to distinguish itself in the works of charity." Furthermore, "The Tribunals of the Consulado, Minería, and other corporations . . . will do no less."[96]

---

[94] *Ibid.*, Vol. VI, Exp. [7], fol. 376.
[95] *Ibid.*, Vol. XVI, Exp. 7, fol. 6.
[96] *Ibid.*

Replies to the Viceroy's letters were deceptively prompt, for some plainly showed that when pesos were involved other people could be as coy as Branciforte. The Consulado, for example, promised "the most visible signs" of support, but it said nothing about spending money. Its chief contribution was to venture the opinion that as few virolentos had entered the hospitals, surely most such persons must have ample private means; the implication was that all the recent talk of the need for money for the poor had been exaggerated. Otherwise the merchants skirted the thin ice of finances. The reply of the prior of the Convent of San Hipólito must have been somewhat more encouraging to Branciforte. The convent announced its decision to make a positive contribution in the fight against smallpox. It was, for its part, prepared to make available valuable burial space from the cemetery in its courtyard. The only stipulation was that the bodies must be those of "respectable persons." Furthermore, the convent was prepared, if necessary, to open its infirmary for public use—presumably for the benefit of the same social class that would patronize the courtyard.[97]

While busily dispensing praise and collecting money, Branciforte paused to inquire of Mier about progress in the matter of public inoculations. The Judge reported that certain inoculations had already been performed, and that he was still optimistic that the city would escape the outbreak which the doctors had forecast. This opinion was based upon the assumed capacity of inoculation to blunt the onward course of the epidemic. It was a hopeful sign, said Mier, that respectable people had widely sought the operation. Certainly their example should commend it to the lower classes, who were generally unpersuaded of its value.[98]

García Jove supplied additional information on public reaction to inoculation. At Hospital de San Andrés members of thirty families had submitted to the operation, but these had all been from the upper classes. The task now was to convince the poor that they ought to be inoculated. García Jove suggested that the Archbishop prepare a pub-

[97] *Ibid.*, Vol. XVI, Exp. 6, fols. 75–76.
[98] *Ibid.*, fol. 80.

lic statement "so that the people . . . incapable of understanding the advantages of inoculation would accept its benefits."[99]

It was announced on September 6 that Luis José Montaña had composed a guide, described as a revision of Bartolache's pamphlet of 1779, for the administration of inoculation. Mier, before endorsing it, took the precaution of asking the Protomedicato to call a meeting of physicians "who merit your satisfaction and confidence" to pass judgment on its value. The meeting was held, and the guide was approved, but the Protomedicato, not to be outdone, announced it would also prepare one of its own.[100]

Archbishop Núñez de Haro took the lead in making inoculation freely available to the public. Hospital de San Andrés, which was under his control, offered the operation without charge to all persons, regardless of their class or standing. The Archbishop reported that by September 15 a total of 373 persons had been inoculated there.[101] Núñez de Haro unhesitatingly used his superior authority to persuade clerics of lesser rank, who were sometimes less voluble in their endorsement of inoculation, that it would be well for them to favor the operation. He learned, for example, that it had been necessary for Mier pointedly to remind Father Matías José Rodríguez, provincial of the Convent of Santiago de Predicadores, that not only was inoculation approved by the Viceroy but that he had rescinded his previous requirement that inoculados must remain in quarantine. The Archbishop advised Mier that it was his understanding that the priests of the convent were "now prepared to comply with their obligations." [102]

Mier was delighted with such effective cooperation from the Archbishop, which was invaluable in securing popular and clerical support for inoculation. As of September 11, Mier informed Branciforte that inoculation was being widely practiced among all classes of people in the capital. This fact, in his opinion, had been instrumental in holding the epidemic within reasonable bounds. Another reason for such containment, said the Judge, was the heavy and unseasonable rains falling

[99] *Ibid.*, Vol. XI, Exp. 2, fols. 24, 32.
[100] *Ibid.*, fols. 49, 51, 54, 56v.
[101] *Ibid.*, fol. 88.
[102] *Ibid.*, fol. 61.

on the capital. As long as this providential downpour continued, the air would be fresh and clean, but with the return of fair weather the atmosphere might become "infected," and this could well cause a resurgence of the disease. Mier was firmly, albeit vaguely, convinced that infection of the air was the chief cause of the epidemic. At the moment the rains were falling, so Mier was optimistic, but he cautioned Branciforte that preparations for an impending epidemic ought to go forward.[103]

The chief need was for an accelerated program of inoculation. Many persons found it too inconvenient to go to the center at Hospital de San Andrés and they remained uninoculated. By September 9 at least one other center, located on San Homobono Street (today Avenida Juárez) in Mier's own district, was in operation. The Judge, in fact, equipped it from his own pocket with beds, mattresses, sheets, and other furnishings.[104] It was open for service between seven and and eight o'clock in the morning, and between four and five in the afternoon. Montaña was the doctor in charge,[105] and he was aided by a custodian who had, as one responsibility, the duty of keeping a register of all persons inoculated and of all expenditures. By September 14 Montaña reported that 136 persons had been inoculated at the center. [106] Mier suggested that the seven other members of the Ayuntamiento who, like himself, were responsible for the major districts should also sponsor centers; it appears that none did so. A public-spirited citizen, Bernardo Miramón, offered the free use of a house in San Pablo ward as an inoculation center and provisional hospital.[107] Miramón's offer was gratefully accepted by the Viceroy, but Mier

---

[103] *Ibid.*, Vol. XVI, Exp. 9, fol. 16v; *ibid.*, Exp. 6, fol. 8.

[104] *Ibid.*, Vol. I, Exp. 7, fol. 487v.

[105] *Ibid.*, Vol. XI, Exp. 2, fol. 81. There is one report that Montaña operated an inoculation center in Mexico City as early as August 13; it is not known whether this was the same as the one on San Homobono Street. See *ibid.*, Vol. VI, Exp. [7], fol. 290.

[106] See *ibid.*, Vol. I, Exp. 7, fols. 492, 497v, 500v, 501v. On October 14 the center on San Homobono Street reported that there had been performed 177 inoculations during the past two weeks. Elsewhere in the city (presumably at Hospital de San Andrés) 596 inoculations were reported. Of the total of 773, only 5 inoculados had died. On October 28 there were reported 104 more inoculations. *Ibid.*

[107] *Ibid.*, Vol. XVI, Exp. 9, fol. 33.

still considered that the number of centers was inadequate. He accused García Jove of obstructing the program by making contradictory statements about the value of inoculation.[108]

Mier also received an unflattering report about the president of the Protomedicato from Dr. Montaña, who charged that a quack inoculator was obtaining pus for his illicit operations from Hospital de San Andrés, where García Jove was a member of the staff. Montaña wrote: "There is a report of an inoculator who makes cuts between all the fingers of the hands, and applies to the wounds the serum squeezed from smallpox pustules, charging one peso for each operation."[109] Montaña thought it strange that García Jove had no knowledge of this practitioner, but the President of the Protomedicato staunchly denied the accusation and disclaimed any knowledge of an unlicensed inoculator "who performs the operation between all the fingers." Furthermore, he considered the report to be sinister and deliberate.[110]

The Archbishop advised Branciforte on September 4 that he had reconsidered his earlier opinion on the assignment of burial sites for virolentos. He now felt that it was not sensible to transport the bodies of lower-class virolentos from all parts of the city to the cemetery at Hospital de San Andrés. Such an involved procedure was an especial hardship on the outlying parishes of the city—San Sebastián, Santa Cruz (y Soledad), La Palma (known also as Santo Tomás), San Pablo, and Santa Cruz Acatlán. So much carrying about of the bodies not only delayed their burial but also tended to infect the air. Similar objections could be raised, as well, to the requirement that bodies of respectable persons must be buried at either the Church of San Cosme or the Church of San Hipólito.

The Archbishop suggested that it would be more feasible to inter the virolentos from the five outlying parishes in a cemetery near Hospital de San Lázaro. To relieve congestion in the traffic of the bodies of respectable persons, the Archbishop suggested that three new cemeteries be approved. These would be at three churches: Santiago Tla-

[108] *Ibid.*, Vol. XI, Exp. 2, fol. 81. A more valid reason for the delay was no doubt the fact that the Ayuntamiento had to date been unable to find any means satisfactory to Branciforte of raising the money for municipally operated inoculation centers.

[109] *Ibid.*, fol. 113.

[110] *Ibid.*, fol. 144.

telolco, San Pablo, and San Antonio Tomatlán. These sites would advantageously serve the purpose, since they were all well ventilated, infrequently visited, and far removed from the more populous parts of the capital.

The Archbishop also made the practical suggestion that before burial the bodies of all virolentos should be covered with quicklime—to hasten decomposition and to lessen the risk of contamination. Generously Núñez de Haro offered to assume all costs involved in the use of this precaution when it was applied to the Indians, or to the poor of other groups.[111] The use of quicklime, as well as all the other suggestions related to burial sites, was approved by Branciforte.

The orders of the Archbishop and the Viceroy regarding the use of designated burial sites were not invariably obeyed. On one occasion it was necessary for Branciforte to remind even Mier himself that "the burials of victims of smallpox, or those who have been inoculated, must be carried out only in the designated churches, without exception of circumstances, or of persons . . . since nothing outweighs the public health and common good."[112]

The Epidemic Begins

At the same time that Mier was expressing confidence about stopping the epidemic, new reports of its further spread were received in the capital. On September 3 several cases were reported from Tacuba, a city quite close to the capital. No physician was in attendance there, and the Protomedicato recommended that Dr. José Villareal be sent. He was furnished with necessary supplies by Mier, and upon his arrival in Tacuba he conferred with the local priest and the subdelegate, Luis Miqués, on ways and means of aiding those virolentos who lacked resources. The three men agreed that it would be unwise to impose either quarantine or inoculation on the people of Tacuba: "We have found no other way to aid them except with medicine and food, because to do otherwise would be simply to harm them. They not only hide their children, but remove them, and carry them off to the mountains . . . where not only they might die, but also their parents."[113] Dr.

---

[111] *Ibid.*, Vol. XVI, Exp. 6, fol. 82.
[112] *Ibid.*, Vol. XI, Exp. 2, fol. 141.
[113] *Ibid.*, fol. 33; *ibid.*, Vol. XVI, Exp. 6, fol. 71.

Villareal sent word to García Jove that the lack of a horse made it difficult for him to visit all his patients. Several lived in the village of San Juan, more than three miles from Tacuba. Proper attention to their needs depended upon the availability of a horse, and García Jove was asked to have one sent immediately.[114]

On September 5 Sebastián de Henas y Soto, whose official position, if any, is unknown, wrote that the epidemic had spread throughout Mexico City.[115] Two days later it was learned that the outbreak in Tacuba had spread to the neighboring village of Azcapotzalco. Branciforte advised the priests of the Convent of Santo Domingo of that village to begin collecting alms for the needy, and he said that the citizens were obligated to contribute to such a worthy cause.[116]

Several days earlier Mier had told Branciforte that there were few signs the epidemic was spreading. Since reports were, at that time, so openly contradictory, the Viceroy took immediate steps to ensure a much-needed, accurate estimate of the real progress of the epidemic. He enlisted the cooperation of the Archbishop and the Protomedicato in the preparation of separate weekly reports on the number of virolentos and deaths. This seemed to be the only reliable method by which he could be kept advised of the epidemic's progress.

The Protomedicato was asked to require weekly reports from the doctors and surgeons of the city, who were to list the total number of persons of all ages who had contracted smallpox during the preceding week. There were to be two major classifications: those persons who acquired smallpox in the natural manner (*naturales*), and those who contracted a virulent form of the disease through inoculation—the inoculados. The total number of deaths of both naturales and inoculados was also to be included.[117]

On September 25, in his first weekly report, García Jove advised Branciforte: "The smallpox now propagates itself rapidly, as is known from the admissions to the hospitals, and it is to be expected, if God does not remedy it, nor inoculation limit it, that the infection will

[114] *Ibid.*, Vol. XI, Exp. 2, fol. 95.
[115] *Ibid.*, fol. 41.
[116] *Ibid.*, fols. 1v, 8, 10–11.
[117] *Ibid.*, Vol. XVI, Exp. 7, fols. 8–9.

move forward."[118] He admitted that a few inoculados had died, but their deaths were running less than 1 per cent. According to García Jove, this figure compared most favorably with the death rate of 4 to 5 per cent which was reported from Europe for inoculados.[119] Furthermore, it was possible, although perhaps unknown even to García Jove, that an inoculado who had died might have been suffering from the very early stages of virulent smallpox at the time of inoculation, and that the operation was only the apparent cause of death.[120] The well-documented résumé of the epidemic, as prepared by the Archbishop with the aid of the parish priests, listed the deaths of only twenty-one inoculados.[121]

The parish priests were asked to specify in their reports the burial sites of virolentos, in addition to the type of information specified above. The curate of the parish of Salto del Agua, Eugenio José García, advised Branciforte that it would not be possible for him to submit an accurate report of the number of virolentos from his parish: "In the past week the Holy Sacraments have been administered to only eighteen individuals [in my parish] infected with smallpox. . . . [However, I know] of some small children who are sick because of the said disease, but since nobody has asked for the Holy Sacraments for them their number is unknown [to me]."[122]

The plan for compiling the weekly reports was well conceived, but the execution was faulty. The Protomedicato, like the priests, found it impossible to guarantee the accuracy of its report. García Jove believed that the total number of virolentos—both naturales and inoculados—was actually much higher than the number he reported. The figure for inoculados was underweighted because of the presumably large numbers of illicit inoculations which quacks performed in se-

[118] *Ibid.*, Vol. VI, Exp. [7], fols. 204–204v.
[119] *Ibid.*, fol. 204v.
[120] Humboldt, *Political Essay*, I, 112.
[121] AGN, "Bienes Nacionales," Leg. 873, Exp. 180, fol. 3v.
[122] *Ibid.*, "Epidemias," Vol. I, Exp. 1, fol. 45. It would appear that relatively few of those persons who had contracted smallpox and had asked for and received the last rites actually died of the disease. García reported again on October 23: "Although in the past week the Holy Sacraments have been administered to more than seventy persons who are suffering from the epidemic of smallpox, only three have died." *Ibid.*, fol. 13.

cret, and the total number of naturales was underweighted since many of them had fled, or had been carried away, to the countryside.[123]

Another reason for the inaccurate totals was that some doctors failed to submit any report. This omission was, of course, subject to corrective action. On one occasion Branciforte sent a stinging rebuke to Dr. Montaña for neglecting his secretarial responsibilities. Branciforte considered Montaña's negligence as a personal insult to himself —the Viceroy. He ordered Montaña to appear before the regent of the Audiencia, Ladrón y Guevara, to explain why he had ignored the Viceroy's directive on prompt reporting. Branciforte said, without elaborating, that if the summons before the judge did not persuade Montaña to do as required, he was prepared "to take another measure which will make him understand his obligations."[124] In any event, the Protomedicato was not always given full information by the physicians, and its report naturally reflected the accuracy of its sources.

Branciforte accepted as valid the statistical problems which confronted his assistants in the preparation of their weekly reports, but he realistically observed that once death had occurred the bodies could be concealed only with considerable difficulty, and thus the total number of deaths would provide a reasonably accurate gauge of the spread of the epidemic.[125] Some persons, however, did try to conceal the fact that death had occurred as a result of smallpox. The curate of the parish of San Pablo reported, for example, that in his parish "they carry away the dead with the face covered, and with gloves on the hands, so that the sickness from which they have died will not be discovered." The priest said this was done because "of the fear which they have of being punished for not warning [the authorities] in time of the sickness which attacked their children and relatives."[126] Thus even the figure reported for the total number of deaths was lower than it should have been, but it was still the most accurate of all the various indices used to gauge the course of the epidemic.

Mier reported to Branciforte that he had completed a study of the

123 *Ibid.*, Vol. VI, Exp. [7], fols. 206–206v.
124 *Ibid.*, Vol. XI, Exp. 2, fol. 175.
125 *Ibid.*, fol. 207.
126 *Ibid.*, Vol. I, Exp. 1, fol. 19.

records of the epidemic of 1779, and he had discovered that economic conditions in the city were quite different during the previous great visitation of smallpox: "In that year there were more resources in this capital; housing, food, and supplies were moderately priced; commerce and wages mutually balanced. . . . [But] today everything is different."[127] Mier concluded that since fewer people could now provide for themselves a much greater reliance would have to be placed on public and private charity. He acted quickly to order the preparation of a list of those citizens from each of the eight major districts who were thought to be well-to-do. The donations which they would be asked to provide would be in addition to those already solicited from the Church and the corporations.

Mier thought it unlikely that private charity could shoulder the entire burden of relief in a major epidemic. But the expedient by which the Ayuntamiento (and other groups) could amass the funds necessary to render aid to the needy was still pending. Mier, who served both the Ayuntamiento and the Viceroy, was in the difficult position of needing to serve simultaneously two powerful masters— currently at odds with each other over money. In a discreetly worded letter, signed first by Mier, and addressed to "the true Father of the Kingdom," the Ayuntamiento held fast to its earlier plan of raising money for relief by curtailing public works. The municipal council went further, boldly reintroducing the sensitive question of using royal funds from the pulque tax for relief of the sick-poor. But such stalwart persistence moved neither the heart nor the mind of the Viceroy; once again he spurned the Ayuntamiento's favorite scheme. The impasse continued.[128]

Although stymied over the matter of money, the Viceroy received somewhat more welcome news from Mier concerning the crucial question of inoculation. On October 2 Mier reported that the total number of inoculations known to have been performed in the capital had recently exceeded 3,000. Nevertheless, in spite of such success, the operation continued to arouse a considerable and militant opposition. Grossly exaggerated rumors and innuendos, defaming inoculation as

[127] *Ibid.*, Vol. XVI, Exp. 9, fol. 20v.
[128] *Ibid.*, fol. 33.

exceedingly dangerous or fatal, circulated about the city. It was Mier's opinion that certain priests were partly responsible for this surreptitious misinformation: "It is not the people . . . but certain regular and secular ecclesiastics who . . . sow and scatter opinions and doctrines contrary to inoculation. . . . [The Archbishop should advise the priests] that for no reason should they engage in conversations . . . nor give opinions or advice contrary to inoculation, whose fundamentals . . . require a knowledge different from that provided by their studies and experience."[129]

José Inojosa, a priest who was the choir director at the metropolitan cathedral, was reported to be the author of some little verses which crudely satirized both the operation and the doctors who performed it. After an extended investigation (involving both Mier and Branciforte) had been held to determine their authorship, the priest denied, under oath, that he was responsible.[130] The authorship of the verses, several of which are given below in free translation, was never officially determined.

Inoculations have been invented by the most poor and needy doctors.
But it is said that those who receive inoculation are walking with death.
Those who are inoculated have no judgment; they think they will stay healthy; this is a trick.
And this is so certain that they remain scarred, and some die.
I give you the very wise counsel not to be inoculated, since you would be making a mistake.
One sees that the inoculados are infected.
[O] unfortunate Mexico, one regrets that the poor doctors have infected you.
With experience one sees the evidence for this.
The very poor and hungry doctors who bring the smallpox have invented [inoculation].

129 *Ibid.*, Vol. XI, Exp. 2, fol. 139v.
130 *Ibid.*, "Historia," Vol. XLIV, Exp. 14, fols. 1v, 36. Each line of the translation represents one stanza of the original. The poem has thirty-eight stanzas, with alternating stanzas of four lines and three lines. The poem is without literary merit but it has the virtue of being an interesting curiosity in the literature of the history of medicine.

Salazar,[131] worried, and without money, goes about inoculating, but without understanding it.

Flores[132] goes about fancying himself an inoculator, but he is a jackass.

The stupid doctors of San Andrés inoculate anybody who wants it [but] without understanding it.

They say that Contreras[133] is the most clever [of all] but he is a beast.

In addition to writing scurrilous verses, the enemies of inoculation also spread rumors which greatly exaggerated the number of inoculados who had died. It was widely rumored, for example, that a child of Fausto de Elhuyar,[134] the famous Spanish mining engineer and director general of the Tribunal de Minería, had died as a result of inoculation. The report was false: "He has only a small daughter who, [having been] inoculated, has been happily free of smallpox."[135]

The rumors were considered particularly vicious since the operation had met with almost complete success. The fiscal of the Treasury Department, Lorenzo Hernández de Alva, commented forcefully upon this point. After reporting that four children of one Gabriel de Iturve had been inoculated, he continued: "[They have recovered] with the same ease and good results that all the inoculados have generally had until now, and these have been the families of the most important citizens of this capital, who take warning from the fearful destruction that resulted from the past epidemic of smallpox of 1779, which left a memory of mortality forever sad."[136]

Mier advised Branciforte on October 19 that after two months of

[131] Probably Licentiate Pedro Ignacio Salazar y Urrea, who received his Licentiate in Medicine in 1785. See Guillermo S. Fernández de Recas, *Medicina: nómina de bachilleres, licenciados y doctores, 1607–1780, y guía de méritos y servicios, 1763–1828*, p. 123. The Licentiate is a degree intermediary between Bachelor and Doctor of Medicine.

[132] Probably Manuel José de Flores, who was assigned to assist the virolentos of District No. 2. See AGN, "Epidemias," Vol. XIII, Exp. 6, fols. 125v–130.

[133] Possibly Dr. José María Contreras, Suárez Canseco y González. The date on which he received his Doctorate in Medicine is unknown, but in 1818 he composed a paper listing his "méritos y servicios." Fernández de Recas, *Medicina: nómina de bachilleres*, p. 137.

[134] Haring, *The Spanish Empire*, pp. 265–267.

[135] AGN, "Historia," Vol. XLIV, Exp. 14, fols. 22v–23.

[136] *Ibid.*, fol. 23.

relative quiesence the epidemic was spreading rapidly. Although it did seem to be less virulent than previous outbreaks, Mier believed that the charitable societies should be organized at once to coordinate relief activities. The Ayuntamiento was of the same mind, and it instructed the commissioners of the districts to complete their lists of well-to-do citizens who would sponsor the societies. The city also named four men to discuss with the Archbishop the most effective means of using the charitable donations. They agreed that in general the measures used in 1779 should be used again. Branciforte supported this approach, and agreed with the other powerful men of the city that the services of the charitable societies were needed without delay.

Various interested parties in the city were notified of the Viceroy's plans. The Cabildo of the cathedral promised that it would support the relief program in a manner befitting its status, and it requested responsibility for the poorest and most needy section of the city. Furthermore, the Cabildo promised to aid the virolentos generously with its rent moneys—its only expendable source of revenue.[137]

The Consulado reported on October 22 that "the considerable increase of the smallpox is now obvious to all." In the Consulado's view, the disease could be expected to intensify in relation to the cooler temperatures of autumn and winter. The Consulado was confident that the joint decision of the Viceroy and the Archbishop to follow the plan of 1779 was wise; so confident was it that it was prepared to follow "blindly" the leadership of these two officials. Nevertheless, the Consulado on this occasion did mildly chide Branciforte for his extended absence from the city. Relief operations were bound to suffer, it said, since "we now have the misfortune that His Excellency, the Viceroy, finds himself absent; his presence would overcome the greatest difficulties."[138]

The considerable increase in the epidemic, which the Consulado had observed, was evident in the nearby town of Azcapotzalco. The parish priest, Mariano José de Ocio, reported on October 21 that eighty-two deaths from smallpox had occurred in the town. Nevertheless Ocio felt that the situation was being properly handled. Funds

[137] *Ibid.*, "Epidemias," Vol. I, Exp. 2, fols. 352–353, 364–364v.
[138] *Ibid.*, fols. 367–367v.

had been collected and entrusted to a local merchant who, aided by his wife, supervised the daily distribution of food and medicine; virolentos who were without shelter were given a place to stay. No necessary form of assistance had been spared, "and God being served it will continue until the end of the epidemic." Nor had spiritual assistance been neglected. Ocio's superior had sent two additional priests to Azcapotzalco. "I am able to say with confidence," said Ocio, "that never have they [the people of this village] seen themselves so well cared for."[139] By October 29 a total of 105 deaths had occurred in Azcapotzalco, 6 in Tacuba, and the epidemic had spread to neighboring towns.

The hospitals of Mexico City were so crowded by October 23 that they could receive no more virolentos, and those who had already been admitted were in one respect, at least, receiving inferior care. Ladrón y Guevara said that the hospitals refused to issue cotton sheets to virolentos because sheets which had been used by infected patients were not supposed to be used again.[140] Fortunately, Mier was able to advise Branciforte that relief for the suffering virolentos would soon be forthcoming from another and more important source than the overcrowded hospitals, as by then the lists were almost complete of those well-to-do citizens who would contribute to charity.

Three days later, the lists ready, Branciforte announced the establishment of the Chief Council of Charity, whose main function would be to coordinate the activities of the various neighborhood societies. A total of 180 of these smaller units were organized on the basis of squares, or blocks of houses, with a respected citizen in charge of each.[141] Archbishop Núñez de Haro was the presiding officer of the Chief Council, and he was ably assisted by other prominent men. These included two priests from the Cabildo of the cathedral; the

[139] *Ibid.*, Vol. XI, Exp. 2, fol. 14. For further data on Azcapotzalco, see *ibid.*, fols. 21, 69v–70, 75, 102, 189, 208.

[140] *Ibid.*, Vol. I, Exp. 1, fol. 78.

[141] Originally 184 local societies were to be organized. Each of the eight major districts was to have the following number of local groups: (No. 1) 17, (No. 2) 39, (No. 3) 26, (No. 4) 32, (No. 5) 14, (No. 6) 18, (No. 7) 27, and (No. 8) 11, a total of 184. See *ibid.*, Vol. I, Exp. 7, fol. 496v. The figure of 180 was given by Antonio Basoco, treasurer of the Council, who wrote a long résumé of its financial operations. See *ibid.*, fol. 479.

superintendent of the Ayuntamiento, Cosme de Mier y Trespalacios; and also two aldermen from the Ayuntamiento; and one member each from the Tribunal de Minería and the Tribunal de Consulado. There was no representative from the Protomedicato.[142]

The Cabildo of the cathedral promised to contribute 10,000 (soon raised to 12,000) pesos from various rent moneys. It said also that it was prepared "to contribute in proportion to the public need, even to the point of selling, if it should be necessary, the chalices of the church, and the furniture of our houses."[143]

The Consulado offered to assume independent responsibility for relief operations in four of the eight major districts. This would be done with the understanding that the merchants would be relieved of any further financial obligation, including any donations to the four remaining major districts or to the local collections sponsored independently by the neighborhood societies. This curious proposal was disallowed by Mier on the grounds that "it would expose the unfortunates of the remaining four districts to ruin and the lack of assistance." Since "the foremost citizens of this city are the merchants," said Mier, their assistance was needed throughout the city and not merely in a part of it. Mier's refusal to endorse this offer did not endear him to the merchants, who accused the Ayuntamiento of wishing "to deprive the unhappy sick of the benefits and assistance which this Consulado would like to give them."[144] Within a few days, however, the Consulado donated 12,000 pesos to the operations of the Chief Council.[145]

The Tribunal de Minería stated: "Although the funds of Minería are now found insufficient to support other expenses in addition to those related to past and present wars, [nevertheless], for its part, this Tribunal has offered 12,000 pesos because of the urgency of this calamity."[146] The Viceroy believed that the powerful mining Tribunal, despite its pledge, was not giving in proportion to its ability to pay. Branciforte suggested that the miners should give still more for the

[142] *Ibid.*, Exp. 2, fols. 375–376, 380.
[143] *Ibid.*, fol. 382v.
[144] *Ibid.*, Exp. 7, fol. 497v; Exp. 2, fols. 384–384v.
[145] *Ibid.*, Exp. 7, fol. 498v.
[146] *Ibid.*, Exp. 2, fol. 387v.

reestablishment of the public health. He warned: "It will be appropriate for you, as for the others, not to hold back any resources."[147]

Núñez de Haro announced that he was pledging 12,000 pesos in addition to meeting expenses for eight hundred beds for virolentos in Hospital de San Andrés. By October 30 a total of 48,000 pesos had been pledged to the Council from these four sources. The Ayuntamiento interpreted this fact to mean that no donation would be needed from its own funds; however, within a few days, Branciforte generously gave the Ayuntamiento "permission" to donate 6,000 pesos to charity.[148]

The Protomedicato advised Branciforte on October 29 that recent sufferers from smallpox had experienced a more virulent form of the sickness than had the first victims. García Jove called an extraordinary session of the most competent physicians of the city to discuss this new development. They recommended that the Protomedicato announce a simple, effective, and general method of preventing smallpox, to be based on experience and facts.[149] Several days later the Tribunal recommended the following:

bonfires [to purify the air]; a general cleaning [fumigation] of the city and its houses by the use of sprinklings and vapors of vinegar; the complete separation of the clothing of the well from that of the sick; the burning of the trash which is daily taken from the city, so that its exhalations will be consumed by fire, and so that rags will not be gathered up and brought back into the city [for reuse]; the fostering of ventilation by means of fires; and above all the restoration of inoculation because of the value which it had.[150]

It would appear from the Protomedicato's emphasis on the urgent need for the "restoration" of inoculation that the administration of this aid had been halted in the city. Such was not the case, although by November the number of persons asking to be inoculated was indeed substantially reduced. On November 13 Branciforte advised the Protomedicato that his policy on inoculation was that "of allowing complete liberty to heads of families and guardians of children on

---

[147] *Ibid.*, fols. 390–390v.
[148] *Ibid.*, fols. 403–404.
[149] *Ibid.*, Vol. VI, Exp. [7], fol. 372v.
[150] *Ibid.*, Vol. I, Exp. 7, fols. 499–499v.

whether or not to use inoculation."[151] This statement would indicate its continued availability on an optional basis, although no further activity was reported by the inoculation center after November 20. For the center's final month of operation only 39 inoculations were reported.[152] The reasons for the ending of inoculation at that time are not clear, but only the upper classes had adopted it enthusiastically, and by the midpoint in the epidemic most of them would already have been inoculated.

Mier learned that some of the city's foodsellers had become infected with smallpox. Two Indian children, both victims of the disease, were found dead in a canoe which brought vegetables for sale in the capital from the neighboring town of Ixtacalco. This place, and several others nearby, was an important source of the city's food supply. In view of the threat of general contamination, Mier took prompt action and ordered that a careful search be carried out in all the houses of Ixtacalco. Any vegetables found at the homes of known, or suspected, virolentos were destroyed. Tax officials were alerted to inspect all canoes bringing foodstuffs to market, and in each case where smallpox was discovered the occupants of the canoe were denied permission to enter the city.[153]

The Chief Council of Charity in Command

The Chief Council of Charity, meeting on November 5 in the conference room of the Archbishop's palace, discussed a variety of matters related to the epidemic. Its first act was to thank Branciforte for "permitting" the Ayuntamiento to donate 6,000 pesos to charity. Although much money had already been pledged, the Council thought that more was needed since nearly all parts of the city were having to be assisted by the charitable societies. Specifically, it recommended that the lists of the city's well-to-do citizens, which had been compiled by the district commissioners, be carefully rechecked. Some persons whose names were on the lists were found to be sick, out of the city, or for some other reason unable to contribute. One person who did

[151] *Ibid.*, fol. 501.
[152] On November 11 only 17 were reported, and the center's final report on November 20 listed only 22. *Ibid.*, fols. 492, 497v, 500v, 501v.
[153] *Ibid.*, Vol. XI, Exp. 2, fols. 202, 211.

respond to the Council's plea for more money was Branciforte himself, who donated 4,000 pesos of viceregal funds. This sum, he mentioned, was in addition to the generous contributions he had already
made to help fight smallpox in Orizaba.[154]

The Council reported that some physicians had been negligent in
their service to the sick, a charge which was promptly and vigorously
denied by the Protomedicato. The Tribunal, in defense of the physicians' performance, said that in view of the multitude of sick who
clamored for attention, they had been properly professional, and that
"all of them have done their best in the present circumstances."[155] In
the opinion of the Protomedicato the public was being well served.
Rather grandly García Jove proclaimed, "The Tribunal of the Protomedicato continues, and will continue, with the same efficiency and
zeal [it has followed] until now regarding the public good."[156]

The Council, on which no representative from the Protomedicato
sat, answered with specific examples the Tribunal's blanket denial of
any negligence on the part of the physicians. It cited the cases of
Dr. José Rojas and Dr. José Navarette, who had contracted to care
for the virolentos of District No. 1 at the salary of 70 pesos per month.
Despite repeated warnings from the Council these two doctors had
persisted in leaving their patients unattended. They had received a
hearing in the presence of the Council where their justifications were
heard with disapproval, and the cancellation of their contract was
followed by a forewarning never to submit a claim for payment to the
Council.

In another case, Dr. Ignacio Segura had asked the Council that he
be excused from serving the virolentos by reason of his advanced age
and infirmities, but he was promptly informed that it would be "prudent" to report for duty without delay.[157] Segura had received his
Doctorate in Medicine forty years previously.[158] He was, in 1797,

[154] *Ibid.*, Vol. I, Exp. 2, fols. 404, 413.
[155] *Ibid.*, fols. 426–426v.
[156] *Ibid.*, Vol. XVI, Exp. 6, fol. 90.
[157] *Ibid.*, Vol. I, Exp. 2, fols. 404v–405, 409v.
[158] Secretaría de Hacienda y Crédito Público, *Guía del archivo histórico de
hacienda: siglos XVI–XIX*, "Doctores en medicina," Leg. 267, "Annata," fol. 9.

sixty-eight years old—a very advanced age for that time—and it is clear that the shortage of physicians was severe if the services of such an elderly doctor were so essential.[159]

At the same time, the Council praised those physicians who in a time of public crisis had offered their services to the sick with dedication and disinterest. But it also reported that certain physicians "have excused themselves for various reasons, or have tried to charge exorbitant fees . . . so that for this purpose alone there is needed a very large amount of money which is not available, and [which, if paid in fees,] would cause a shortage of the many essential aids of which the sick themselves have need."[160]

The doctors had no income other than that provided by their fees, but all of them had taken an oath to assist the indigent poor without charge. The Council therefore decided not to enter into any further contracts with the doctors, surgeons, and phlebotomists, since such agreements were "opposed to the divine precepts of charity, and the obligations to which they have sworn." This meant that during the course of the public emergency the doctors would receive no payment for their service to charity patients, but the Council promised that once the crisis had passed they would receive "a gratification according to the number of [charity] patients they had assisted, and the extent and effectiveness . . . of their Christian zeal."[161]

The Council decided that the best way to coordinate medical services would be to appoint a prominent physician to oversee medical affairs in each of the major districts. Each of the three members of the Protomedicato was given such an assignment, as was also Luis José Montaña. These men, and the four other physicians who were also named, were expected to contact and assign the doctors and surgeons needed for their own district. The physicians would at least have the advantage of working directly with one of their own profession, who would be conversant with their needs and problems. But if any one of them, when asked to serve, made "excuses or the like

---

[159] Fernández de Recas, *Medicina: nómina de bachilleres*, p. 76, entry F. 314. Segura was born in Mexico City on October 29, 1729.
[160] AGN, "Epidemias," Vol. I, Exp. 2, fol. 404v.
[161] *Ibid.*

of them," the commissioner of each district was instructed to take the reluctant doctor to the district chief of police.[162]

In further actions the Council announced its decision to distribute printed forms to wealthy persons to facilitate their donations to the city relief chest (*caja de socorros*). This was a special fund, administered separately from the moneys collected by the neighborhood charitable societies. It was, in effect, a central fund, administered directly by the Chief Council for use in those areas which had insufficient local resources. The final action of this lengthy meeting was to ask the Protomedicato to evaluate a new prescription for "putrid fevers" the use of which had been advocated by one Barón de Carondelet.[163] The new preparation was thought to be most effective against yellow fever.[164] But the Council felt that its potency against smallpox ought to be investigated.[165]

After each meeting of the Council a detailed report of proceedings was sent to the Viceroy, and Branciforte, in his reply, completely endorsed the Council's firm stand against uncooperative physicians. He made it clear that if necessary he would use his superior authority to ensure that all physicians attended the sick-poor during the period of public crisis. Branciforte also condemned the damnable actions of certain shopkeepers, who were accused of renting out or selling sheets and clothing previously used by virolentos. This pernicious practice, obviously a factor in the spread of contamination, had also been followed in the epidemic of 1779, and with very serious consequences to the public. Branciforte contemplated issuing a proclamation forbidding this dangerous traffic in contaminated clothing.[166]

The Ayuntamiento informed Branciforte that it did not have 6,000 pesos to give to charity. The city government was faced with many

---

[162] *Ibid.*, fol. 405.

[163] Max Moorhead has suggested that in all probability this was François Hector, Barón de Carondelet, who had just completed a term as Spanish governor (1791–1797) of Louisiana, where such fevers frequently posed a public problem.

[164] In 1796 José Antonio Alzate also recommended a new treatment for yellow fever to Branciforte. He had read in the *Mercurio Peruano* that "the juice of pineapple mixed with water is the true antidote . . . for [that] fever which depopulates the coasts of America." *Ibid.*, Vol. XIII, Exp. 2, fol. 19.

[165] *Ibid.*, Vol. I, Exp. 2, fol. 405v.

[166] *Ibid.*, fol. 407v.

outstanding financial obligations, including salary payments of 3,500 pesos to its own members. It had interest payments to meet, plus the usual monthly upkeep on the city jail. Considerable sums were needed for the purchase of corn (the sale of corn was carefully regulated by the government) which was then in short supply. Little additional income from any sources was anticipated before the following January. The only feasible source of income at that time was the royal tax on pulque, the use of which Branciforte had already forbidden several times in the past. But once again Mier raised the question, and he repeated his promise that as soon as possible the city would repay every centavo of the King's money. Perhaps convinced at last by Mier's repetitious logic, or perhaps simply wearied to persuasion, Branciforte finally gave in. The pulque tax, he said, would go to aid the sick-poor.[167]

By early November the epidemic had become widespread and so lethal that available burial sites were insufficient. Núñez de Haro reported on November 6 that more than 200 bodies of "respectable persons" had been buried at San Hipólito. Since no more could be accommodated, the Archbishop advised the parish priests not to schedule any more burials at this site. He suggested to Branciforte that several other locations might be used, including grounds at the Apostolic College of San Fernando, the Convent of San Diego, the Monastery of Monserrat, and the College of Mercedarians of Belén. Since 400 persons had died of smallpox in Mexico City during the past week, the burial situation was critical; this in spite of the fact that two bodies were often placed in the same grave.[168]

Because of the worsening state of the epidemic there developed throughout the city strong support for holding a novena. On November 6 the Ayuntamiento advised Branciforte that it had delegated two of its members to discuss the arrangements with the Archbishop. The city's representatives thought it best to honor the Virgin of Los Remedios, but the Archbishop, on the basis of experience gained from the epidemics of 1779 and 1783,[169] advised honoring the image of

[167] AGN, "Epidemias," Vol. I, Exp. 2, fols. 417–419v.

[168] *Ibid.*, Vol. XVI, Exp. 6, fols. 100, 104.

[169] Since nothing is known about an epidemic in Mexico City in 1783, it seems likely that the Archbishop meant 1784.

Santísimo Christo Renovado de Santa Teresa. He agreed, however, to leave the final decision to Branciforte. He emphasized the necessity of these special prayers since on that same day the curate of the parish of Santa María had reported 1,135 virolentos in his parish alone—a parish of somewhat less than 3,000 parishioners.[170]

Branciforte announced three days later that since he wanted the city to have all possible help in easing its afflictions, he had approved the holding of a novena to honor the image of Santísimo Christo Renovado de Santa Teresa. Simultaneously he announced a second novena to honor the image of the Virgin of Guadalupe—venerated since the sixteenth century as the patron saint of New Spain and especially beloved by the Indians. In order that the novena for the Virgin of Guadalupe might be held with the customary solemnity, the Viceroy generously offered to defray all costs for the first day's proceedings, while his wife would sponsor the second of the nine-day celebration.

The novena for Santísimo Christo began on November 17. The saint was asked to obtain "divine assistance in the present epidemic of smallpox, which afflicts the inhabitants." The public procession, which bore the image through the streets of the city, "was made with the greatest solemnity. The Most Excellent and Illustrious Archbishop, his Venerable Cabildo, various priests, the Royal Audiencia, the Ayuntamiento, and other corporations, tribunals, and distinguished persons took part."[171] Many people watched the colorful proceedings from sidewalks, balconies, and windows.

The beginning of the novena honoring the Virgin of Guadalupe had to be postponed until December 4 because of a scheduling conflict with the "Fiesta of the Indians." This eight-day holiday, or octave, was authorized by a royal decree requiring that the Shrine of Guadalupe be reserved exclusively for worship by the Indians during this period. The Ayuntamiento considered the delay unfortunate and told Branciforte that "not a moment should be lost in carrying out the measures relative to imploring, in the name of the public welfare, the mercies of the Most High, as a remedy for the present epidemic."[172]

[170] AGN, "Epidemias," Vol. VI, Exp. 1, fols. 1–2.
[171] *Ibid.*, fols. 7, 9.
[172] *Ibid.*, fols. 13–13v.

The Chief Council of Charity submitted on November 11 another of its periodic reports to the Viceroy. It said that a new method for treating smallpox (which was not described) had been devised by Licentiate Juan de Dios Miguel de Miranda. Thirteen virolentos at Hospital de San Andrés had been placed in a special ward to receive the new treatment, where they were visited three times daily by Miranda. At first the new method seemed to be working well, but within a week it was said to cause grave damage to the patients. Two of the original group of thirteen had died, and the others had been transferred to the general smallpox ward at San Andrés.[173]

The Council said that various problems had arisen regarding the distribution of relief funds and supplies to the sick-poor. It was known that various of the poor passed from district to district, soliciting aid in each. In some of the more impoverished districts special allotments had been made available from the central relief chest. But the commissioners of those districts which had not received such help were accused by some of the residents of neglecting the local interests. It was difficult for the Council to lay down general rules to handle such situations because of the disparity of customs and resources in the various parts of the city. However, a few general rules were announced: "Nobody would be allowed to die for lack of food and medicine. The shelter which is given to the sick should be in keeping with their [previous] conditions and customs." Those persons accustomed to the use of cheaper fabrics should not be given wool "if woolen fabric would harm them." If a local society received no support from the relief chest—i.e., if it was spending its own money—it could proceed in all respects as it thought best. The Council also reported that it had received complaints that certain unscrupulous parents, and other persons, had been guilty of "selling or pawning the bed clothing, and other [items given by the Council, thereby] . . . leaving the sick in their former nudity and frustrating the purposes of charity."[174]

Several days earlier Branciforte had contemplated issuing a proclamation prohibiting traffic in clothing which had been worn by virolentos. After receiving the above information from the Council,

---

[173] *Ibid.*, Vol. I, Exp. 2, fols. 408–408v, 429v.
[174] *Ibid.*, fols. 408v, 410.

he issued it on November 16. It prohibited the selling, or pawning, of items of clothing which had been issued to, or used by, virolentos. Conviction on the first offense brought a fine of 10 pesos, plus confiscation of the clothing. The second offense brought a 20-peso fine, plus confiscation. For the third offense there was to be imposed "the most severe penalty permitted for such obstinate disobedience."[175]

The Council reported further difficulties with certain physicians. Dr. Montaña said that three doctors from his district had been "disobedient," and that he had reported them to both the Protomedicato and the district chief of police. The Council expressed its concern about the "grave, positive, and irreparable harm resulting to the public from the excuses, resistance, and forgetfulness of the physicians." The doctors, however, had some just complaints of their own. Some were said to be so poor that they had asked the charitable societies for a daily ration of food. Others were not paid for their services to certain well-to-do persons who had had to be reminded by the Viceroy that only the sick-poor were entitled to free treatment. Those who could pay must do so, and Branciforte asked the Council to impress this fact upon the citizenry.[176]

García Jove advised Branciforte on November 20 that he believed the epidemic would soon begin to run its course. He reasoned that after its presence in the city for nearly four months few persons could be left who had not already been exposed to smallpox.[177] It was not likely that numerous new cases would be reported. After receiving this opinion, Branciforte ordered that as soon as the epidemic had in fact ended, a résumé should be prepared showing its exact extent. This should list the total number of virolentos aided by the relief societies and also the total number from this group who had died.[178] This résumé, to be prepared by the commissioners of the local charitable societies, was in addition to the two compilations solicited previously from the Protomedicato and the parish priests. In all, three separate (and conflicting) résumés were prepared.

Dr. Montaña asked that the Council provide funds from its relief

[175] *Ibid.*, Vol. VI, Exp. 2, fol. 33v.
[176] *Ibid.*, Vol. I, Exp. 2, fols. 424, 427v–428.
[177] *Ibid.*, Vol. VI, Exp. [7], fol. 576.
[178] *Ibid.*, Vol. I, Exp. 2, fols. 432, 434, 439.

chest to aid virolentos from the town of San Angel, to the south of the capital. On the grounds that this town was not officially within its jurisdiction, the Council refused to make available to it any money or supplies. On the same day it took action to ensure that convalescents from smallpox would not be denied entrance to the public baths, as some reported to have been the case. The Council decreed that bathing was essential for convalescence from smallpox. Owners of public baths were ordered to reserve a special section of their facilities for the exclusive use of convalescents. Any person denied permission to bathe because he had recently suffered from smallpox was instructed to take his complaint to the district chief of police.[179]

It was announced on December 10 that the epidemic was declining. García Jove advised Branciforte that the outbreak had diminished so much during the past week that many districts had reported no new cases. The president of the Protomedicato generously attributed these happy results to the fine efforts of the Viceroy and the Council, especially its president, Archbishop Núñez de Haro. "If only all the towns and cities of the Kingdom," he added, "might have had the assistance enjoyed by the people of this city!"[180] It was too early to announce the extinction of the epidemic, and the Protomedicato reported that a few virolentos had contracted an especially virulent form of the sickness. The Council authorized the transfer of such persons to the hospitals for special care. It also announced its plan for reimbursing physicians for their services during the epidemic. Rather than pay each of them at the fixed rate of 2 pesos per day, as had been suggested, it had decided to keep to its original plan to base payment on the total number of charity patients whom they had treated. Some had seen as many as 200 per day.[181]

The Council reported on December 27 that many of the neighborhood charitable societies had submitted their final report, thus indicating the extinction of the epidemic in their districts. The Council also took note of the fact that although it had been organized to serve the people of Mexico City, many families had come from the provinces in search of aid. Furthermore, many of these uprooted people

[179] *Ibid.*, fols. 439–439v.
[180] *Ibid.*, Vol. VI, Exp. [7], fol. 576.
[181] *Ibid.*, Vol. I, Exp. 2, fols. 448v, 455–455v.

moved from place to place, and because of their desperate circumstances, they sometimes neglected, or abandoned, members of their
own families.[182]

The Council had hoped to terminate its responsibilities by the end
of the year, but this was not accomplished. However, by January 12,
1798, it was able to advise Branciforte that the epidemic had reached
a "happy state," and that its account books were being closed out.
Finally, on January 18, Branciforte declared that the epidemic was
over.[183] The Viceroy stated that a full report would be sent to the
King; meanwhile, he approved the actions which the Council had
taken during the course of the epidemic.[184] He seems to have inter-
fered very little in its operations, although he kept a watchful eye over
all its proceedings. It was the members of the Chief Council of Charity
who made the basic decisions about fighting the epidemic, subject
only to the usually automatic approval of Branciforte. However, Branciforte deserves commendation (and he has received very little of it
from historians) for his forceful leadership in a time of crisis.

The Council held its final meeting on February 20, 1798, to collate,
summarize, and prepare for distribution the data submitted in the
reports of the various districts. At this meeting the Council expressed
its appreciation to all persons and groups who had aided the cause
with money or service. The eight physicians who had served as co-
ordinators of medical care in the major districts were singled out for
special recognition, and each was given a gratuity of 200 pesos. The
three members of the Protomedicato and Dr. Luis Montaña, all of
whom had served in this capacity, were among those honored.[185]

On February 22 the Ayuntamiento wrote to Branciforte to thank
him for "the incalculable benefits which it [Mexico City] has just
received from the wise and prudent measures of Your Excellency for
extinguishing, or reducing, the terrible effects of that [epidemic], by
which it was so greatly terrorized and afflicted, and which recalled the
dreadful time in the year of 1779." The city also thanked Branciforte
for having given his permission to spend some of the King's money.

---

[182] *Ibid.*, fols. 458v, 460.
[183] *Ibid.*, Exp. 1, fol. 329. (Marginal note.)
[184] *Ibid.*, Exp. 2, fols. 457, 460, 463.
[185] *Ibid.*, fols. 466–466v.

Furthermore, in a wryly expressed compliment, the Viceroy was lauded because he "had agreed to sacrifice all his rents, and even those of the Ayuntamiento, in the public service, and in the relief of the poor." The Ayuntamiento praised the system of aiding the sick-poor, as supervised by the Chief Council of Charity, and assisted by the neighborhood charitable societies: "Your Excellency may with all confidence inform His Majesty that in the event the use of the principal and auxiliary Councils of Charity merits his royal approval . . . it would be worthy of him [in future need] to order the formation and use of them at the first sign of the disease."[186]

On February 28—exactly one year to the day after he issued his important edict on smallpox—Branciforte sent a letter to the Ayuntamiento acknowledging that he had received its final formal report on the epidemic. He endorsed the report completely (much of it was in praise of himself). The Viceroy agreed that the system of local charitable societies, headed by a Chief Council, had proved successful. He promised that in his next letter to the King he would suggest that His Majesty endorse the method for use in future epidemics. Warm words of commendation, which came "more from the Marqués de Branciforte than from the Viceroy," were bestowed upon the Ayuntamiento. Cosme de Mier y Trespalacios, who had discharged the double, and sometimes conflicting, role of viceregal Delegate and Superintendent of the Ayuntamiento, received special and well-deserved praise. In the Viceroy's view, these city officials had fulfilled their obligations, complied with viceregal directives, and had done so with competence and zeal. The King would be so informed. The epidemic was over and, officially at least, the Viceroy laid to rest his heated fight with the city over money. On March 8, the Ayuntamiento sent its "most heartfelt and humble thanks" to the Viceroy, to whom the members characteristically and wisely attributed most of the credit for the final victory over smallpox.[187]

A Glance at the Monterrey Outbreak

Many other cities of New Spain had fought the same battle at the

---

[186] *Ibid.*, fols. 469v–470.

[187] Ex-Ayun., "Actas de Cabildo (1796–1802)," Vol. 380, pp. 81–83, session of March 8, 1798.

same time. Puebla, Orizaba, and Monterrey, among many others, were all attacked by epidemics of smallpox in 1797–1798. All these provincial outbreaks were part, of course, of that same great visitation of epidemic disease which swept across the land, killing thousands, in cities great and small throughout the kingdom. Events in Mexico City form but one peak in a vast range of outbreaks, although a peak of lofty magnitude. Some day the story of these provincial epidemics will be written, for their history is of interest and importance. Numerous sources still exist for the study of some of them.[188] But since the account of the onslaught of the smallpox epidemic of 1797–1798 in the provinces is for the most part beyond the scope of this volume, only one example—valuable for comparative purposes—has been included from the outlying regions.

In Monterrey the epidemic struck later than it had in Mexico City, or not until early in 1798. The Ayuntamiento of Monterrey met on January 17 to discuss proper actions for handling the crisis. It asked Father Antonio de la Vera y Gálvez (the only doctor present in the city) to prepare a plan for combating the disease, and it voted to divide the city into twenty districts, with one or two wealthy citizens from each to be named as commissioners. Another measure proposed was the establishment of a provisional hospital to care for the "many

---

[188] The *ramo* of "Epidemias" of AGN (17 vols.) contains considerable material on the outbreaks of 1796–1798 in Puebla and Oaxaca, lesser amounts for Guadalajara and Orizaba, and scattered references to other places. S. F. Cook has compiled a useful guide to the ramo of "Epidemias," and to those of "Protomedicato" (5 vols.) and "Hospitales" (76 vols.) as well. These contain the titles of the various expedientes which comprise these three ramos. A copy of this guide is kept at AGN, and microfilm copies are on file at the University of California (Berkeley) and at the Latin American Collection of The University of Texas. Volumes 530 and 531 of the ramo of "Historia" of AGN, both thick volumes, are devoted to the smallpox epidemic of 1796–1797 in Oaxaca, and to outbreaks in several other provincial centers, such as Vera Cruz, for the years 1810–1816. S. F. Cook and Heinrich Berlin have both informed me of the probable existence of considerable amounts of material on health and medicine in the archives of Puebla. For a published account of the effect of the epidemic of 1797 in Puebla, see J[osé] Joaquín Izquierdo, *Raudón: cirujano poblano de 1810: aspectos de la cirugía mexicana de principios del siglo XIX en torno de una vida*, pp. 63–74. Izquierdo states (p. 70) that in Puebla 3,099 persons died as a result of the epidemic. It is likely that careful search would provide ample sources for a detailed study of the effect of the epidemic of 1796–1798 throughout New Spain.

poor who live in shacks, and who will certainly suffer from the epidemic." The city officials appointed a representative to confer with the local bishop, the dean and Cabildo of the Cathedral of Monterrey, and certain parish priests, to discuss ways and means of raising money for relief. With the money to be collected, blankets, clothing, food, and medicine would be distributed. Corn would be taken from the public supply to feed the needy *virolentos*. Finally, the Ayuntamiento decided to call a meeting of the wealthy townspeople to allow them to "volunteer" their financial assistance. It seems that the measures employed in Monterrey were similar to those used in Mexico City, although no further data is known for this particular epidemic, including the mortality which it caused.[189]

Final Report of the Chief Council of Charity

Antonio Basoco, treasurer of the Chief Council of Charity, wrote a highly informative report of its financial operations. He said that the average expenditures in relief funds per *virolento* assisted (for the entire period of aid) had varied considerably from district to district. Some had averaged as much as 6 pesos for each person, while the district of the Count of Regla, where 2,500 persons had been "adequately" cared for, averaged only 2.5 pesos for each. Most districts averaged more than this minimum amount. Wages for hired help at the relief centers, particularly for cooks, breadmakers, and custodians, had considerably inflated the costs. Much money spent on food had been wasted, said Basoco, since those persons who could be hired as supervisors were sometimes not well informed about the purchase or distribution of supplies. Some centers gave out food on plates—an obvious waste, since many of the poor refused to use them. Basoco concluded that the entire operation of the Chief Council could have been handled at less expense with comparable efficiency.

He suggested that in the future the number of neighborhood relief centers, which had been organized by subdivisions, or "blocks,"

---

[189] Carlos Pérez-Maldonado (ed.), *Documentos históricos de Nuevo León, 1596–1811*, I, "Disposiciones del Ayuntamiento para contrarrestar una epidemia de viruelas, 17 de enero de 1798," 139–141. Ramo of "Epidemias" of AGN contains no material on this outbreak in Monterrey.

be reduced from 180 to 64. Reducing the large number of centers, Basoco predicted, would substantially reduce labor costs. In a report which was to be sent to the Viceroy, and ultimately to the King, Basoco grasped the wisdom of outlining future economies, particularly since certain royal funds had just been spent.[190]

Approximately 6,000 persons had been assisted in each of the eight major districts. None had assisted more than 7,000. There had been four blocks in which more than 2,500 persons had been assisted satisfactorily through just one distribution center—proving thereby the feasibility of handling that many people through one outlet. Basoco commented unfavorably on the supervisory personnel who had been employed at the various centers; most of these ill-trained persons had performed their duties with little enthusiasm or economy. But their services had been necessary since few members of the charitable societies had had sufficient free time to assume the work load personally.

Basoco stressed the necessity of organizing the charitable societies in the very early stages of any future epidemic. He pointed out that experience had shown that smallpox usually made its first appearance in the city in late summer, but that it did not begin to be rapidly propagated until the cooler months of autumn. Therefore, at the first sign of an outbreak, usually to be observed in July or August, preparations should go forward at once to organize the societies. By no later than the first of September they should be in full operation. Such an early start would give ample time to list those persons who might be potentially susceptible to smallpox, i.e., those born since the last outbreak or those few who might have escaped infection during previous epidemics. At the same time, and for obvious reasons, a list should be prepared of the "wealthy subjects of greater and lesser means." From this number, six persons should be chosen to provide money for each small district, although these six should not be expected to assume all the costs for their neighborhood. Another six persons should also be chosen from among the responsible citizens to contribute not money but their personal service. This would obviate the necessity of hiring ill-qualified workers, and, besides reducing the outlay for wages, this arrangement would reduce the amount of fraud in the distribution of

[190] AGN, "Epidemias," Vol. I, Exp. 7, fol. 477.

supplies. There had been a considerable amount of such fraud, said Basoco, especially in the distribution of clothing. Once the twelve respected citizens had been selected, the local ward chief should be instructed to give them all possible assistance, and preferably he should be an ex officio member of the local council, which the twelve citizens would comprise.[191]

Basoco suggested that a further advantage in reducing the number of auxiliary societies, suggested earlier in his report, would be a more efficient use of medical personnel:

Under the former method there were 180 [units] soliciting doctors, surgeons, and phlebotomists, and since there were not enough for all, this resulted in their taking advantage of necessity. Seeing themselves sought by many they asked exorbitant fees, but by reducing the societies to 64 . . . the doctors and surgeons would appeal to the societies, and not the societies to them. . . . [Also there would be] no necessity of using students and apprentices [*practicantes*] of medicine and surgery, who, lacking the necessary knowledge and experience, one may assume would send an infinite number to the grave.[192]

Basoco said that the shortage of qualified physicians had been severe, even though some doctors had come to the capital from other communities. He reported that 24,200 pesos had been spent in payment of salaries to physicians and surgeons, and that each phlebotomist received 50 pesos for two months' work.[193] In all, approximately one-third of all money spent by the Council had been paid in salaries to the physicians, surgeons, and phlebotomists.

Nearly as much—23,500 pesos—had been spent on drugs. Basoco considered this amount excessive, since in many of the societies the

[191] *Ibid.*, fols. 477v–478.

[192] *Ibid.*, fol. 479.

[193] Bloodletting, the specialty of the phlebotomist, while increasingly under attack, was still practiced in 1797. Dr. José Francisco Rada, who was not a phlebotomist but was a member of the Protomedicato, reported that bloodletting might have helped one of his patients: "If he had been treated with the most efficacious measures, that is to say, if . . . he might have received bloodletting, and the antifebrile medicines [he might now be recovered]." Dr. Rada sought to administer his favorite treatment, but unfortunately the "bad disposition" of his patient (a *Meco* Indian) made this impossible. *Ibid.*, Vol. XI, Exp. 2, fol. 112.

medicinal preparations of "whey, barley water, and vinegar tonic" were prepared in the homes, at no cost to the Council. He estimated that perhaps half the amount spent on drugs might have been saved, "since the best way to treat smallpox is with few medicines."[194] For the future, Basoco believed that the ideal way to handle distribution of drugs would be to establish a provisional pharmacy in each major district, and these could well be in the same places set up to distribute food and clothing. Since the pharmacists who would be employed in these provisional centers would be serving largely as a public accommodation, they should receive wages slightly in excess of their usual salary.

Basoco had strong opinions on the distribution of food and clothing. In his view, experience had shown that the effective treatment of smallpox did not necessitate much clothing, and the items given to the poor should be in keeping with their previous condition and customs. It also seemed to him that some virolentos had been given more food than their condition called for, since "an excessive sustenance . . . may also be harmful."[195] In his final statement, Treasurer Basoco reported that as of March 28, 1798, a total of 92,895 pesos had been raised for purposes of relief, of which only 77,902 had been spent. The balance of 14,993 pesos was to be returned to the contributors according to a percentage of their original donation.[196] Basoco's figures do not agree with those published in a separate report by the Chief Council of Charity. In its *Resumen General*, dated February 17, 1798, the Council indicated that the total expenses for the epidemic had come to 127,897 pesos, of which 59 per cent (75,244 pesos) had been raised for the relief chest, while 41 per cent (52,653 pesos) had been raised locally by the various neighborhood affiliates.[197]

The terrible epidemic of 1797–1798 was at last over. The exact mortality which it exacted can never be known precisely. Three sets of figures exist for the number of deaths, all of which have some claim to official recognition. One of these was in the *Resumen General*, referred to above. It gives 4,451 deaths from among that restricted

[194] *Ibid.*, Vol. I, Exp. 2, fol. 478v.
[195] *Ibid.*   [196] *Ibid.*, fol. 480v.
[197] Ex-Ayun., "Policía, Salubridad, Epidemia Viruela," Vol. 3678 (P. 255), Exp. 5, fol. 5.

group of 44,516 persons who had been assisted by the various charitable societies. Although a copy was sent to the King, this report does not constitute an accurate estimate of the total deaths that resulted from smallpox during the epidemic in Mexico City. This fact is clearly recognized within the report itself, as it states that it does not include those deaths which occurred in hospitals, community houses, or in the homes of well-to-do citizens. Its estimate of the total number of deaths from smallpox from all places was 7,068.[198]

A second estimate of the total number of deaths was prepared by the Protomedicato and was based on the weekly reports submitted to the Tribunal by the various physicians. Its accuracy may well be questioned since on various occasions the physicians, and the Protomedicato itself, were accused of submitting incomplete and irregular reports. It lists two separate categories of deaths: in the "convents, colleges, hospitals, and community houses" of the city there had occurred 585 deaths; "in the rest of the 180 blocks into which the city is divided" there had occurred 5,366—a combined total of 5,951.[199]

The third estimate was compiled from weekly reports submitted to the Archbishop by the curates of the fourteen parishes of Mexico City. It is very detailed, as it shows the deaths which occurred in *each* parish, as well as the combined total in *all* parishes, during a given weekly period. The records are complete for all parishes of the city over a span of twenty weeks from September 9, 1797, through January 26, 1798. The total number of deaths from the epidemic is given as 7,143, although information from another source adds 4 more deaths after January 26—a total of 7,147.[200] This report is clearly more reliable than either of the preceding two.

198 *Ibid.*, n. 1.
199 AGN, "Epidemias," Vol. VI, Exp. [7], fol. 587.
200 AGN, "Bienes Nacionales," Leg. 873, Exp. 180, *passim*, esp. fol. 4. The precise dates of the twenty weekly reports are not given, but on folio 1v there appears the statement, "Hasta 16 de Octubre van muertos de viruelas naturales 135, y de inoculadas, 11." It is appended to the report of the "5ª semana." By accepting October 16 as the terminal date of the fifth report, it is possible to establish September 9, 1797, and January 26, 1798, respectively, as the beginning and the terminal dates of the report. The final summary gives 7,131 as the total number of deaths, but 12 deaths for the twentieth week were not included. The corrected total would therefore be 7,143. Evidence from another source indicates 4 deaths during the week of January 27 to February 3, 1798, giving a

Had it not been for the effective work of the Chief Council of Charity, headed by Judge Cosme de Mier y Trespalacios, and Archbishop Núñez de Haro, and ably supported by Viceroy Branciforte (with some important assistance provided by the timely use of inoculation), the death toll would certainly have been much higher. Nevertheless, the decimation resulting from the epidemic of 1797 had been considerable—nearly one resident out of sixteen in the capital was left dead in its wake.[201] Except for inoculation, the use of which was largely confined to the small upper class, few of the preventive or curative measures of the day were of much value. Nevertheless, the Viceroy and his staff, the various arms of the Church, and the city government, assisted by many others, worked diligently and effectively to bring food, medicine, clothing, shelter, and (for those who wanted it) inoculation to the sick-poor of the capital. They treated the symptoms if not the cause of the disease. The obligation of society to assist these unfortunates during the public crisis was never challenged. It was assumed that during this fearful epidemic the welfare of the group was directly related to the well-being of its individual members.

The years to come would bring other epidemics to Mexico in their train. But their unbridled sweep through city, hamlet, and countryside was retarded, if not stopped, by the dawn of modern medicine which came with the nineteenth century. No medical discovery was more vital to colonial Mexico than the introduction of vaccination, which, although a discovery of the late eighteenth century (1798), did not come to Mexico until 1803. This wondrous discovery, which was the

---

total of 7,147. For data on the 4 additional deaths, see *ibid.*, "Epidemias," Vol. XI, Exp. 2, fol. 391.

[201] Humboldt gives the population of Mexico City in 1794 [*sic*]—just four years before the outbreak—as 112,926. Assuming the mortality to have been approximately 7,000 persons, this would give a ratio of one death per sixteen persons. See Humboldt, *Political Essay*, I, 97. (Humboldt obviously got his figures from the census of 1790, ordered drawn up by Viceroy Revilla Gigedo, which showed the population of Mexico City for that year as 112,926.) It should be emphasized that such a ratio is, at best, only an approximation—no precise figure is possible. It is certain that more than 7,147 persons died of smallpox, since those officials who compiled the reports which formed the basis for this figure stressed that for various reasons many deceased persons could not be included.

glory of Francisco Xavier Balmis[202] to disseminate to the far corners of the Spanish world, was capable of banishing smallpox from the land. This happy result has even today not been completely achieved,[203] and it certainly was not accomplished in the nineteenth century. It was tragedy that human ignorance and caution thwarted for a time the general use of vaccination, and in 1840 the ghost of smallpox returned with a vengeance to kill nearly 3,000 people in Mexico City.[204] But even so the mortality was greatly reduced as compared with that of 1797.

But vaccination was not available in 1797 and inoculation, its predecessor that might have saved innumerable lives, was not without a certain danger and so was little used. These were years of great sorrow for the people of New Spain. A simple people, warm-hearted and spiritually inclined, was crippled by a foe that some called providential, and others natural but unknown. Its origins and source of power were both mysterious, though it had come and come again for many generations. Some grieved in humble resignation as they said their prayers, and buried their dead. Others cursed the killer smallpox, and

[202] Perhaps no phase of the medical history of colonial Mexico has been so thoroughly studied as the Balmis expedition. The best account is that of S. F. Cook. See "Francisco Xavier Balmis and the Introduction of Vaccination to Latin America," *Bulletin of the History of Medicine*, XI [Pt. I] (May, 1942), 543–560; XII [Pt. II] (June, 1942), 70–101. The activities of this expedition in Mexico City (it traveled throughout the far-flung empire of Spain, even to the Philippine Islands) are described in Pt. II, pp. 70–78.

[203] Cook reports: "The disease is to this day [1939] quite prevalent in the relatively backward and remote regions of Mexico despite the most energetic efforts on the part of the government to eradicate it." See Cook, "The Smallpox Epidemic of 1797," *Bulletin of the History of Medicine*, VII (October, 1939), 937, n. 1.

[204] There were 2,878 deaths in a population of 205,430. José Alvarez Amézquita *et al.*, *Historia de la salubridad y de la asistencia en México*, I, 235. Tome IV of Vol. 3678 (P. 258) of the ramo of "Policía, Salubridad, Epidemia Viruela" from Ex-Ayun. is devoted entirely to this epidemic. A brief comparison with the history of vaccination in the United States is instructive: "The introduction of vaccination into the United States almost wiped out smallpox by 1830. Subsequently, as memory of the disease receded, people became careless and the incidence of smallpox rose steadily until the 1880's and 1890's. It was not until the 1930's that smallpox was virtually eliminated from the United States." Personal communication, John Duffy to Donald B. Cooper, December 10, 1964.

buried their dead. In the end it was the same: there was little one could do. Through generations lost in time this foe had come and gone, and though some said that this would change, or could be changed, few believed it. But it was true. But for many broken families, impoverished by the death of their breadwinner or mourning the loss of a beloved child, the saving grace of vaccination had come too late. Such luckless persons would long remember the terrible epidemic of 1797, which, while snuffing out the lives of some 7,000 people, had for six tragic months paralyzed with deadly sickness the largest city of the New World.

chapter seven

The Year of Mysterious Fevers
(1813)

THROUGHOUT much of 1813 Mexico City and many other parts of New Spain suffered a mysterious epidemic of "pestilential fevers."[1] The physicians were reluctant to give a specific name to this disease; some simply referred to it as the "fevers of 1813."[2] One doctor, Faustino Rodríguez of Puebla, who was bolder than his colleagues, believed that the sickness was yellow fever: "The epidemical fever which we are presently experiencing is . . . contagious, and according to my latest observations it is the same true yellow fever that appeared endemically in Philadelphia, Veracruz, Havana, and the Windward Islands, [and was also] known in Cádiz and Seville in 1800, [and] in Málaga in 1803 and 1804."[3] Yellow fever had for centuries been endemic in the hot and humid coastal regions of the colony, but it rarely spread to the temperate highlands. The baffling variety of symptoms

---

[1] The best published discussion of the epidemic of 1813 is contained in José Joaquín Izquierdo's excellent volume, *Montaña y los orígenes del movimiento social y científico de México*. See especially Chap. XIII, "Comisionado por el primer Ayuntamiento de elección popular para combatir la epidemia de 1813," pp. 279–297, and Chap. XIX, "Observaciones y dictamen sobre las fiebres de 1813," pp. 369–386. Chap. XIII is based mainly on the *Diario* and Vol. XI of AGN, "Epidemias." (The present chapter is based upon independent study of these same two important sources, plus various others not cited by Izquierdo.) Chap. XIX is a valuable discussion of contemporary views, particularly those of Dr. Montaña, on the clinical aspects of the epidemic of 1813. It is based mainly on Montaña's booklet of 1817, *Avisos importantes sobre el matlazahuatl, o calentura epidémica manchada que pasa a ser peste, y que es frecuente en esta N[ueva] E[spaña]* (Mexico City, 1817), but a few other works are cited.
[2] Alvarez Amézquita *et al.*, *Historia de la salubridad y de la asistencia en México*, I, 189.
[3] AGN, "Epidemias," Vol. XIII, Exp. 6, fol. 42.

reported by all observers in 1813 suggests that several diseases were commonly responsible for the epidemic of that year, and it is remotely possible, although improbable, that yellow fever was among them. However, it is not possible that yellow fever was solely responsible, and it is probable that typhus was the chief offender. Dr. José Olvera of Mexico City, writing in 1884, stated that the fevers of 1813 were typhus, but he also gave them the separate and unique designation of "spotted fever."[4]

The outbreak did not attain epidemic proportions in Mexico City until April, but in late January the newspaper *Diario de México* reported the beginning of an epidemic in an unspecified place said to be close to the capital.[5] As a public service the *Diario* began to publish various articles related to public health and epidemics. In the first of these, Dr. Florencio Pérez y Comoto warned of the dangers to public health posed by certain funeral customs. In particular, he assailed the *luterías*—a kind of store, or pawn shop, which rented biers, shrouds, and special clothes for use during the time of mourning.[6] For the occasion the body was wrapped in a special shroud, the room where it lay was bedecked with dark draperies, and family and friends donned the black garb of mourning. Such items were used during the wake, or death watch (when relatives and friends watched over the body of the deceased on the night before burial), the funeral procession, and the ceremony of interment. Since some of these rented items actually came in contact with the corpse, while others were close at hand, they became—when death had resulted from a contagious disease—a prime focus of contamination, since again and again they were rented out to new customers by the shops. Pérez y Comoto saw no need to abolish these shops if their owners agreed to forgo the "dirty and dismal" practice of rerenting "the biers, pillows, sheets, and whatever

---

[4] José Olvera, "Memoria sobre el tifo," *Gaceta médica de México*, XVIII (May 15, 1883), 185. A contemporary of Olvera's, José María Reyes, wrote: "The epidemics of matlazahuatl, according to the data I have been able to gather, were nothing but typhus." See Reyes, "Importancia de los estudios médicos locales," *ibid.*, XIV (September, 1879), 340.

[5] *Diario*, 2d Ser., I (January 28, 1813), 157.

[6] Florencio Pérez y Comoto, "Informe de los perjuicios de las luterías, [a]targeas, y cementerios dada al Sr. Superintendente de policía," *ibid.* [Pt. I], 157–160.

else might have had immediate contact with the corpses."[7] If this precaution was carefully observed, he argued, there would be no need to enforce the law of the preceding year that these shops could be operated only in the suburbs. On February 20, 1812, the intendant at Mexico City, Ramón Gutiérrez del Mazo, had issued the following statement on these shops:

With attention to the public health, I have determined that within four days the above-mentioned shops shall be moved to the outskirts of this capital, where it is to be made certain that the bier, sheets, pillows, or anything else which was used close to the body, must not be rented out again for use during times of mourning.[8]

Pérez y Comoto believed that it was not in the best interests to move the shops to the outskirts of the city, since the people of these areas, because of their unfortunate circumstances, already suffered a strong predisposition to disease: "The poverty, lack of education, and the scant cleanliness which the inhabitants of the outskirts usually have, make them more disposed to contract epidemic and contagious diseases, and, unfortunately, the orderliness [*policía*] of their streets, if not in complete abandonment, is in a very imperfect state."[9]

Another funeral custom which Pérez y Comoto considered a menace to the public health was the ancient tradition of entombing the bodies of the dead inside churches. They were disposed in crypts in various parts of the churches, as in niches in the walls of the naves, in the undercrofts, or, on occasion, in the area of the sanctuary. As mentioned earlier, entombment within the church was a privilege reserved for those persons who had been distinguished patrons of the church, or who had led lives judged to have been especially meritorious.[10] But despite such restrictions it seems that many of the faithful were found worthy of being so honored. Pérez y Comoto thought it "intolerable" that such a practice should have persisted into the nineteenth century:

[7] *Ibid.*, p. 159.
[8] Ex-Ayun., "Policía, Salubridad," Vol. 3668 (P. 245), Tome I, Exp. 6, fol. 2.
[9] *Diario*, 2d Ser., I (January 28, 1813), 159–160.
[10] AGN, "Ayuntamientos," Vol. II, Exp. 11, fol. 146. This cédula relates some of the "history" of burial customs.

These magnificent temples, consecrated to God, . . . are being converted into stinking cemeteries which profane the sacredness of the sanctuary and endanger the public health.

It is time the government . . . put a stop to this fertile source of sickness. . . .

In the [revolutionary] convulsions which we have unfortunately suffered, and which are still not ended, we have seen agriculture destroyed, industry damaged, and commerce in the most pitiful paralysis. . . .

Hunger and epidemics are the direct sequents of such a scourge, and they will unquestionably be more terrible and harmful so long as there exist other causes which effectively contribute to their formation and growth.[11]

Early in February the editor of the *Diario* predicted that an epidemic would soon strike the city. He also stated that the article by Pérez y Comoto, and a similar one by Dr. Rafael Sagaz, proved conclusively that the effects of the rental shops and church burials were sufficiently harmful, in and of themselves, to cause a multitude of illnesses.[12] The following month of March is almost a hiatus insofar as information about the epidemic is concerned. But the one piece of evidence indicates unmistakably that the city had already became afflicted with "fevers": Dr. Manuel Gómez published an announcement in the *Gaceta del gobierno de México* that because of the current shortage of thermometers he had constructed several which were being offered for public sale.[13]

After several weeks of relative quiescence—indicated by the absence of pertinent data—Viceroy Félix María Calleja (1813–1816) formally announced on April 12 the appearance of an epidemic of fevers. He asked the Ayuntamiento to inform him what measures, if any, had been taken "to impede the propagation of the fevers which have begun to manifest themselves in this capital."[14] The Ayuntamiento disclaimed any knowledge of a true epidemic, although it had heard indirectly that Dr. Sagaz had learned of certain fevers. It was

[11] *Diario*, 2d Ser., I (January 28, 1813), [Pt. I], 160; (January 29, 1813), [Pt. II], 161.

[12] *Ibid.* (February 3, 1813), 181–182, n. [1]. Sagaz' article echoed that of Pérez y Comoto. It is printed on pages 181–191.

[13] *Gaceta del gobierno de México*, 2d Ser., IV (March 18, 1813), 292.

[14] AGN, "Epidemias," Vol. IX, Exp. 16, fol. 1.

said that he had attributed their origin to the mixing of good and spoiled wheat and to the public sale of diseased mutton. Both practices were, of course, strictly forbidden by law, and Sagaz, after being questioned, denied having made any such statements. Seeking to confirm elsewhere the rumor of fevers, a member of the Ayuntamiento visited Hospital de San Andrés, where he was told that the patients there were suffering not from pestilential fevers but from ordinary seasonal ailments.[15]

The Ayuntamiento's next step was to appoint a committee of five members composed of two aldermen, two physicians, and a notary. It was asked to authenticate the rumors, and to determine, if possible, whether these fevers were yellow fever, or some other kind of contagion. The curate of the parish of Santa Cruz y Soledad, Félix Flores Alatorre, reported that he had administered the sacred viaticum, or last rites, to more than 200 of his parishioners who were sick with fevers but that few of them had died. The two physicians, seeking to determine the exact nature of the fevers, personally examined 27 patients. They proudly reported that while conducting their professional examinations they had managed "not to lose themselves in the effects of the misery in which these wretched people live." The fevers were diagnosed as "simple, customary, . . . without signs of malignancy, and with no indication of being contagious."[16] The doctors supposed that if the patients were given expert medical care, good food, and proper medicines most of them would recover, although unfortunately none of them enjoyed such advantages at the time, nor were they likely to acquire them.

In its report to the Viceroy the committee said that it had found no evidence of a true epidemic. Calleja was quick to reply that even though the fevers might not be malignant they were certainly contagious as proved by their rapid propagation among the poorer people, and he advised the Ayuntamiento to take such actions as would be considered appropriate.[17] In so doing, however, it found that its freedom of action was severely limited because of the total lack of funds in the city treasury. Thus it was decided to solicit do-

[15] *Ibid.*, fols. 2–3.
[16] *Ibid.*, fols. 13–13v.
[17] *Ibid.*, fol. 4.

nations from certain wealthy corporations and private individuals. In the expectation of obtaining revenue from such sources the city hired four physicians, who agreed to succor the sick with daily visits for the salary of 4 pesos per day. The city also agreed to pay for such drugs as the physicians considered indispensable in treating their indigent patients. A Health Commission, composed of five members of the Ayuntamiento, was established to oversee the distribution of food, clothing, and medicine, but considerable autonomy was retained by the commissioners of the small districts who made the actual distribution of supplies.[18]

The Ayuntamiento sought the advice of Dr. Luis José Montaña, who was asked to write a report which would bring together all his thoughts on the epidemic.[19] It clearly shows Montaña's belief that both medical science and public sanitation were relatively advanced in his own day, and that the common people, because of their special needs, were worthy of assistance and compassion:

All of New Spain has been subjected periodically . . . to this fever, and the [epidemic] of the years of 1737 and 1738 marks an epoch in these annals, but since one observes . . . that in those former years neither public sanitation nor [the practice of] medicine was advanced, and that effective measures were lacking which are not lacking now . . . I believe that today such problems may be solved with plain and common measures, and that we can prevent the destruction which has taken place so many times in the past.[20]

Montaña's rationale was secular and scientific, and he drew upon the records of the past to show the progress inherent in his own times.

Montaña emphasized that although the fevers were not necessarily malignant great numbers of people were sick, and that if these were denied immediate assistance many of them would die. He conceded that in some cases the victims had themselves largely to blame, since

[18] *Ibid.*, fols. 7–8.

[19] Montaña divided his report into two parts, the first of which deals with the "yellow fever of Veracruz," which he did not believe was the cause of the epidemic in Mexico City. This part dwells upon clinical matters and has not been cited in the present study. For a discussion of its contents, see Izquierdo, *Montaña y los orígenes*, pp. 280–282.

[20] AGN, "Epidemias," Vol. IX, Exp. 16, fols. 9v–10.

on occasion they had refused all manner of public aid. He cited, for example, the obstinate villagers of Ixtacalco, who would "not give up their errors and prejudices, nor submit themselves completely to the [recommended] method of treatment, and a considerable number of them have died."[21] His impatience with the traditionalism of the village is understandable, since he saw it as a barrier to the adoption of "modern" innovations.

Montaña's explanation of the source of the epidemic, if characterized in terms of present-day disciplines, seems more akin to sociology than physiology. He mentioned, as if in passing, the influence of the unseasonably cold weather of that spring in bringing on the fevers. But he argued that the chief reason people became sick lay in the deficiencies of their social rather than physical environment. This idea is, of course, a fundamental premise in the modern practice of public health, and its corollary, which is no less basic, is that such deficiencies can be corrected by rational means. In Montaña's view, those persons who wilfully clung to irrational traditions, such as the Indians of Ixtacalco, could not be helped, and they deserved little sympathy. But certain other impersonal factors in the intricate complex of the social causes of disease were definitely subject to amendment, and Montaña's listing of these was at once a call to action and a social indictment of his own times.

From all reports the lower classes were most severely affected by the epidemic, and in Montaña's opinion their inadequate diet predisposed them to sickness. An example was "the scarcity, high cost, and poor condition of the meats in a city where the vegetables are more watery than nutritious." Furthermore, the housing and clothing of the lower classes did not provide them sufficient protection from the elements. Because of their collective social disadvantages the members of the lower classes were frequently sick and their general condition jeopardized the health of all members of the community. Montaña championed the cause of the disadvantaged primarily because they were sick and in need, and secondarily because of their impersonal threat to society. But realistically he overlaid his basic humanitarianism with a gloss of self-interest so that persons of means

[21] *Ibid.*

who helped the poor would feel that they were, in fact, helping themselves. He wrote:

Although the lower class, because of its apathy and for other reasons, views with equanimity the disturbances in the kingdom, or feels that these are only passing disorders, it is extremely sensitive to its own problems and disasters. Many persons and families have been terrified by criminals, or seized in uprisings. Such circumstances have . . . diminished their means of subsistence in such calamitous times. It cannot be doubted that these unfortunates are disposed to take sick during the epidemic, and perhaps dangerously so; and that each family more or less influences the healthfulness . . . of a street or of a neighborhood. A poor family that has been reduced [to living] in indigent circumstances, even when the family is not in poor health, provides a focus from which the epidemic can attack relatives, friends, or anyone who is nearby.[22]

Montaña closed his report with the recommendation that charitable societies be established to help the poor, who "live like prisoners in shacks hidden away in a maze of alleys and [vacant] lots, which are surrounded by rubbish, manure piles, and puddles."[23] Montaña saw no evidence that these slum dwellers had been the object of any human compassion.

Near the end of April the Ayuntamiento finally decided that a true epidemic was in progress, and the number of doctors hired for emergency medical care was increased from four to eight. None was appointed without the approval of Montaña, who agreed to act as coordinator of the physicians and also to assume personal responsibility for District No. 1. Since the city was nearly bankrupt, four wealthy citizens from each of the major districts were asked to organize a relief society in their own neighborhood. The city officials hoped that the sight of such widespread misery among the poor would stimulate the charitable instincts of these wealthy patrons, but since these persons had, in effect, been drafted for the purpose there were grave doubts among the councilmen that this would in fact be the case. The organizers of the relief societies were to be advised, as needed, by a commissioner appointed by the Ayuntamiento. Each commissioner

---

[22] *Ibid.*, fols. 11–11v.
[23] *Ibid.*, fols. 11v–12.

was made responsible for two of the small districts and, in all, sixteen of these officials were appointed.[24]

The Ayuntamiento was so desperate for funds that it asked Calleja's permission to confiscate the balance of the treasury of two Indian communities within Mexico City—San Juan and Santiago Tlatelolco. Their treasury contained "6,000 pesos, which were coveted by the city because of the scant hopes . . . of good results from the charitable collections."[25] Its seizure would be legal, argued the Ayuntamiento, because the "spirit" of the Constitution of 1812 suggested that Indian communities should no longer be accorded any separate or special status and recognition, and it would therefore be proper to transfer the funds of such communities to the city treasury. Calleja found this constitutional exegesis startling, but it was buttressed by the nimble argument that if the Indians' money was taken from them it would after all be spent in their own best interest: "The suburbs are the places most frequently attacked by epidemics, and these are for the most part inhabited by Indians."[26] After receiving the consent of the second-ranking fiscal of the Treasury Department (*fiscal menos antiguo de Hacienda*), who enjoyed the designation of "Protector General of Indians," Calleja consented to the confiscation of the Indians' treasury in the name of the public welfare. But he made it clear that this action was taken only because of the financial crisis and should in no way be construed as setting a precedent, or of approving the Ayuntamiento's peculiar interpretation of the Constitution.[27]

The *Diario* was utilized to publish official notices concerning the epidemic, including the names of the commissioners, the physicians who had been hired by the city, and the four affluent citizens from each of the small districts who had been asked to organize local relief societies. It was announced that food and medicine would be made available to persons who presented tickets signed by one of the city physicians.[28] A further announcement was that Juan Díaz González

[24] *Ibid.*, fols. 15–19.
[25] *Ibid.*, fol. 19v.
[26] *Ibid.*, fols. 19v–20.
[27] *Ibid.*, fols. 20–27.
[28] *Diario*, 2d Ser., I (April 30, 1813), 2, 4. These references are taken from a special supplement to the regular issue of April 30, 1813.

had been designated by the Ayuntamiento to receive all contributions for the epidemic.[29] The public was informed through the *Diario* that any suspected case of the fevers should be reported to the local ward chief, who would notify the ward physician to attend the sick person immediately. Medicine was provided free of charge to the indigent sick, but an exact accounting of all expenditures for drugs was kept by the ward chief in a register. When the supply of any drug was exhausted the request for replacements was sent to Dr. Montaña. The *Diario*, in an outspoken article, strongly attacked the practice of bloodletting, to which it attributed many deaths. The phlebotomists were accused of taking advantage of the ignorance of the Indians in order to perform unnecessary and harmful operations. The newspaper reminded its readers that indiscriminate bloodletting was prohibited by law, and that before any blood could be taken from a patient a physician must first specify in writing the precise number of ounces to be withdrawn.[30]

A reader of the *Diario* urged that, as in previous epidemics, the divine intercession of the Virgin Mary should be implored by means of a novena. Several such celebrations were in fact held before the end of the month to honor the Virgin and various other saints. For example, in the parish of Santa Veracruz, a seven-day "novena" (*septenario*) was held to honor the image of Cristo Crucificado so as "to implore the mercies of the Lord in the present epidemic of fevers." The people gave generously to defray the costs of the celebration, which concluded "with a devout procession of penitence which took place . . . amid a vast concourse of people." Also honored was the martyr San Sebastián, described as "the special mediator of the pest."[31] Another reader called attention to the fact that the terrible typhus epidemic of 1737 had not ceased until after the divine assistance of the Virgin of Guadalupe had been formally requested. Assuming a causal relation in these two events, the reader advocated that her assistance again be requested:

[29] *Gaceta del gobierno de México*, 2d Ser., IV (May 4, 1813), 458.
[30] *Diario*, 2d Ser., I (May 7, 1813), 556; (May 8, 1813), 557, 559–560.
[31] *Ibid.* (May 11, 1813), p. 571; (May 16, 1813), pp. 591–592; (June 13, 1813), p. 722.

In the . . . terrible [epidemic] which the entire Kingdom suffered in 1737 . . . there died in Mexico City about 100 persons every day, [and] ultimately there perished during all the period of the pest about 60,000 persons in Mexico City alone, and about 200,000 throughout the Kingdom. It did not stop until the sovereign Mother of Mercies, in her aspect of Guadalupe, was solemnly reaffirmed to be the patron of the Kingdom, on April 27 of that year. . . .

Since our circumstances are the most calamitous which America has seen since the Conquest, flooded on all sides by the blood of her own sons, . . . threatened with hunger, and attacked by devastating epidemics . . . [we must again honor the Virgin] since there is no peace for the impious.[32]

One nonconformist writing in the *Diario* considered as pointless the frantic concern of so many people about an epidemic since in his opinion, none existed. He was convinced that the fevers were nothing but the "fermentations of nature" so commonly seen at that time of year. It was a bewildering sight, he said, to see so many people going about seeking and selling cures. Certain misinformed people, he reported, who claimed that they could read and think, had even gone so far as to label these "innocent fevers" as "putrid." Such a charge could not be true since the fevers were not a "true pest" and hence were not dangerous.[33]

One of those persons who went about suggesting a cure for the fevers was José Joaquín Fernández de Lizardi (1776–1827), the Mexican *littérateur* who is better known by his pseudonym, "El Pensador Mexicano." His purpose was to spare the public certain complicated, but worthless, remedies which others were peddling about town. Fernández suggested the use of a concoction of "tartar of potash and antimony," called *masdevall*, whose virtue was simplicity. He wrote: "No antidote nor method is for this case more certain, quick, or convenient in its effect than the one which they call masdevall. It is simple . . . and by its very nature it ought to be more of our choosing than the complicated formulas which bother equally the sick person who takes them and the pharmacist who prepares them. . . . The per-

[32] *Ibid.* (May 18, 1813), "Rasgo moral sobre la fe y confianza con que debemos implorar las misericordias del Señor ante su portentosa ímagen de Santa Teresa," pp. 599–600.
[33] *Ibid.* (May 20, 1813), pp. 605, 607.

son who prescribes complicated formulas sins either through gross ignorance or through detestable fraud."[34] Fernández warned that in preparing the medicine the formula must be precisely followed. One should take pains to avoid the mistake of "certain reckless idiots" who used masdevall indiscriminately for all types of illnesses, and as a part of the most disagreeable combinations, while possessing no knowledge of the sickness, the medicine, nor the circumstances of the patient. But many other sick persons who had used the medicine discreetly had been "snatched from the claws of the pest."[35]

It is likely that many of the poor turned in desperation to the quacks and the peddlers since assistance from official sources was inadequate and uncertain. The Ayuntamiento advised Calleja on May 28 that so little money was available it feared that all relief operations, including the distribution of food, medicine, and clothing, would soon have to be stopped. Many individuals and some corporations (unidentified) had refused to make any donation.[36] By that date 13,099 pesos had been collected, but 12,002 pesos had been spent, leaving only 1,097 pesos to underwrite the expensive program of public relief.[37] The commissioners of the major districts invited prominent residents from their districts to meet with them to discuss new economies and ways of raising money. Half of the small districts operated provisional lazarettos, but it was feared that the lack of funds would force them to close down.

In June the physicians of the city were still fiercely debating the mysterious nature of the fevers. One reader of the *Diario*, Pedro Clara Cobos, mocked their indecision: "Some characterize it [the fever] as of slight importance, others as serious, and even the same doctor says sometimes that it is benign, other times that it is like yellow fever, or it is of harmful character, and finally . . . he calls it *matlazhuatl*."[38]

---

[34] [José Joaquín Fernández de Lizardi], *Receta, o método curativo, propuesto por medio del pensador en la presente peste* (Mexico City, [1813]), p. 5. "Masdevall" was named for its popularizer—the eighteenth-century Spanish physician José Masdevall. See Izquierdo, *Montaña y los orígenes*, p. 379.

[35] [Fernández de Lizardi], *Receta*, pp. 1, 7.

[36] AGN, "Epidemias," Vol. IX, Exp. 11, fols. 3–3v, 16.

[37] *Gaceta del gobierno de México*, 2d Ser., IV (May 28, 1813), 602.

[38] *Diario*, 2d Ser., I (June 2, 1813), 657. Izquierdo states that "Pedro Clara Cobos" was the assumed name of an anonymous enemy of Dr. Montaña, who

The common people had become so terrified by the unidentified fevers that a reader suggested in a letter to the *Diario* that the priest who made rounds administering the sacred viaticum ought to refrain from ringing the small bell which he used to announce his passing. So many persons had died that the familiar sound of the *Sacramentado*'s bell served to remind the living of such grimly serious matters as the last rites and death. At the same time, and for the same reason, the reader also suggested that the porters who carried bodies to the cemetery ought to stop ringing their small bell which foretold that still another corpse was about to be laid away.[39]

Calleja requested that the Protomedicato provide him with certain vital information on the nature of the disease, the number of sick persons, the preferred method of treatment, and the measures which ought to be adopted to stop the outbreak. The doctors' reply noted that the fevers had first been observed in Mexico City near the end of March; by June 12 all parts of the city, especially the suburbs, had been affected. Persons of both sexes and all ages reported symptoms of high fevers, severe headaches, sharp pains in the shoulders and legs, bitterness of the tongue, decreased appetite, occasional vomiting, and general malaise. The Protomedicato thought it best not to dogmatize on the manner of treatment, especially in view of the bewildering variety of symptoms. It could not supply precise information on the total number of sick persons because the physicians had not kept exact records. Montaña, however, was thought to have certain papers in his possession from which a list of the sick might be prepared, but he had refused to release them "until he received what he had asked for to fight the epidemic."[40]

The Protomedicato was downcast about the possibility of stopping the spread of the fevers; in fact, it then seemed impossible to do so by human means. The doctors made note of the fact that both the virulency and extension of the disease had substantially increased. From

---

had that physician in mind when he ridiculed the medical profession. Izquierdo considers Cobos' remarks "libelous." See Izquierdo, *Montaña y los orígenes*, pp. 291–292.

[39] *Diario*, 2d Ser., I (June 8, 1813), 692. The reader signed his letter "*el pobre de las tres efes.*"

[40] AGN, "Epidemias," Vol. IX, Exp. 8, fols. 2, 5, 6v–7.

their great store of knowledge they explained that such changes could have resulted either from "the irregularity of the atmosphere" or from "the predisposition of the population more than from the fever."[41] Calleja's soul may still be pondering the meaning of this sage information from the colony's medical experts.

The Ayuntamiento's relief efforts continued barely afloat, but the rapid evaporation of its financial sources threatened to run aground the entire operation. Even though half of the small districts had established lazarettos,[42] these were neither large enough nor sufficiently well supplied to accommodate the enormous number of sick people. It was hoped that certain other places, such as the Convents of San Hipólito, San Juan de Dios, and Belén, might be pressed into service, since this would make it possible to treat the sick with greater convenience and with less expense.

The Protomedicato made several suggestions to the Ayuntamiento which were more specific than the data it had recently supplied to the Viceroy: (1) All places where the sick were housed must be fumigated regularly to prevent harmful "emanations" arising from their bodies; (2) The method of cleaning the city must be improved so that garbage and rubbish would not be scattered about; (3) No refuse should be collected until after curfew had sounded, or until the people were off the streets and their windows and balconies closed; (4) The vendors who brought food from neighboring villages, such as Ixtacalco and Santa Anita, must be instructed not to store it in their homes prior to marketing; (5) All the city's rubbish heaps, "of which there are a great number in the suburbs," plus all articles which had been in contact with victims of the fevers, such as clothing and mattresses, must be burned; (6) The bodies of victims of the epidemic should be taken outside the city immediately after death so as to be given a deep burial in a cemetery—none should be entombed inside churches.[43]

On June 10 the Ayuntamiento announced its decision to hire doc-

[41] *Ibid.*, fol. 7v.

[42] Seventeen lazarettos were in operation by June 18. One of these, identified in the document only as "San Cosme," is known to have been a lazaretto, and it has been included in the total of seventeen. See *Ibid.*, Vol. XIII, Exp. 6, fols. 78–78v.

[43] *Ibid.*, Vol. IX, Exp. 8, fols. 8–9.

tors to work in each of the city's thirty-two small districts; previously only eight had been hired for the entire city. The doctors were instructed to hold joint meetings each week to compare procedures and prepare notes for use in future epidemics. It was also announced that 3,000 pesos had been borrowed from city funds to finance poor relief, since the scheme of drafting for this purpose four wealthy persons from each small district had largely failed. Unfortunately, those persons who had found their names on the list of proposed public benefactors made "innumerable excuses," and it had been necessary for the city to prod them a second and a third time. From all sources a total of 27,000 pesos had been scraped together, but by June 10 most of it had been spent. None of the doctors or druggists had been paid a peso.[44] At the very time the relief operations were collapsing, the need for such assistance multiplied. Félix Flores Alatorre reported that in the first ten days of June "the epidemic is three times greater with respect to what is was in May."[45] The problems of the epidemic had become so overwhelming that the city's best efforts were largely unavailing.

A priest from the parish of the Sagrario reported 265 deaths from fevers between April 26 and June 10. Of this number only 49 had received a burial service for which a proper payment had been made to the priest; the 216 others had received a burial service paid for (if at all) by alms.[46] It is clear that many victims of the epidemic were unceremoniously consigned to an anonymous grave.[47] The total burials of fever victims in Mexico City by June 10, as reported by the parish priests, was 3,640.[48]

A provisional hospital was established for treatment of the sick-

[44] *Ibid.*, Exp. 11, fols. 20–22.
[45] Ex-Ayun., "Policía, Salubridad, Epidemias," Vol. 3674 (P. 251), Tome 1, Exp. 12, fol. 159.
[46] *Ibid.*, fol. 2.
[47] AGN, "Epidemias," Vol. XIII, Exp. 2, fol. 11v.
[48] Ex-Ayun., "Policía, Salubridad, Epidemias," Vol. 3674 (P. 251), Tome I, Exp. 12, fol. 170. This reference shows 2,918 deaths through June 10 for all parishes *except* those of Sagrario and Santa Catarina; they are given elsewhere. See *ibid.*, fol. 2, for statement of 265 deaths in Sagrario by June 10. See *ibid.*, fol. 25, for information of 357 deaths in Santa Catarina through May 30, and 431 for *all* of June. I have allowed 100 deaths through June 10, arriving at a grand total of 3,640 deaths through June 10.

poor at the College of Santiago Tlatelolco. The administrator reported that "in this district there is a considerable number of people and almost all of them are found in the greatest misery and abandonment, as the physician can testify . . . who visits them daily . . . from five in the morning until seven in the evening."[49] Francisco Crespo Gil reported that nearly half of the sick in his district were suffering relapses, and that this misfortune would have been less likely to occur if they had been given ample quantities of fruit, tamales, and meat. His district operated a relief kitchen which, because of the lack of adequate funds, was forced to serve somewhat less appetizing foods. But what was served was of good quality, and the kitchen was kept as neat and clean as possible, he said. *Atole*, a porridge or gruel made from corn meal, was served both morning and afternoon. *Puchero*, a dish of meat and vegetables, was also prepared. (The cook's recipe for puchero called for lamb fat, pork, chickpeas, and rice.) Bread, mutton, and pulque were also available, but the specific ration which a person received depended upon the meal ticket signed by a physician. One of the chief problems connected with the kitchens was the difficulty in hiring women to grind the corn and chickpeas used in making bread (*tortillas*) and porridge. Crespo Gil said that he offered an "excessive" wage for this work, but that few women were willing to do it. Furthermore, the commercial vendors of atole refused to make deliveries to the relief kitchen, and all such difficulties greatly increased its operating expenses.[50]

One employee who played an important but unheroic role in the operation of the relief kitchen was the assistant (*sobresaliente*). He had numerous duties, and for the performance of these he was not adequately compensated:

Daily he accompanies the doctor who visits the sick to collect the expired meal tickets, and to give new ones to those who have taken sick; he collects the sick who are going to the hospital; he assists in the kitchen in the morning at the hour when porridge is given out; he gives out broth (*caldo*), soup, and meat . . . at 4:00 P.M.; porridge at 4:00 for the hos-

[49] *Ibid.*, fol. 264.
[50] *Ibid.*, fol. 270v.

pital . . . and, at night, another porridge for the hospital; this person earns one peso daily, well-earned since he works incessantly all day long.[51]

Kitchens from other districts gave food of similar type and quality.

Despite the assistance of these kitchens numerous people went hungry (one case of starvation was officially reported),[52] although Joaquín Altamirano wrote that some persons, obviously in need of help, had spurned public charity. Some of the districts distributed emergency bedding supplies to the sick—a sleeping mat and a baize sheet.[53] The *Diario* reported on June 14 that the prognosis for the epidemic was bleak, and two days later the Ayuntamiento announced: "We have exhausted all our resources. . . . Today we find ourselves compelled to suspend assistance, and one after another of the kitchens of the districts have had to close."[54]

On June 22 the Ayuntamiento submitted a lengthy report to Calleja on the state of the epidemic. A major problem had been the refusal of the hospitals of the city, with the exception of Hospital Real de Indios, to accept patients suffering from the fevers. One hospital had refused outright to accept any of them, and others had imposed unsatisfactory conditions. The city officials declared that as a "lesser evil" several more provisional hospitals, or lazarettos, had been established for the sick, since in their own homes, where otherwise they would be forced to stay, there was seldom any competent person to care for them. The paucity of lazarettos, however, created a major risk: "The simple comparison of the number of deaths in the lazarettos with those [of patients] who are attended outside [of them] shows that lazarettos are harmful to humanity. It would therefore be most desirable to increase their numbers considerably . . . so that fewer people would need to be crowded into [each of] them."[55] Special houses for convalescents were also needed; a great many persons,

[51] *Ibid.*, fols. 275–275v.
[52] Montaña reported, "Of four dead children, one died solely of hunger." *Ibid.*, fol. 263v.
[53] *Ibid.*, fol. 284.
[54] *Diario*, 2d Ser., I (June 14, 1813), 724; AGN, "Epidemias," Vol. VIII, Exp. 7, fol. lv.
[55] *Ibid.*, Vol. IX, Exp. 8, fol. 18v.

apparently recovered, later suffered serious, even fatal, relapses. Unfortunately the lack of funds invalidated both of these suggestions.

The Ayuntamiento urged that the lazarettos be fumigated frequently to prevent "overloading of the atmosphere," which was said to occur when large numbers of sick persons were crowded together. The most efficacious fumigants were nitric or sulfuric acids, but these were scarce and expensive because of military priorities in the fight against the rebels. Therefore the Protomedicato had suggested, as substitutes, a mixture of garlic and vinegar, which could be sprinkled over the ground, or of dried cow dung, which could be burned to achieve the purpose. Not only had the doctors' suggestions not worked, but, in the opinion of the city officials (who were not, of course, physicians), they were a positive menace to the sick. Conclusive proof of this was the fact that "the wretched inhabitants of the huts and shacks of the *barrios* who . . . use no other fuel [than dried cow dung] for cooking, or for other domestic uses, are those who are most frequently attacked and become ill."[56] Fortunately, Calleja agreed to release two *arrobas* (about fifty pounds) of nitric acid for civilian use in fumigating.[57]

The Ayuntamiento also reported to Calleja that the cleaning of sewers and dungheaps "has been going forward for some days, although by degrees, and not with the acceleration which *we* would like."[58] The reason for the delay was the reluctance of many workers to avail themselves of this employment opportunity. Many of the regular crew of workers (*excrementeros*) who had performed this service had taken ill, or had died, from the fevers. Replacements could not be hired even with the inducement of a triple wage. Nor had the city, for lack of workers, been able to drain certain noxious swamps. But the problem was eased when Calleja instructed that convicts might be assigned to such chores.[59]

One of the city aldermen, Ignacio Adalid, took the trouble to investigate personally the working routine of the excrementeros, who, by popular demand, pushed their carts about the city sometime after

[56] *Ibid.*, fol. 20.
[57] *Ibid.*, fol. 29.
[58] *Ibid.*, fols. 20v–21. (Italics mine.)
[59] *Ibid.*, fols. 21, 29.

curfew, usually beginning around 10:00 P.M. Adalid reported to Calleja that he had executed this civic responsibility not so much as a precautionary measure against the epidemic, but for "physical reasons which cannot but be known to Your Excellency."[60] His investigation was sufficiently thorough that he could report that despite the shortage of workers the carts continued to roll. Unfortunately many citizens, less concerned about their civic responsibilities than was the alderman, were careless in their cooperation with the department of sanitation, and by daybreak, according to Adalid, the city streets were usually once again found to be intransitable. Another function of the Ayuntamiento's crew of sanitary specialists was to collect for disposal those items which had been in contact with the bodies of fever victims. These items were called for at the hospitals and, along with "the infinite filth which the common people throw in the streets and other public places by night," were carted away for burning.[61]

By early June deaths from the fevers were multiplying so rapidly that many bodies were buried in huge common graves. The "big ditch" at the cemetery of Santa María was large enough to accommodate 500, and other sites in the area could receive 200 more. The city officials ordered two special carts to haul bodies from the provisional hospitals to the cemetery. Some bodies were still being placed in vaults inside churches, and the Ayuntamiento again asked that the Archbishop expressly forbid this ancient practice which was so inimical to the public welfare. The crux of the problem, according to the Ayuntamiento, was "the unyielding obsession of the people, common and not common, to be buried in church (*en sagrado*)." The hardpressed city officials would have preferred to cremate the bodies, though this more sanitary method seems not to have been used at all: "If only . . . in the time of this Ayuntamiento [we] would see established this beneficial measure [of cremation], which would save us money."[62]

Contrary to the report of the public-spirited alderman two police commissioners informed the Ayuntamiento on June 26 that the excrementeros had in fact been inexcusably lax in the performance of their

[60] *Ibid.*, fol. 22.
[61] *Ibid.*, fols. 22v–23.
[62] *Ibid.*, fols. 25v–26.

public duties, and that "the citizenry demand the immediate correction of a defect which in part propagates the fever." There was scarcely a street in the city which was not in need of immediate cleaning. It was true that many of the experienced workers had contracted the fever, and that replacements were hard to find. But the chief problem had been that the contractor, despite repeated warnings and fines, had refused to take proper measures for the cleaning of the city. The Ayuntamiento had succeeded in breaking the contract in court and had itself assumed supervisory responsibility for public sanitation. Thirty new cleaning carts were ordered, and it was promised that proper sanitary measures would be observed "day and night with the least possible imperfection."[63]

A writer in the *Diario* denounced the gravediggers for gross negligence in the performance of their duties. "[I point out] the scant regard of the gravediggers in not burying the mats on which the dead are carried. . . . It sometimes happens that other poor people find these mats and take them for their own use . . . as I have seen in the [cemetery of] La Candelaria . . . [where] there is not only carelessness with these articles, but anybody who cares to look will see the open ditch and the bodies only half-buried."[64]

Félix Flores Alatorre, curate of the parish of Santa Cruz y Soledad (and also a physician), after seeing that 1,550 of his parishioners had died of the fevers by June 10, took the liberty of sending his views on the causes of the epidemic to Calleja:

The practitioners of medicine will be able to inform you about the causes of this frightful multiplication [of disease]; I lay great stress on the lack of assistance in these [areas]: The scarcity of food and the complete lack of clothing for the sick; filth in the suburbs; such crowding of the sick in the lazarettos that these [persons] heartily despise them—the results being relapses and inevitably [*sic*] death; and lastly the corruption from the innumerable corpses that have been dumped in the cemetery of San

---

[63] *Ibid.*, fols. 35v, 39–41. John Duffy writes that "getting the street-cleaning contractors to perform their duties was a major problem in every American city in the nineteenth century." Personal communication, John Duffy to Donald B. Cooper, December 10, 1964.

[64] *Diario*, 2d Ser., I (June 29, 1813), 792.

Lázaro; since this place is to the east of Mexico City the winds which blow [from there] ... bring the pest to the city.[65]

One curious result of the epidemic was that it created a shortage of aguadores, men paid to carry jugs of water. One citizen complained: "I have suffered greatly because of the shortage of aguadores, since some are sick, others have died, and many have hired themselves out as paid mourners (*trinitarios*)." In normal times an aguador was supposed to make four roundtrips for payment of one-half *real*. But owing to their scarcity they were charging one-half *real* for each trip, and many refused to serve the poorer and more distant districts at any reasonable price.[66]

It was reported by the commissioners of the small districts that 54,119 persons (from among those aided by public relief) had contracted the fevers by July 31. Of this number 38,491 had recovered, 7,304 remained sick, and 8,324 had died.[67] Since many persons, including some in dire necessity, had not received, or had refused to accept, public assistance, the various totals for the entire population of the city would have been somewhat higher. After the middle of the summer, the availability of public relief was severely limited by lack of funds. After July 31, for example, sick persons in two of the small districts received no assistance except atole, and in another all public assistance ceased completely after August 6.[68]

Hospital Real de Indios was forced, because of lack of funds, to turn away many sick Indians, including some who came from great distances and who had no other source of assistance. Joseph Alegría, the administrator, reported that the hospital's usual sources of funds had suffered "the same progressive decadence which all the [dependencies] of the public treasury have suffered." Before the start of the rebellion, in 1810, the hospital had enjoyed an average income of 52,000 pesos per year. Two-thirds of this amount came from a small

[65] Ex-Ayun., "Policía, Salubridad, Epidemias," Vol. 3674 (P. 251), Tome I, Exp. 12, fol. 259v.

[66] *Diario*, 2d Ser., II (July 17, 1813), 3–4.

[67] Ex-Ayun., "Policía, Salubridad, Epidemias," Vol. 3674 (P. 251), Tome I, Exp. 12, fol. 259v.

[68] *Ibid.*, fols. 183, 241.

annual tax of one-half *real*, which the Indians paid as a part of their tribute. The remaining third came from such other sources as rent from urban real estate, interest on capital, gifts from the king, private donations, and ticket sales at the hospital's theater. By 1813 the income of the hospital had dropped to approximately 15,000 pesos, and at the very time when demands for its services were greatest. It was Alegría's hope that the Viceroy would find it possible to give some money since, among his many other titles and designations, he was vice-patron of the hospital. Usually some additional income had also come from certain bishoprics outside the capital, such as Valladolid (Morelia), Guadalajara, Oaxaca, and Monterrey. But none of these could be expected to contribute further until "the provinces have recovered from the paralysis which affects their agriculture."[69]

Throughout the epidemic the physicians could never agree on the proper name of the mysterious fevers which wrought such widespread havoc. On August 31 a conference of leading physicians met in the chapter hall of the Ayuntamiento to decide whether the numerous symptoms of the fevers might be equated with the syndrome of a specific disease.[70] Dr. Manuel de Jesús Febles acted as secretary, and many members of the Ayuntamiento were present as interested listeners. It was the consensus of the physicians that the epidemic was more severe in the smaller settlements, as in the villages and haciendas, than in the larger towns and cities, and also that it was more severe in cooler regions than in warmer ones.[71] In order of seniority the physicians were asked to elaborate upon these premises.

Dr, Rafael Sagaz, a surgeon, spoke first. He took issue with the position that held Puebla responsible for spreading the fevers. It was

---

[69] AGN, "Hospitales," Vol. XLVIII, Exp. 14, fols. 1–1v, 5v.

[70] AGN, "Epidemias," Vol. XIII, Exp. 6, fol. 72.

[71] That the disease was confined to the cooler highlands is a clear indication of typhus: "[Typhus occurs] in most colder areas of the world where appreciable groups of people live under unhygienic conditions and are lousy. Endemic centers exist in mountainous regions of Mexico . . . [but not in] the humid tropics. Prior to modern methods of control, epidemics were frequent among military and refugee populations and in areas suffering famine or war." American Public Health Association, *Control of Communicable Disease in Man*, p. 204.

true that Puebla had suffered greatly from fevers, and that an epidemic had started there somewhat earlier than the one in the capital. But placing the blame on Puebla was pointless, according to Sagaz, since he had observed fevers like those in the capital in the village of Cuauticlan for more than six years. This village was much closer to Mexico City than was Puebla, and its inhabitants, said Sagaz, were not above reproach in causing the spread of the epidemic. They had refused, for example, to accept proffered help for the fevers, and they had retained certain disgraceful and harmful customs, such as drinking alcoholic beverages and the practice of bleeding the sick. The result of such scandalous behavior was that "before long the epidemic swallowed them up, spread to other villages, and from there to the capital."

Sagaz explained that one reason why the epidemic had taken such a fierce hold was the general poverty of the people. Other reasons were that some persons, such as the villagers of Cuauticlan, had refused to accept help, and also that certain physicians had been remiss in promptly visiting the sick. But unlike Montaña, Sagaz dwelled mainly upon the unseasonableness of the weather rather than the social misery of the people as the chief cause of the sickness:

The unseasonable variation from the hot to the cold season has had the effect of bringing together certain gases so that the system is weakened and enervated. This diminishes the flow of certain secretions, whose humors flow to the cavities of the body, and from these into the volume of the blood, where they distribute themselves in greater or lesser quantity, [thereby] producing in certain parts hemorrhages, petechiae, and the whole series of nervous anomalies which are observed [in conjunction] with these fevers. I have proved this with my own observations, and with those of other professors made in Andalucía.[72]

Such was the discourse of Dr. Rafael Sagaz as paraphrased at the time by Dr. Febles. Dr. Sagaz, for all his display of popular medical theories, still refrained from assigning a specific name to the fevers, and he was no more precise in explaining why colder regions were chiefly affected: "I say that these places and their inhabitants are af-

---

[72] AGN, "Epidemias," Vol. XIII, Exp. 6, fols. 72v–73.

fected more by the atmospheric airs, and consequently they must suffer in their variations. The cold being a powerful debilitant, and enemy of the nerves, it must produce an abundance of fevers."[73]

Dr. Antonio Serrano seconded the learned analysis of Dr. Sagaz, but added that, in his own opinion, the real cause of the fevers was "suppressed perspiration." Dr. Francisco Selma remarked that he had observed variations of the present fevers in Mexico City for thirty years. Dr. José Gracida y Vernal, a member of the Protomedicato, explained that the harmful gases which were thought to contribute to the fevers were caused by emanations from cemeteries, sewers, and rubbish. The concluding remarks in this early nineteenth-century medical symposium were delivered by the venerable president of the Protomedicato, José Ignacio García Jove:

[He] wisely summarized the history of the different epidemics which had attacked other nations, and the causes to which they had unjustly been attributed, concluding therefore that it would be difficult to determine the cause of the present epidemic, and for its true cause he attributed it to the scourge of God, which he proved exactly with various texts from the Holy Scriptures, [while] also referring to, and approving as causes, the . . . things said by the other gentlemen.[74]

It is not known precisely when the epidemic of 1813 finally played out. It is known that this epidemic caused a greater loss of life in Mexico City than any previous one since the outbreak of 1761–1762. Furthermore, none since that time has rivaled it in terms of loss of life. More than 20,000 people died in Mexico City from the "fevers of 1813":

According to the census . . . [of Revilla Gigedo of 1790] Mexico City had at that time 112,926 persons. . . . In 1811 . . . there were counted 168,846, including 16,179 Indians attached to the Indian communities of Santiago Tlatelolco and San Juan, and the many families who emigrated from towns occupied by the rebels; but in the year 1813 the population of the capital was reduced to 123,907 persons, according to enrollment which the constitutional Ayuntamiento made at the order of the government. This decrease was due in very considerable part to the epidemic of fevers

[73] *Ibid.*, fol. 73.
[74] *Ibid.*, fols. 73–73v.

which was then being suffered, from which there died 20,385 persons, as is shown by the necrological statement which the same Ayuntamiento sent to the superior [government] on January 18, 1814.[75]

In spite of its great toll of destruction, the epidemic of 1813, insofar as the record shows, quickly faded into obscurity after August of that year. Administratively there was less activity, hence less to record, since by midsummer the exhaustion of funds had forced the stoppage of public relief. In November, Calleja issued a proclamation enjoining foodsellers from taking advantage of "the present circumstances" to enrich themselves at the expense of the poor. It is possible that the epidemic forced the issuance of the proclamation, since it appeared after the submission of a report to Calleja by José Francisco Villanueva, the Ayuntamiento's deputy for Health and Public Welfare. It required that all foodsellers, upon entering the city, report directly to a royal scribe, who would list the kind, quantity, and value of the foodstuffs. The sellers were required to sell their products at the price, and in the place, established by law. After the goods were sold, the scribe issued a pass showing compliance with the law. No foodseller could pass through the city gates to return home until the pass had been collected by a sentry at one of the checking stations. The products included within the scope of the proclamation were all those "which are necessary for human sustenance," as, for example, beans, rice, salt, cheese, eggs, fish, charcoal, firewood, and chile peppers.[76]

The last contemporary references to the epidemic of 1813 are found in two lawsuits which sought to recover money that the claimants had spent during the outbreak. On November 11, 1814, the treasurer of the Ayuntamiento paid to Juan Ignacio Orellana the sum of 1,236 pesos for expenses incurred "in the past epidemic of fevers in District [small] No. 28."[77] On April 9, 1815, the administrator of

[75] Fernando Navarro y Noriega, "Memoria sobre la población del reino de Nueva España," *Boletín de la Sociedad mexicana de geografía y estadística,* 2d Ser., I (1869), 282, n. 1. See also AGN, "Epidemias," Vol. XIII, Exp. 6, fol. 81.

[76] *Diario,* 2d Ser., II (November 11, 1813), 1–2.

[77] Ex-Ayun., "Policía, Salubridad, Epidemias," Vol. 3674 (P. 251), Tome I, Exp. 10, fol. 7.

Hospital de San Andrés claimed 2,629 pesos as payment for drugs dispensed by the hospital pharmacy. The claim was not honored until September, 1819, and even then the settlement was reduced to 1,899 pesos. The Ayuntamiento held that in some cases the pharmacy had dispensed medicine to persons who were not truly indigent, and that such as these were not entitled to public charity.[78]

The epidemic of 1813 was prosecuted much less successfully than was the previous major outbreak—the smallpox epidemic of 1797. In the former epidemic there had been close and effective cooperation between higher and lower authorities, both civil and ecclesiastical. The Archbishop, the Viceroy, and the superintendent of the Ayuntamiento all played important roles. In 1813 little is heard about the Viceroy, and almost nothing about the activities of the Archbishop. Local authorities, chiefly the Ayuntamiento, had to do the best they could with whatever resources were at hand—meager and inadequate at best. The highly successful agency of the Chief Council of Charity which, in 1798, Viceroy Branciforte had recommended to the King for use in future epidemics, was not reinstituted in 1813. Neighborhood charitable societies of a sort were set up in the small districts, but they were short of funds, loosely organized, and almost totally inadequate in the face of overwhelming privation, hunger, and disease. In 1813 each small district had to raise its own funds locally, whereas in 1797 provision had been made, through the agency of the central relief chest, for the wealthier ones to help the poorer ones.

In the face of overwhelming political and economic upheavals throughout the colony in 1813, the problems of the epidemic tended to be shunted aside. The result was the most calamitous onslaught of epidemic disease to the capital in that century. The epidemic of 1813 was a major human disaster, but only one among many in a time when famine, pestilence, rebellion, and death swept almost unbridled across the beautiful Valley of Mexico.

[78] *Ibid.*, Exp. 15, fols. 1, 5, 8v.

PART III

THE CYCLE OF SICKNESS

chapter eight

Conclusions

THROUGHOUT the colonial period New Spain was subjected repeatedly to mass invasions of epidemic disease. Such visitations were so varied in character, and so widely dispersed in time and space, that all residents of the colony, white or Indian, rich or poor, young or old, ran the risk of premature death from smallpox or typhus or some equally dangerous malady. It may be assumed that the relative isolation of persons living in rural areas or small towns would have lessened their chances of being exposed to a contagious disease, whereas the residents of a large municipality, especially Mexico City, could hardly escape being exposed once an epidemic had broken out. But the residents of the larger centers enjoyed the advantage of greater resources at hand for fighting the outbreak. Mexico City was incomparably the richest and most sophisticated city in the colony, and if any place in New Spain had the doctors, medicines, hospitals, and money for helping the sick in their fight for recovery it would have been the capital. Nevertheless, in spite of the greater abundance of these resources there, some of them were only moderately effective, others were useless, and they were not uniformly available to all the people according to the relative seriousness of their illness.

It is beyond dispute that even in the most advanced and richly endowed metropolis of the colony, human life was repeatedly threatened by various kinds of epidemic diseases. In the period of primary concentration of this study—1761 to 1813—Mexico City was attacked by five deadly epidemics which—by a conservative estimate—

claimed a minimum of 50,000 lives.[1] Indeed, epidemics occurred there with such regular frequency that this very fact made them seem inevitable, and, given the conditions which prevailed at the time, perhaps they were. The historian may well ask what were the conditions which permitted such a sustained and terrible onslaught against human life. In general, the causes of these outbreaks may be categorized as (1) administrative, (2) social, and (3) medical. Each of these categories will now be considered in turn.

Administrative Conditions: A successful program of public health demands close and effective cooperation between administrators on both local and national levels. Local authorities must assume responsibility for most of the burden of maintaining adequate environmental sanitation, implicit in such matters as refuse disposal and a potable water supply, but it is also true that since epidemics are oblivious to political boundaries, only regional or national authorities can cope effectively with mass outbreaks of epidemic disease. In Mexico City we have seen that all levels of government, national and local, civil and ecclesiastical, were involved in varying degrees in maintaining public health. But the general effort, which sporadically was successful and praiseworthy, suffered over the long run because of the wide dispersion of authority. The basic failing in the area of administration lay in the fact that there was no single person or office in New Spain sufficiently cognizant of the diverse problems of public health to cope with them within a national or regional range. This lack of any overall supervision or coordination resulted in considerable confusion, overlapping of authority, and duplication of effort.

---

[1] This total has been arrived at by adding together the *minimal* (except for 1797) figures on mortality from the four out of five of the major epidemics for which such figures exist. These figures are: (1761), 14,600; (1779), 8,821; (1797), 7,147; and (1813), 20,385. This gives a grand total of 50,953 deaths from epidemic disease in Mexico City from 1761 to 1813. No mortality figures exist for the epidemic of 1784–1787 except for the record of 711 deaths among patients at Hospital de San Andrés during this period. Since these figures are so fragmentary they have not been included. If one accepts Alzate's estimate for the epidemic of 1761—25,000 deaths—or Mier's estimate (probably the most accurate of the four which exist) for the epidemic of 1779—18,000—this gives a grand total of 70,532 deaths. I have accepted the highest of the three recorded estimates for 1797—that of 7,147 deaths—because there is no doubt in my mind that it is the most accurate of the three.

In retrospect, it would appear that the Tribunal of the Protomedicato would have been the logical authority to have functioned as a kind of "National Board of Health." But this was not the case. The Tribunal's role was restricted mainly to the tasks of licensing medical specialists and inspecting pharmacies; otherwise its influence was confined to offering advice on those occasions when this might be solicited by the viceroy, city government, or the courts. Since the colony's medical Tribunal did perform only a limited, albeit important, function, the role of coordinator, or supervisor, of the public health fell perforce upon the viceroy. This official was in one sense eminently qualified to perform such duties since he acted in the king's name, and, all things considered, he was the most powerful man in the colony. But he was overburdened with innumerable responsibilities. Most viceroys served terms of about five years, and by the time a man had learned his job sufficiently well to grasp its myriad details, it was usually time to start thinking about the trip back to Spain.

It was clearly recognized by the eighteenth century that the viceroy was overworked to the point that his effectiveness was impaired. A major reason for the introduction of the intendancy system to New Spain in 1786 had been to reduce the work load of the viceroy. But in Mexico City the intendant never got out from under the thumb of the viceroy, who may have preferred long working hours, or inefficiency, or both, to a powerful rival. In the area of public health little is heard of the work of the intendant in Mexico City; in the extensive records of the epidemic of 1797 this official is never mentioned once. In fact, the only agency in New Spain of which it could be said that it was ever powerful enough to rival, or occasionally dominate, the viceroy was the audiencia. But in the area of public health the intervention of the high court was occasional and tangential, and it was never concerned with formulating or enforcing policy matters in this area.

The only two important areas where it was understood that the viceroy did not enjoy primary authority, at least theoretically, in public-health administration (aside from the limited role of the Protomedicato, as mentioned) were hospitals and cemeteries, both of which were controlled, of course, by the Church. But aside from these few exceptions, the viceroy clearly had the legal right to intervene in almost any area related to the public health, even at the municipal level.

But the possession of the authority and the exercise of it were hardly one and the same thing. The fact is that in view of more pressing obligations elsewhere, such as in political, military, religious, and financial affairs, public health was neglected by the only agency, i.e., the viceroyalty, that had the authority to cope with problems of health on a regional or national basis.

In a time of crisis, notably epidemics, when a situation threatened the general welfare, the viceroy was usually motivated to take strong action; Branciforte, for instance, performed such a role well in 1797. But whereas a time of crisis might temporarily divert the viceroy away from his customary obligations, and the outbreak then in progress could be effectively prosecuted, the viceroy, as top authority, failed in the less dramatic but more important area of preventive medicine. In other words the dispersion of authority in the area of public-health administration made it difficult for any official other than the viceroy to take effective action with regard to mass outbreaks of disease. When he failed to act, as was generally the case except in a time of crisis, it was nearly impossible to anticipate, or in effect to prevent, those problems which contributed to the spread of disease and epidemics. To say that the viceroy "failed to act" is not to overlook the fact that periodically there was issued through his office a host of sensible edicts on such matters as public works, food and water, and sanitation. But the point is that these edicts were widely, almost characteristically, ignored, and the viceroy seemed to regard the flouting of his authority as one of the inexorable facts of life.

Many of these edicts were admirable in their intent, and remarkable for their advanced understanding of the nature of the problems to which they addressed themselves. Two examples of such viceregal efforts are Croix's edict of 1769 on municipal sanitation, and Branciforte's edict of 1797 on smallpox. But noteworthy as these pronouncements were (and similar examples could be cited), the real determinant is that in spite of his superior authority the viceroy intervened only irregularly in matters of public health, especially in the area of preventive medicine. Lacking any adequate viceregal supervision or coordination, the various local and municipal authorities of the colony usually went their own way and at their own pace, secure in the knowledge that they would be free to act as was convenient or seemed best.

It would thus appear that a prime cause of the chronic endemic sicknesses and the recurrent epidemics in New Spain was the absence of an effective central government capable of enforcing its edicts in the area of public health. Yet it must be recognized also that the lack of enforcement was due in large part to the backward social conditions of the time. As S. F. Cook has written: "If their [the edicts'] enforcement left a good deal to be desired this was due to the inherent difficulty of administering drastic legislation among an ignorant and backward people . . . [and] where the actual administration of an edict devolved upon minor officials of the most diverse qualifications."[2] If administrative irresponsibility caused failure to act, or failure to follow through once an action had been announced or initiated, this was but one horn of the dilemma. The social conditions of the times represent the other.

Social Conditions: Two great and widely divergent socioeconomic classes embraced nearly all the population of colonial Mexico City— the rich and the poor. While this is a gross oversimplification it is nonetheless useful, since this central fact represents the logical starting point in any consideration of the historical interrelation between disease and social welfare. It has long been recognized that poverty produces disease and disease in turn produces poverty and destitution. In colonial Mexico City the vast majority of the population chronically suffered a poverty-stricken existence characterized by malnutrition and inadequate shelter and clothing. In a time of general public crisis, such as an epidemic, many of them would have starved to death without the fruits of charity. Conversely it may be assumed that many of those who did die of disease had contracted their ailment because of their disadvantaged condition. This was the thesis of Luis José Montaña, the most influential physician of his time. Through the centuries poverty and disease have walked hand in hand as partners in a disabling and recurring cycle. For the historian the most logical way to understand the effects of this cycle is through the study of the

---

[2] See Cook, "Smallpox in Spanish and Mexican California: 1770–1845," *Bulletin of the History of Medicine,* VII (February, 1939), 155.

sick-poor, since their misfortune has traditionally been the common meeting ground of both of its phases.[3] The records of the disastrous epidemics of colonial Mexico City have furnished new and dramatic illustrations of this ancient cycle, which through the years has constituted one of the greatest social problems confronting mankind.

It is obvious that the capacity of Mexico City to assist its sick-poor during any given epidemic was closely related to its economic prosperity at that particular time. It would appear, however, that even in relatively prosperous years the existence of a majority of the population was marginal. For example, in 1779, a year when the material prosperity of Mexico City was at a high level, more than 80 per cent of those persons who contracted smallpox during the epidemic were forced to rely entirely or in part on the assistance of charity.[4] And many of those who died were so poor they had to be buried at public expense. One should keep in mind that smallpox is not a chronic disease, but runs its course over a span of only two or three weeks. This short period is telling evidence of the marginal resources of most of the people, since the destitution of the sick-poor was almost immediate. With 80 per cent of the sufferers from smallpox relying on charity in 1779, such assistance had to be provided quickly. The affluent groups in society, including the Church, certain corporations, and various wealthy individuals, had such ample reserves that even a surplus of funds for charity was raised. In that year of relative plenty the upper class did not question its obligation to give assistance to the sick-poor. This was a duty inherent in its exalted position in the community. But in 1797 ample funds for charity were raised only with considerable difficulty, and the assistance which was given to the sick-poor was minimal. The raising of ample funds required all the peculiar skills of Branciforte, who artfully blended threats and praise. Furthermore, in 1797 money which traditionally had been sent to Spain had to be locally retained to fight the epidemic. This is ample

[3] Albert Deutch, "Historical Inter-Relationships between Medicine and Social Welfare," *Bulletin of the History of Medicine*, XI (May, 1942), 485.

[4] Viceroy Mayoraga reported that by December 27, 1779, a total of 44,286 cases of smallpox had been reported; of this number only 7,566 persons had the resources to care for themselves. See Chap. Four, n. 40.

evidence of the general scarcity of funds, since customarily the use of royal moneys for charitable purposes was not permitted except in dire emergencies.

In 1813, during the last great epidemic of the colonial period, the sick-poor were rendered cruelly vulnerable to their ailment because of the disappearance of their traditional source of aid. Foreign wars and domestic insurrections had shattered the local economy, and the customary dole from the rich to the poor was woefully inadequate in 1813. Only one person is officially known to have died of starvation, but many thousands of unfortunates were destitute of food, clothing, and shelter. The fruits of charity had dried up and withered away. Many of the rich had joined the poor, and before the epidemic finally ran its course more than 20,000 people were left dead in its wake. No greater tragedy has befallen the capital of Mexico since that time. We now come to the last of the three prime factors responsible for these vicious onslaughts against human life.

Medical Conditions: Even by the end of the eighteenth century, the practice of medicine in New Spain had few aspects that were truly scientific and professional. Physicians were only vaguely aware of the causal relation between microorganisms and disease, although they sensed that in some mysterious manner contagion could be trans- mittted by means of air, water, or personal contact. The chief cause of disease was thought to be "infection of the air," but of course no phy- sician anywhere in the world had yet succeeded in equating a particu- lar microorganism with a specific disease. If physicians thereby could not treat the actual cause of a disease, they could, and did, treat its symptoms, and to this extent some of their prescriptions for rest, spe- cial diets, medicinal teas, tonics, poultices, warm clothing, and even some of the drugs, were no doubt appropriate and helpful. But certain of their treatments were useless or worse, such as bloodletting, purga- tives, scatological prescriptions, and comparable drastic measures.

In seeking to curb the spread of contagious diseases, particularly smallpox, considerable stress was placed on the ancient and still essen- tial method of quarantine. In New Spain, however, despite the best efforts of public officials, an effective quarantine was rarely if ever achieved. According to the law, which was reiterated time and time again, all virolentos had to be confined—forcibly if necessary—to lazarettos. Ordinarily, during major epidemics there were never enough of these provisional hospitals to accommodate the vast throngs of sick-poor. Those which did operate tended to be overcrowded, understaffed, and pestiferous. Nothing about them inspired the patients housed there to hope for a speedy recovery. In the public mind lazarettos were not viewed as treatment centers but as "death houses," and families took extreme measures to hide their virolentos from the spying eyes of doctors, pharmacists, and priests who would endeavor to place them there. It would appear that the popular dread of such places was well justified; in 1813, for example, the Ayuntamiento purchased two new carts for the express purpose of transporting corpses from the lazarettos to the cemeteries. In view of the massive public resistance, the lazaretto was of doubtful value as a means of halting an epidemic.

Nor did other measures which were intended to diminish the threat of contagion have any great success. Despite repeated prohibitions issued by secular and ecclesiastical authorities, the practice of burying corpses in churches continued. During epidemics, the law notwithstanding, shopkeepers rerented the sheets, pillows, biers, shrouds, and coffins used in the burial of virolentos; there were even reports of heartless or desperate guardians and parents who sold the clothes provided by charity for their sick children. Public authorities clearly understood the danger to public health posed by the movement of contaminated persons and objects, but neither by quarantine nor by other measures were they able to achieve a satisfactory level of control.

In eighteenth-century New Spain, as indeed in the rest of the world, the frontiers of medical knowledge were obviously quite restricted. But in New Spain, in contrast to more enlightened medical attitudes elsewhere, not much interest was shown in the kind of innovation which might have broadened them appreciably. No evidence has been found of any deep-seated opposition to experimentation of a medical nature, but neither was very much of it done. Autopsies, including the dissection of diseased organs and the preservation of samples, were performed occasionally to learn more about the cause of disease. Caesarian sections are known to have been performed on the bodies of deceased pregnant women, but under barbarous conditions, and for theological rather than medical reasons. New treatments of the sick were sometimes devised, such as those recommended by Miranda and Carondelet for smallpox in 1797. The Protomedicato made an effort to collect information on new herbs, plants, and drugs of possible medicinal value. Sporadically various physicians would meet together to exchange opinions, and frequently notes were taken for the specific purpose of ensuring the continued availability of such information. But in spite of the commendable effort made to gather and preserve important data of medical interest, no record has been found of any significant advance in medical science which resulted from experimentation conceived and carried out in New Spain during the years of this study. In all classes of society traditionalism was a barrier to the acceptance of new ideas, and by and large the physicians were no exception to this rule. There was only one Luis José Montaña, and this modern-minded doctor won his greatest fame in the early years of the nineteenth cntury. It is interesting to compare the ideas expressed in the same year—1813—of the secular, rational-minded Montaña, who recognized environmental influences on disease, and the superannuated García Jove, who still sought to explain epidemics as a ·'scourge of God."

The physicians of the day seem to have followed no very exact methods of diagnosis, and various diseases were not at all well differentiated. Smallpox and chicken pox were frequently confused, as were also yellow fever and typhus. Because of the historic changes in medical nomenclature, and because the same disease will have different manifestations in different patients and at different times, the assigning of modern names to diseases of the past is frequently conjectural. It is clear, however, that two diseases—typhus and smallpox—were about equally responsible for the major epidemics in Mexico City between 1761 and 1813. These were the twin scourges of New Spain. Other diseases known to have been present endemically, and perhaps epidemically from time to time, include yellow fever, typhoid fever, diphtheria, pneumonia, influenza, dysentery, chicken pox, measles, leprosy, scurvy, and venereal disease. In spite of the relative scarcity of data on diseases other than smallpox and typhus, it may be safely assumed that they were responsible for considerable loss of life. Insofar as is known, however, no deaths from any of these other diseases are included in the estimate of 50,000 deaths from epidemic disease in Mexico City between 1761 and 1813. This is further evidence that this minimal figure is indeed a conservative estimate.

As already pointed out, the Tribunal of the Protomedicato was responsible for maintaining and raising the standards of the medical profession, but it did not succeed in doing much more than to eliminate some of the more flagrant abuses. Outside the capital it had little influence, and in Mexico City it seemed more interested in defending the good intentions of physicians than in cracking down relentlessly on quacks and incompetents. Once a physician was licensed the Tribunal left him alone; it seemed to assume that there could be no such thing as a licensed quack. The wrath of the Tribunal was usually visited upon the pharmacists, who were frequently merited such attention. The Protomedicato deserves much credit for championing inoculation in 1797 in the face of opposition from the Viceroy, the lower ranks of the clergy, and the common people, but customarily it did not provide vigorous leadership. On occasion a member of the Tribunal advocated or defended ideas which at the time were considered antiquated by most doctors. In 1797 José F. Rada praised the use of bloodletting when this harsh procedure was being widely condemned by numerous physicians. In 1813, as we have seen, the venerable president of the Protomedicato, José Ignacio García Jove, on the occasion of a distinguished medical symposium, interpreted an epidemic of typhus as "the scourge of God." This influential doctor had formed his opinion after a careful reading of Holy Scriptures—a diagnostic aid which may have been no less useful to the physician than were the still-popular medical authorities of that time, Hippocrates and Galen.

Throughout the period covered by this study, medicine and theology were rather closely related. Persons who were sick customarily sought supernatural assistance in overcoming their physical disabilities. Many people believed that a host of saints—including the much beloved and revered Virgin of Guadalupe, the Virgin of Los Remedios, the Virgin of Loreto, San Sebastián, Santa Rosalía, and numerous others—enjoyed some special competence in the affairs of medicine. No person could be licensed by the Protomedicato to practice medicine until he had sworn under oath to uphold the mystery of the immaculate conception of the Virgin Mary. Despite the chronic shortage of funds during major epidemics, invariably substantial sums of money were spent at these times for the purpose of appeasing divine wrath or of winning divine protection.

Another form of supernatural influence on medicine, which, however, had no connection with orthodox theology, was the popular belief in "evil winds" as a cause of disease, and some persons attached great significance to the relative positions of the earth, sun, and moon. It may be assumed that much of the reason sick people in New Spain turned so readily to the supernatural world of religion and astrology was the general ineffectiveness of the "natural" world of medicine. The Indians, in particular, had very little confidence in Spanish physicians, and preferred some traditional native remedy, or appeal to some supernatural power, to the prescriptions of the licensed doctors. The common people, mainly out of necessity, relied on curanderos and quacks for medical attention.

The greatest advance in the practice of medicine that occurred in New Spain during the period of this study was the introduction of vaccination in 1803. For the first time the medical profession could guarantee protection against one of the common contagious diseases, a fact which was not properly appreciated until some years after the event. Since the story of vaccination, including its introduction into New Spain, has been so ably presented in other works, the present study has focused primarily on the use in New Spain of its forerunner —inoculation. It is true, of course, that inoculation was never accepted widely in New Spain. But in spite of certain hazards the operation, at least by 1797, was generally effective and reasonably safe. Considering the extent and perils of smallpox at the time, the life of a nonimmune person was safer with inoculation than without it. By 1797 there is no record of any physician of Mexico City who opposed the use of inoculation on medical grounds. It is quite possible, however, that the physicians' despair over the failures of quarantine accounts in large part for their vigorous endorsement of inoculation. They knew it was dangerous, but in the absence of any practical alternative it seemed well worth the risk. In the epidemic of 1797 when more than 7,000 persons died of smallpox in Mexico City only 21 of this number were inoculados.[5]

That inoculation was completely ignored in 1779, and accepted by only the small upper class in 1797, was probably due more to the general lack of confidence in the medical profession than to the fear of hazards inherent in its use. This view is substantiated by the fact that the virtually foolproof preventive of vaccination encountered the same kind of militant opposition in 1803 as had inoculation when it was introduced into New Spain in 1779. But both of these preventives were innovations, and the manner of their "magic" was to most persons mysterious and incomprehensible; consequently they preferred to curse what they could not understand.[6] Nevertheless, in spite of the rejection of inoculation, and the cautious acceptance of vaccination, an effective answer had at last been found for the age-old scourge of smallpox, and this advance marks the faint beginnings of modern medical science in Mexico.

Although smallpox had been overcome, at least potentially, with the introduction of vaccination, that other scourge of New Spain—typhus—was fully as dangerous in 1813 as it had been in 1761. No progress at all was made within the period of this study in controlling the ravages of this louse-borne disease. Such failure is not surprising in view of the wretched sanitary conditions of the times, which were particularly faulty in a metropolis such as the capital. Public and private regard for matters of hygiene was deficient in the extreme. It should be pointed out, however, that the medical profession itself had no understanding of typhus, so one can scarcely blame public-health authorities for their failure to prevent the disease. Public health nec-

[5] AGN, "Bienes Nacionales," Leg. 873, Exp. 180, fol. 3v.

[6] See Cook, "Smallpox in Spanish and Mexican California: 1770–1845," Bulletin of the History of Medicine, VII (February, 1939), 168. Cook cites a letter from Dr. Fray Francisco Rouset de Jesús, bishop of Sonora, Sinaloa, and the Californias, to Fray Estevan Tapis, which is dated November 27, 1804. The letter refers to difficulties which Rouset had encountered in the introduction of vaccination: "But since men in their ignorance pretend to curse what they do not understand . . . we find that those who have the smallest comprehension of the matter are accustomed to spread over the country pernicious ideas which are capable of nullifying and disintegrating the most efficacious measures for the public welfare." Ibid. Translation is by Cook.

essarily operates on the prevailing medical concepts, for it is concerned essentially with applying existing medical knowledge on a broad scale.[7] But in a day when the best physicians of the city attributed the cause and spread of disease to such diverse factors as "infection of the air," "overloading of the atmosphere," "suppressed perspiration," "degenerative dispositions of the humors," plus a host of mysterious fermentations, emanations, vapors, miasmas, and "putrid exhalations," it is no wonder that public officials were often as perplexed as the physicians. But although many of the physicians' explanations of the cause of disease were wide of the mark, and although the causal relation between filth and disease (as with the body louse and typhus) was imperfectly known in 1813, all competent authorities, including the ayuntamiento, the viceroy, and the physicians, clearly recognized a general if not a specific need to maintain adequate environmental sanitation in the interest of protecting the public health. The failure to do so was a major cause of epidemics in New Spain.

Finally, it would appear that epidemic disease (with the probable exception of infant mortality) constituted the single most common cause of premature death throughout the history of New Spain. It cannot be doubted that this was true of Mexico City during the final years of the colonial period. Certain advances were made on all fronts during these years, but in general the challenges posed by epidemics were simply too powerful and too little understood to be dealt with effectively. The ignorance of physicians was compounded by the failings of administrators; this was particularly true in the all-important area of environmental sanitation, an indispensable adjunct of preventive medicine. Administrative deficiencies in this regard, especially on the municipal level, were chronic and disastrous. Public works of vital interest to the health and general well-being of the community, such as aqueducts, water lines, roads, and canals, were inadequately maintained, and many fell quickly into disrepair or disuse. The interior-drainage system of the city was totally inadequate, and only partial solutions were found for the chronic threat of floods. Public services,

[7] Personal communication, John Duffy to Donald B. Cooper, December 10, 1964.

such as the cleaning of streets and canals, the collection of garbage and refuse, and the maintenance of cemeteries, were inadequate to say the least. Private sanitary facilities were nonexistent in most dwelling places. In such an unfavorable physical environment the people were prime targets for a filth-begotten disease such as typhus.

The lack of education of the common people made it difficult for them to appreciate the importance of sanitation to health. Many of the Indians knew no Spanish. The appearance of newspapers during the period of this study, for those persons who could read or had the money to buy them, represented a notable advance in public education. The *Gazeta de México* was published from 1784 to 1821, and the *Diario de México*, which was used effectively to publish official notices about the epidemic of 1813, was published from 1805 to 1817. But most of the people were illiterate, and communication between the various social groups of the city was highly ineffective. Tensions were heightened because of legal discriminations. For example, persons who were not of good family, legitimate birth, and of "Spanish" blood could not be licensed to practice medicine or surgery, and persons from the lower classes could not be buried in the same cemeteries with "respectable persons." The law favored the rich and influential in alloting private fountains. It would appear that mutual respect and understanding between the two extremes of the social order could hardly be said to have existed. It is true that during an emergency the common people were entitled to enough aid—when it was procurable—to keep them alive, but generally they seem to have impressed themselves on the consciousnes of the well-to-do only when they posed some real or fancied threat to the ruling classes, such as by their inability to work or as carriers of a contagious disease. Humanitarian sentiments, like those expressed by Montaña, were uncommon, and the poor were often held to be chiefly responsible for their own misfortunes.

It is obvious that the failures in public-health administration were deep-seated, and that they cannot be adequately understood without reference to the social and intellectual currents of the time. Standards of public health are but a reflection of, and are largely determined by, the cultural conditions of the particular period under study. But there are certain absolutes as well as variables in this matter, for an effective program of public health demands a strong central government capable of enforcing its edicts, and a reasonably enlightened population with sufficient civic pride that its cooperation is voluntary and dependable. Neither of these requisites was present in New Spain; here lies a prime cause of the recurrent epidemics.

A distinguished historian of medicine, Dr. George Rosen, has written concerning disease and death and social criticism:

Criticism of society is so often framed in terms of unnecessary disease and death. In every age the impetus to social criticism, and eventually to reform or revolution, springs from a realization of the contrast between the observed state of society and the standards recognized as valid by the individual. Since disease is very often one of the most striking examples of social and economic injustice, it becomes in the hands of the social dissenter an instrument for criticism of the existing social order.[8]

Yet in colonial Mexico City, where more than 50,000 people died of epidemic disease in approximately half a century, the absence of social criticism concerning this is indeed surprising. It is true that the rebellion (1810–1821) which led to the independence of Mexico was in progress during the final great epidemic in 1813. But the sources used in this study have revealed no evidence that "unnecessary disease and death" was ever included in the justifications for political revolution. The destruction of human and natural resources which occurred in the Valley of Mexico and its leading city during colonial times was enormous. The contrast between the splendor of the original natural setting, the "wooded, watered, and verdant Valley of Mexico —the valley full of promise," and the disease-ridden annals of the later settlers, ought to have pricked the consciousness of numerous dissenters unwilling to accept other social conditions.

Further study must be directed to the paradox between the enormous deprivation and mortality among the people and their apparent resignation to a social and political order which seemed incapable of materially improving their lot. It would appear, if Rosen's generalization is valid, that the social and political reaction of the people of Mexico City to the challenge of disease must have differed signifi-

[8] George Rosen, "Disease and Social Criticism: A Contribution to a Theory of Medical History," *Bulletin of the History of Medicine*, X (June, 1941), 11.

cantly from what has been observed to be the usual reaction of people from other areas in similar situations. In the field of medical history, as in all other areas of interest to historians, the records of all the major cultures and regions of the world, including those of Latin America, must be made available and taken into account. Only then will it be possible confidently to set forth historical generalizations of the widest possible validity. When this is done in the area of Latin American social and medical history, the dramatic cycle of sickness which plagued Mexico City at the end of the colonial period should not be disregarded. With the emphasis in our own day on the eradication of social evils spawned by poverty, the epidemics of Mexico City furnish useful insights and dramatic illustrations that are of more than historic interest.

BIBLIOGRAPHY

Manuscripts[1]

A. Archivo General de la Nación. (Cited in the footnotes as AGN.) Mexico City, Mexico.

(1) Ramo de Audiencia
  a. Vol. II, Exp. 2. "Qüenta y razón de los gastos erogados en la casa del hospital que de orden del Exmô. Señor Virrey de este reino se ha formado para la curación de los enfermos de la Real Cárcel del corte, que a el passan de la presente epidemia del mal de matlasagua [matlazahuatl] cita en el puente de Manzanares"
(2) Ramo de Ayuntamientos
  a. Vol. I, Exp. 1. "Carta de Virrey Félix Berenguer de Marquina al señor Presidente y Cabildo Sede Vacante de esta Santa Yglesia Catedral Metropolitana"
  b. Vol. I, Exp. 5. "Sobre traslación de cadáveres del Hospital General de Naturales al Campo Santo del de San Andrés"
  c. Vol. II, Exp. 10. "Sobre que se lleve a efecto la determinación de que se construya una [cementerio] para esta ciudad"
  d. Vol. II, Exp. 11. "Real cédula de 16 de abril de 1819 que manda que los vice-patronos y prelados diocesanos procedan de común acuerdo al arreglo de cementerios y reformar los abusos que se noten"

[1] In listing the titles of manuscripts the original spelling has been retained throughout except in a few cases where abbreviations have been expanded. Modern rules for accenting have been observed. Several manuscripts cited in the text could not be listed in the bibliography alphabetically because they have no title; however, in lieu of a title, I include below a complete list of the folio numbers of these manuscripts. From the Archivo General de la Nación I have cited the following untitled manuscripts: (1) Ramo de Arzobispos y Obispos, Vol. XVIII, fol. 1. (2) Ramo de Audiencia, Vol. XII, fols. 325–327v; Vol. XIV, fols. 183, 187, 331, 413; Vol. XX, fol. 79; Vol. XXXI, fols. 21–21v. (3) Ramo de Correspondencia de los Virreyes, Vol. CXXIV, Letter 151; Vol. CXXV, Letter 278. (4) Ramo de Desagüe, Vol. X, fol. 73. From the Archivo Municipal del Ex-Ayuntamiento I have cited one untitled manuscript: "Cedularios," Vol. 451, Tome II, "Cédulas pasta pergamino," fol. 173v.

e. Vol. II, Exp. 13. "Sobre que se señalen cementerios provisionales"

f. Vol. CVII, Exp. 1. "Sobre el alumbrado de las calles de México"

(3) Ramo de Bandos

a. Vol. XII, Exp. 35. "Bando que publica la división de la ciudad de México en 8 cuarteles"

(4) Ramos de Bienes Nacionales

a. Legajo 185, Exp. 59. "Sobre inundación del Convento de San Francisco"

b. Legajo 197, Exp. 1. "Cofradía del Santo Cristo"

c. Legajo 197, Exp. 9. "Cuaderno de recaudos que comprueban la qüenta de gastos del Nuestro Señor de la Salud"

d. Legajo 197, Exp. 13. "Libro de qüentas que pertenese a la cofradía y hermandad del Señor Christo"

e. Legajo 197, Exp. 16. "Patentes, cuentas y actas de la Cofradía del Santo Cristo de la Salud, de San Cosme y San Damián"

f. Legajo 197, Exp. 17. "Cuentas de la Cofradía del Santo Cristo de la Salud, de San Cosme y San Damián"

g. Legajo 197, Exp. 18. "Patentes, cuentas y actas de la Cofradía del Santo Cristo de la Salud, de San Cosme y San Damián"

h. Legajo 266, Exp. 74. "Representación del cura de San Miguel y oficio de S[u] S[antísimo] I[lustrísimo] al Prior de San Agustín, para que por razón de la epidemia den sepultura en el convento a los cadáveres"

i. Legajo 550, Exp. 46. "Cordillera dirijida a los prelados de los conventos sobre el arreglo de campanas en los incendios"

j. Legajo 575, Exp. 35. "Oficio al Dr. Don Joaquín Pío de Eguía y Muro para que renuncie la plaza que sirbe en el Hospital General de San Andrés"

k. Legajo 873, Exp. 119. "Oficio del señor Virrey acompañando exemplares del bando para poner remedio a los incendios de esta capital"

l. Legajo 873, Exp. 155. "Título de cirujano sangrador dado a Don Joseph Anastacio Pardo"

m. Legajo 873, Exp. 180. "Nota de todas las personas que han muerto de viruelas en la presente epidemia, con expresión de los que han muerto de naturales, y de inoculadas, desde principios de Septiembre de 1797"

(5) Ramo de Desagüe

   a. Vol. XV, Exp. 6. "Copia del informe dado al Virrey [Revilla Gigedo] por Don Domingo Trespalacios y Escandón sobre la real cédula para cese la qüartilla aplicada al Real Desagüe"

(6) Ramo de Epidemias

   a. Vol. I, Exp. 1. "Partes de los curas de los cadáveres de virolentos enterrados en sus parroquias y de los hospitales"

   b. Vol. I, Exp. 2. "Orden del Excelentísimo Señor Virrey, Marqués de Branciforte, para que se proceda a la formación de Sociedades para el socorro de los afectados por la epidemia de viruelas"

   c. Vol. I, Exp. 7. "Extracto certificado por el señor Juan Vicente de Vega, Escribano Real, y dé providencia de todo lo obrado en el expediente 'México' a 12 de febrero de 1798"

   d. Vol. III, Exp. 1. "Providencias generales para precaver el contagio de viruelas, y circulares con el mismo objeto"

   e. Vol. III, Exp. 2. "Circular sobre medios para evitar el contagio de las viruelas"

   f. Vol. III, Exp. 3. "Sobre haberse descubierto un meco con viruelas en el Hospital Real de Naturales"

   g. Vol. III, Exp. 17. "El Subdelegado de Tetela del Río [Jalapa] sobre providencias tomadas para socorrer a los enfermos de la epidemia"

   h. Vol. VI, Exp. 1. "Sobre rogaciones públicas"

   i. Vol. VI, Exp. 2. "Bando prohibiendo la venta o empeño de la ropa que se ministra a los variolosos"

   j. Vol. VI, Exp. [7]. "Partes del Protomedicato y sus incidencias; 9 estados y un resumen general de las Sociedades de Caridad que para el socorro de los contagiados de viruelas se formaron en esta capital; Partes semanales que han dado los médicos que asisten a los enfermos de viruela de orden del Dr. Maestro José Ignacio García Jove" (This expediente contains three separate items.)

   k. Vol. VII, Exp. 6. "Sospechas de haber viruelas en México"

   l. Vol. VII, Exp. 7. "Viruelas que se padecen en Tlalnepantla"

   m. Vol. VII, Exp. 8. "Oficio y minutas sueltas del expediente general de viruelas; Método de curación de la viruela del Dr. Don Bernardino Pérez y Arámburu, Bachiller en Filosofía, de Don Gabriel Barreiro y Peñalver y del Dr. Fr. Antonio Manuel Camejo, cirujano recibido en la Habana, ejerciendo en Campeche; Estados que manifiestan el número de enfermos que han habido en el presidio del Carmen y su jurisdicción de la epidemia de viruelas" (This expediente contains three separate items.)

n. Vol. VIII, Exp. 7. "La N[obilísima] Ciudad manifiesta que la peste sigue y se han agotado absolutamente los recursos para socorrer a los enfermos"

o. Vol. IX, Exp. 8. "Orden Superior al Protomedicato para que sin pérdida de tiempo informe sobre la naturaleza de la actual epidemia y del número de enfermos que adolecen de ella en esta capital y sus barrios; Contesta el Protomedicato a la orden de 8 de Junio sobre la naturaleza y síntomas de la epidemia de fiebre; Disposiciones que por bando se publicaron tendentes unas a cortar la epidemia, y otras a minorar sus estragos; Disposiciones de salubridad para evitar la epidemia" (This expediente contains four separate items.)

p. Vol. IX, Exp. 11. "Limosnas colectadas en esta capital para socorrer a los enfermos de la actual epidemia; *Gaceta del gobierno de México* del Sábado, 12 de Junio de 1813; Cuenta de lo colectado y su distribución; Extracto General de los Estados de Salubridad Pública, que de orden de este Nobilísimo Ayuntamiento se han seguido por los señores Regidores y Asociados de Caridad en la actual epidemia; Estado Necrológico de las parroquias de esta capital" (This expediente contains five separate items.)

q. Vol. IX, Exp. 16. "Providencias de precaución para que no se propaguen las fiebres que han principiado en los suburbios de esta ciudad; Dictamen del señor Luis Montaña sobre la enfermedad de las fiebres que se han desarollado en esta capital" (This expediente contains two separate items.)

r. Vol. XI, Exp. 1. "Orden del señor Virrey Branciforte para que se saque copia de la Real Orden fecha en Aranjuez en 15 de abril de 1785, y póngase con este decreto a la cabeza de la *Disertación Físico-Médica sobre el método de preservar a los pueblos de las viruelas,* compuesto por el señor Don Francisco Gil"

s. Vol. XI, Exp. 2. "Incidencia de fiebres petequiales en Azcapotsalco; Continúa la viruela; Partes de los hospitales; Resumen General de las Sociedades de Caridad; Partes originales de Orizaba refiriéndose a la epidemia de viruelas" (This expediente contains five separate items.)

t. Vol. XIII, Exp. 2. "Diligencias practicadas de mandato del Illustrísimo Señor Arzobispado de esta Santa Iglesia sobre la averiguación de las personas que han fallecido de todas calidades desde primero de Septiembre del año pasado en las dos epidemias de viruelas y matlazahuatl, con que dá cuenta el Excelentísimo Señor Virrey de este Reino a Su Magestad"

u. Vol. XIII, Exp. 3. "Certificaciones remitidas con consulta por el Illustrísimo Señor Arzobispo, Obispo de la Puebla, por la que consta el número de personas que fallecieron en aquella ciudad y obispado en las epidemias de viruelas y matlazahuatl, cuyo resumen es de 8,000 muertos"

v. Vol. XIII, Exp. 6. "Los naturales de Zirándaro, jurisdicción de Huetama [Valladolid], sobre enfermedad epidémica; Dictamen del Dr. Faustino Rodríguez sobre los progresos de la enfermedad, curación, establecimientos de lazaretos para enfermos contagiados; Medio de extinguir el contagio. Junta de dirección de policía y salubridad; Estados Generales de los enfermos en el Hospital provisional de San Francisco Javier [Puebla]; Estado Instructivo que por disposición de la Junta de Caridad se imprimió para manifestar al público el resultado de la epidemía" (This expediente contains five separate items.)

w. Vol. XV, Exp. 1. "El Teniente Castellano de Acapulco sobre cuarentena del bergantín *San Francisco de Asís* procedente de Guayaquil"

x. Vol. XV, Exp. 3. "Viruelas en Acapulco"

y. Vol. XV, Exp. 5. "Viruelas en el distrito de Guatemala. Cuarentena a la tripulación, pasajeros y cargamento de la fragata mercante *La Bentura*, procedente de Callao de Lima, conduciendo al Señor Regente de aquella Real Audiencia, Don Ambrosio Cerdá, con cinco hijas de las cuales una había padecido viruelas en Lima y dos en la navegación pocos días antes de haber entrado en Acajutla"

z. Vol. XVI, Exp. 1. "Sobre determinar casa donde se curen los virolentos"

aa. Vol. XVI, Exp. 2. "Extracto del expediente formado para la curación de los enfermos contagiados de viruelas"

bb. Vol. XVI, Exp. 6. "Avisos y providencias sobre haberse descubierto viruelas en México"

cc. Vol. XVI, Exp. 7. "Sobre viruelas descubiertas en México"

dd. Vol. XVI, Exp. 8. "Ejemplar de la circular de 28 de febrero [de 1797] sobre providencias para evitar las viruelas"

ee. Vol. XVI, Exp. 9. "Progreso y estado de la epidemia de viruelas en México, y continuación de las providencias tomadas con dicho motivo. Noticia de las providencias tomados por esta Nobilísima Ciudad acerca de la asistencia de los enfermos, y precaución del contagio para su más puntual ejecución"

(7)   Ramo de Historia
    a.   Vol. XLIV, Exp. 14. "Sobre versos anónimos contra varios médicos de resultas de la inoculación en México. Averiguación del autor de unos versos satíricos sobre la inoculación"

(8)   Ramo de Hospitales
    a.   Vol. XI, Exp. 6. "Entrega del Hospital General de San Andrés a disposición del Illustrísimo Señor Arzobispo para abrirle provisionalmente durante la presente epidemia de viruelas"
    b.   Vol. XLVIII, Exp. 14. "El administrador del Hospital de Naturales proponiendo arbitrios para socorrer a los enfermos por falta de fondos"
    c.   Vol. LIII, Exp. 6. "Real cédula de 19 de Septiembre de 1790 que dispone que el Juzgado del Real Hospital de Indios sea a cargo de los Regentes de esta Audiencia"
    d.   Vol. LVI, Exp. 7. "Pesquiza secreta hecha en razón de los medicamentos que se envian para la curación de los Indios enfermos del Hospital Real"

(9)   Ramo de Protomedicato
    a.   Vol. I, Exp. 1. "Informe a Su Majestad por el Virrey don Manuel Antonio Flores"
    b.   Vol. II, Exp. 5. "El Ayuntamiento de Querétaro suspende una comisión que dió el Real Tribunal del Protomedicato al Dr. Miguel Chacón para que visitase las boticas de aquella jurisdicción"

B.   Archivo Municipal del Ex-Ayuntamiento. (Cited in the footnotes as Ex-Ayun.) Mexico City, Mexico.

(1)   Ramo de Actas de Cabildo
    a.   Vol. 380 (1796–1802), sessions of January 18, 1798, March 8, 1798, and January 16, 1801. Typewritten copies of the original.

(2)   Ramo de Asistencias
    a.   Vol. 368, Tome 1, Exp. 1. "Autos formados sobre lo acaecido con el cabildo ecclesiástico de esta Santa Iglesia en el novenario y missas de Nuestra Señora de Loreto celebrado en el templo de la Casa Profesa por esta Nobilíssima Ciudad por la epidemia"

(3)   Ramo de Historia: Inundaciones
    a.   Vol. 2272, Tome I, no Exp. number. "Diligencias practicadas

para que estén repressas las aguas en la calzada de Nuestra Señora de Guadalupe"

b. Vol. 2272, Tome I, no Exp. number. "Don Francisco Riofrío sobre el mal estado en que se pone con las llubias la calzada"

c. Vol. 2272, Tome I, no Exp. number. "Expediente formado a instancia de la Madre Avadesa, Vicaria, y Definidoras del Real Convento de Jesús María sobre ha verse inundado dicho convento"

d. Vol. 2272, Tome I, no Exp. number. "Fray Miguel Gaviola sobre los perjuicios que causa al Hospital de San Juan de Dios con la agua"

(4) Ramo de Hospitales: Hospital de Naturales

a. Vol. 2309, Tome I, Exp. 1. "Autos formados en virtud de superior decreto de su Excelencia para que esta Nobilísima Ciudad disponga de un hospital para la curación perfecta y convalecencia de los miserables Indios, españoles pobres, y de color quebrado en la presente epidemia y demás que contiene"

(5) Ramo de Ordeñas de Vacas

a. Vol. 3392, Exp. 2. "Varias solicitudes y licencias sobre ordeñas de vacas"

(6) Ramo de Policía, Salubridad

a. Vol. 3668 (P. 245), Tome I, Exp. 1. "Consulta hecha por esta Nobilísima Ciudad sobre la policía y la epidemia experimentada"

b. Vol. 3668 (P. 245), Tome I, Exp. 6. "Oficio del Señor Intendente sobre que se trasladen a los arrabales de esta capital los ataúdes, sábanas, almoadas y camas y demás que sirven a los cadáveres para evitar el contagio"

c. Vol. 3668 (P. 245), Tome I, Exp. 13. "Oficio de la Junta de Sanidad al Ayuntamiento sobre que dé providencia de que sus comisionados para la limpieza de calles hagan se cumpla con ello"

(7) Ramo de Policía, Salubridad, Epidemias

a. Vol. 3674 (P. 251), Tome I, Exp. 4. "Expediente formado sobre la curación de la presente epidemia y precauciones de ellas. Sofocación y pulmonía"

b. Vol. 3674 (P. 251), Tome I, Exp. 5. "Fiebre. Formado sobre providencias para precaver la enfermedad"

c. Vol. 3674 (P. 251), Tome I, Exp. 10. "Cuentas de gastos por socorros a enfermos y pobres"

d. Vol. 3674 (P. 251), Tome I, Exp. 12. "Estado general de parroquias y hospitales desde principio de la epidemia hasta 31 de agosto de 1813"

e. Vol. 3674 (P. 251), Tome I, Exp. 15. "El Hospital de San Andrés sobre que se le paguen 2,629 pesos de las medicinas que ministró para los enfermos de la epidemia de 1813"

(8) Ramo de Policía, Salubridad, Epidemia Viruela

a. Vol. 3678 (P. 255), Tome I, Exp. 1. "Varias providencias para atender y cortar la epidemia de viruelas"

b. Vol. 3678 (P. 255), Tome I, Exp. 2. "Disertación presentada al Ayuntamiento por el Dr. Don Esteban Enrique Morel sobre la inoculación de viruelas"

c. Vol. 3678 (P. 255), Tome I, Exp. 3. "Expediente formado a instancia del Dr. Don Esteban Morel sobre que por esta Nobilísima Ciudad se les satisfaga el costo y trabajo impendido en la inoculación de viruelas"

d. Vol. 3678 (P. 255), Tome I, Exp. 5. "Resumen General de las sociedades de caridad para el socorro de los contagiados de la epidemia de viruelas del año de 1797"

C. Archivo Histórico de la Escuela de Medicina [de la Universidad Nacional Autónoma de México], Mexico City, Mexico.

(1) Ramo de Protomedicato

a. Legajo 1, Exp. 3. "Expediente de Ignacio Esquivel"

b. Legajo 2, Exp. 17. "Expediente de Pedro Prieto Esquivel"

D. Archivo Histórico del Museo Nacional de Antropología. Mexico City, Mexico.

(1) "Legajos de expedientes relativos a exámenes en la facultad de medicina," Vol. "1812," no Exp. number, "Expediente de oficio con motivo a la vicita bienal que dió Don Vizente Zamora"

Primary Sources

Acontecimientos acaecidos en los años de 1784 á 1788. Biblioteca Aportación Histórica. 2d Ser. México, D.F.: Editorial Vargas Rea, 1948.

Alzate, José Antonio. "Proyecto para desaguar la laguna de Texcoco y las de Chalco y San Cristóbal," *Memorias de la sociedad científica "Antonio Alzate,"* III (1889), 185–201. This is the first printing of a work written in 1777.

Beleña, Eusebio Ventura (comp.). *Recopilación sumaria de todos los autos acordados de la Real audiencia y sala de crimen de esta Nueva España, y providencias de su superior gobierno; de varias reales cédulas y órdenes que después de publicada la Recopilación de Indias han podido recogerse así de las dirigidas a la misma Audiencia o Gobierno, como de algunas otras que por sus notables decisiones convendrá no ignorar.* 2 vols. Mexico City: Don Felipe de Zúñiga y Ontiveros, 1787.

Chappe d'Auteroche, Jean. *A Voyage to California, to observe the transit of Venus. By Mons. Chappe d'Auteroche; with an historical description of the author's route through Mexico, and the natural history of the province. Also, a voyage to Newfoundland and Sallee, to make experiments on Mr. Le Roy's time keepers. By Monsieur de Cassini.* London: E. and C. Dilly, 1778.

Esteynef[f]er, Juan de. *Abogados para toda clase de enfermedades del florilegio medicinal, por el hermano Juan de Esteynef[f]er. Impreso en México el año de 1712.* Biblioteca Aportación Histórica. México, D.F.: Editorial Vargas Rea, 1948.

[Fernández de Lizardi, José Joaquín]. *Receta, o método curativo, propuesto por medio del pensador en la presente peste.* Mexico City: M. F. de Jáuregui, [1813].

Fernández de Recas, Guillermo S. (ed.). *Medicina: nómina de bachilleres, licenciados y doctores, 1607–1780, y guía de méritos y servicios, 1763–1828.* Mexico, D.F.: Universidad Nacional Autónoma de México, 1960.

[Gálvez, Joseph de]. [*Despacho de*] *Don Joseph de Gálvez, del consejo y cámara de su Magestad. . . . Hago saber al señor ministro Juez Superintendente, Cavallero Corregidor, Capitulares . . . .* Mexico City, 1771. This despacho has no title, and the above is taken from its first sentence. In the Latin American Collection of The University of Texas.

[Giral, Joseph, Joseph Francisco Rada, and Joseph Ignacio García Jove]. *Públicas demostraciones de celebridad y júbilo que este real tribunal del protomedicato de N[ueva] E[spaña] hace en la gloriosa proclamación y exaltación al trono supremo de las Españas, de los señores Don Carlos Qüarto y Doña María Luisa de Borbón, su muy digna esposa, a quienes Dios Guarde Muchos Años.* Mexico City: Zúñiga y Ontiveros, 1791.

Memoria de los principales ramos de la policía urbana y de los fondos de la ciudad de México presentada a la serenísima regencia del imperio en complimiento de sus órdenes supremas y de las leyes por el prefecto municipal. México, D.F.: Imp. de J. M. Andrade y F. Escalante, 1864.

Memoria económica de la municipalidad de México formado de orden

del Exmô. Ayuntamiento, por una comisión de su seno en 1830.
Mexico, D.F.: Imp. de M. Rivera, 1830.

[Mexico City, Ayuntamiento of]. *Noticia de las providencias tomadas por esta Nobilísima Ciudad* [Ayuntamiento] *acerca de la asistencia de los enfermos, y precaución del contagio, para su más puntual ejecución.* Mexico City: [Printed by the Ayuntamiento of Mexico City], 1779.

Mexico City, Junta directiva del desagüe y saneamiento. *Memoria administrativa y económica que la Junta Directiva del Desagüe y Saneamiento de la ciudad de México presenta á la Secretaría de Gobernación (1896–1903).* México, D.F.: Tip. J. I. Guerrero y Cia., 1903.

Navarro y Noriega, Fernando. "Memoria sobre la población del reino de Nueva España," *Boletín de la Sociedad mexicana de geografía y estadística,* 2d Ser., I (1869), 281–291. This is a reprinting of a work first published in 1820 in Mexico City.

Ordenanzas que se han de observar y guardar en la muy nobilíssima, y leal ciudad de México, del reyno de Nueva España, aprobadas, y confirmadas por el señor rey D. Phelipe Quinto de este nombre (Que Dios Guarde, y ensalce felices años, como la Christiandad ha menester) por su real cédula de qüatro de Noviembre de mil setecientos y viente y ocho años. N.p., n.d. [Mexico City, 1729?]

Pérez-Maldonado, Carlos (ed.). *Documentos históricos de Nuevo León, 1596–1811.* 2 vols. Monterrey, Nuevo León: Impresora Monterrey, 1947.

[Revilla Gigedo, Conde de]. *Instrucción reservada que el Conde de Revilla Gigedo dió a su sucesor en el mando, Marqués de Branciforte, sobre el gobierno de este continente en el tiempo que fue su virey.* México, D.F.: Imprenta de la Calle de las Escalerillas, 1831. This is the first printing of a work written in 1794.

Torre, Ernesto de la (ed.). *Instrucción reservada que dió el virrey don Miguel José de Azanza a su sucesor don Félix Berenguer de Marquina,* No. 1 (January–March, 1960) of *Testimonia Histórica.* México [D.F.]: Editorial Jus, 1960.

Velasco Ceballos, Rómulo (ed.). *La Cirugía mexicana en el siglo XVIII.* México, [D.F.]: Archivo Histórico de la Secretaría de Salubridad y Asistencia, 1946.

Vetancourt, Augustín de. *Teatro Mexicano: Descripción breve de los sucesos exemplares, históricos, políticos, militares, y religiosos del nuevo mundo occidental de las Indias.* 4 parts in 1 vol. Mexico City: Doña María de Benavides, Viuda de Juan de Ribera, 1698.

Viera, Juan de. *Compendiosa narración de la ciudad de México,* prologue and notes by Gonzalo Obregón, [Jr.], México, [D.F.]: Editorial Guarania, 1952. This is the first printing of a work written in 1777.

[Villarroel, Hipólito]. *México por dentro y fuera bajo el gobierno de los vireyes. O sea enfermendades políticas que padece la capital de la N[ueva] España en casi todos los cuerpos de que se compone, y remedios que se deben aplicar para su curación.* México, D.F.: Imprenta del C. Alejandre Valdes, 1831. This is the first printing of a work written in 1787.

Zúñiga y Ontiveros, Mariano de (ed.). *Calendario manual y guía de forasteros en México para el año de 1797.* Mexico City: En la oficina del autor, [1798].

Newspapers

Diario de México (Mexico City), 1813. In the Latin American Collection of The University of Texas.

Gaceta del gobierno de México (Mexico City), 1813. In the Latin American Collection of The University of Texas.

Gazeta de México (Mexico City), 1784. In the Latin American Collection of The University of Texas.

Secondary Sources

Adorno, Juan N[epomuceno]. *Memoria acerca de la hidrografía, meteorológica, seguridad hidrogénica y salubridad higiénica del valle, y en especial de la capital de México.* México, D.F.: Imp. de Mariano Villanueva, 1865.

Alcázar Molina, Cayetano. *Los virreinatos en el siglo XVIII.* Vol. XIII of *Historia de América y de los pueblos americanos,* Antonio Ballesteros y Beretta (ed.). Barcelona, Salvat Editores, S. A., 1945.

Alvarez Amézquita, José, *et al. Historia de la salubridad y de la asistencia en México.* 4 vols. México, D.F.: Secretaría de Salubridad y Asistencia, 1960.

American Public Health Association. *Control of Communicable Diseases in Man.* 8th ed. New York: The American Public Health Association, 1955. Copyright 1955 by the American Public Health Association, Inc.

Barras de Aragón, Francisco de las. "Viaje del astrónomo francés [Jean] Chappe a California en 1769, y noticias de J. A. Alzate sobre la historia natural de Nueva España," *Anuario de estudios americanos,* I (1944), 741–781.

Barrett, John T. "The Inoculation Controversy in Puritan New England," *Bulletin of the History of Medicine,* XII (July, 1942), 169–190.

Blanco M., Gonzalo. "El abastecimiento de agua a la ciudad de México: Su relación con los recursos naturales renovables," *Boletín de la Sociedad mexicana de geografía y estadística,* LXV (March–June, 1948), 199–222.

Calderón Quijano, J. A. "Ingenieros militares en Nueva España," *Anuario de estudios americanos,* VI (1949), 1–71.

Carrera Stampa, Manuel. "Planos de la ciudad de México (desde 1521 hasta nuestros días)," *Boletín de la Sociedad mexicana de geografía y estadística,* LXVII (March–June, 1949), 263–427.

Cook, S[herburne] F. "The Hunger Hospital in Guadalajara: An Experiment in Medical Relief," *Bulletin of the History of Medicine,* VIII (April, 1940), 533–545.

———. "The Smallpox Epidemic of 1797 in Mexico," *Bulletin of the History of Medicine,* VII (October, 1939), 937–969.

———. "Smallpox in Spanish and Mexican California: 1770–1845," *Bulletin of the History of Medicine,* VII (February, 1939), 153–191.

Deutch, Albert. "Historical Inter-Relationships between Medicine and Social Welfare," *Bulletin of the History of Medicine,* XI (May, 1942), 485–502.

Díaz de Yraola, Gonzalo. *La vuelta al mundo de la expedición de la vacuna.* Sevilla: Escuela de estudios hispano-americanos de Sevilla, 1948.

Duffy, John. *Epidemics in Colonial America.* Baton Rouge: Louisiana State University Press, 1953.

Fastlicht, Samuel. *Bibliografía odontológica mexicana.* México, D.F.: La Prensa Médica Mexicana, 1954.

Fernández del Castillo, [Jr.], Francisco. "La inquieta vida del Doctor Bartolache," *El Médico,* Pt. I, Vol. VI (March, 1957), 49–56; Pt. II, Vol. VII (April, 1957), 54–62.

Gibson, Charles. *The Aztecs Under Spanish Rule: A History of the Indians of the Valley of Mexico, 1519–1810.* Stanford, California: Stanford University Press, 1964.

González Obregón, Luis. *Epoca colonial: México viejo: noticias históricas, tradiciones, leyendas y costumbres.* New edition, enlarged and corrected. México, [D.F.]: Editorial Patria, S.A., 1957.

Guerra, Francisco. *Historiografía de la medicina colonial hispanoameri-cana.* México, [D.F.] : Abastecedora de Impresos, S. A., 1953.

Haring, C. H. *The Spanish Empire in America.* New York: Oxford University Press, 1947.

Humboldt, Alexander von. *Political Essay on the Kingdom of New Spain.* Translated by John Black. 4 vols. London: Longman, Hurst, Rees, Orme, and Brown, 1811.

Izquierdo, José Joaquín. *Montaña y los orígenes del movimiento social y científico de México.* México, D.F.: Ediciones Ciencia, 1955.

————. *Raudón: cirujano poblano de 1810: aspectos de la cirugía mexicana de principios del siglo XIX en torno de una vida.* México, D.F.: Ediciones Ciencia, 1949.

Klebs, Arnold C. "The Historic Evolution of Variolation." *Bulletin of The Johns Hopkins Hospital,* XXIV (March, 1913), 69–83.

León, Nicolás. *La obstetricia de México: notas bibliográficas, étnicas, históricas, documentarias, y críticas de los orígenes históricos hasta el año de 1910.* México, D.F.: Tipografía de la viuda de F. Díaz de León, 1910.

Montenegro, Roberto. *Retablos de México (Ex-Votos): Mexican Votive Painting.* México, [D.F] : Ediciones Mexicana, S. A., 1950. The text of this dual-language work is printed in Spanish and English.

Muriel [de González Mariscal], Josefina. *Hospitales de la Nueva España.* 2 vols. Vol. I, *Fundaciones del siglo XVI,* Publicaciones del Instituto de Historia, Primera Serie, Número 35; México, [D.F.], 1956. Vol. II, *Fundaciones de los siglos XVII y XVIII,* México, [D.F.] : Editorial Jus, 1960.

Obregón, Jr., Gonzalo. *El Real Colegio de San Ignacio de México (Las Vizcaínas).* México, D.F.: El Colegio de México, 1949.

Olvera, José. "Memoria sobre el tifo," *Gaceta médica de México,* XVIII (May 15, 1883), 182–196; (June 1, 1883), 204–220; (June 15, 1883), 232–242; (July 1, 1883), 260–263.

Orvañanos, D[omingo]. "De la organización del ayuntamiento de México considerado desde el punto de vista de la salubridad pública," *Gaceta médica de México,* XXXVII (March 5, 1900), 113–118.

Parker, Jean. *Mil plantas medicinales.* México, D.F.: Editorial "Utilidad y Cultura," 1953. The title, as given above, is taken from the title page; on the jacket the title appears as *Mil plantas y yerbas medicinales de América.*

Pasalagua, M[anuel] A. "Algunas observaciones higiénicas sobre la ciudad de México relativamente a los lagos que la rodean," *Gaceta médica de México,* [Pt. I], Vol. VIII (April 1, 1873), 45–48; [Pt. II], Vol. VIII (April 15, 1873), 49–55.

Ramirez, Santiago, "Don Joaquín Velázquez Cárdenas y León, primer Director General de Minería," *Memorias de la sociedad científica "Antonio Alzate,"* I (1887), 227–300.

Reyes, José M[aría]. "Higiene pública: Limpia," *Gaceta médica de México,* [Pt. I], Vol. I (January 15, 1865), 145–152; [Pt. II], Vol. II (April 15, 1866), 113–120.

———. "Importancia de los estudios médicos locales," *Gaceta médica de México,* XIV (September 1, 1879), 337–345.

———. "Panteones," *Gaceta médica de México,* VIII (October 1, 1873), 153–160.

Romero de Terreros, Manuel. "Los acueductos de México," *Anales del museo nacional de arqueología, historia, y etnografía,* 4th Ser., III (April–June, 1925), 131–142.

Rosen, George. "Disease and Social Criticism: A Contribution to a Theory of Medical History," *Bulletin of the History of Medicine,* X (June, 1941), 5–15.

Ruiz y Sandoval, Gustavo. ¿Cuál es la influencia patogénica que tienen los lagos sobre la ciudad de México?" *Gaceta médica de México,* VIII (May 1, 1873), 65–76.

Secretaría de Hacienda y Crédito Público [de México]. *Guía del Archivo histórico de hacienda: siglos XVI–XIX.* México, D.F.: Secretaría de Hacienda y Crédito Público, 1940.

Soriano, M[anuel] S. "Algunos apuntes sobre el Protomedicato," *Gaceta médica de México,* XXXVI (October 15, 1899), 563–589.

———. "Origen de las cañerías de barro para la distribución de las aguas potables en la ciudad de México," *Gaceta médica de México,* 2d Ser., V (September 15, 1905), 233–235.

Téllez Pizarro, Adrián. "Apuntes acerca de los cimientos de los edificios en la ciudad de México," *Memorias de la sociedad científica "Antonio Alzate,"* XIV (1899–1900), [Pt. I], 73–112; [Pt. II], 391–438.

INDEX

164; habits of, 36; aversion of, to hospitals, 75; recommendations of Gálvez on, 76; and famine, 83; susceptibility of, to disease, 84–85, 159; transport of, to hospitals, 117; and inoculation, 122; medical service for, 139; cause of disease among, 163; effect of, on community, 163; proposed charitable societies for, 164; and quacks, 168; in Mexico City, 189; lack of education of, 198; mentioned, 126. *See also* sick-poor

Machincuepa Street: 107, 108
Málaga, Spain: yellow fever in, 157
Márquez, Agustín: 50–51
Martínez, Enrico: 9
Martínez Falcón, Father Francisco: 54
masdevall: 167–168 and n. 34
matlazahuatl. See typhus
Mayorada, Martín de (viceroy): and enlargement of Hospital de San Juan de Dios, 56–57; hospital at College of San Andrés, 57–58; contribution of, for public relief, 61; solicits contributions for public relief, 63; on conditions in Mexico City, 63; on inoculation, 64–65; on epidemic of 1779, 68; and relief for epidemic in Toluca, 68; mentioned, 69
Mazo, José del: 13, 94
measles: 173. *See also* disease
meco: 87
medicine: inspection of, in Querétaro, 32–33; investigation of, at Hospital Real de Indios, 38; expense of, 44; supplying of, by cofradías, 44–45; pamphlet on, 59 and n. 10; printed in *Gazeta,* 73–74; used by poor, 80; for smallpox, in Tlalnepantla, 91–92 and n. 14; expenditures for, by charitable societies, 151–152; effectiveness of, 154–155, 191, 195; paid for by Ayuntamiento, 162; distribution of, 162, 165, 168, 182; advances in, in New Spain, 192–193; relation of, to theology, 194–195;

failure of, 197–198; history of, 200; mentioned, 35, 37, 149, 166, 196. *See also* bloodletting; inoculation; *masdevall;* medicine, preventive; pharmacies; pharmacists; purgatives; vaccination
—, preventive: delegation of authority for, 16; failure of viceroy to act on, 188; effectiveness of, 197–198; mentioned, 154
Mexico City: relation of location of, to public health, 3; lakes in, as cesspools, 7; suggested relocation of, 9, 10; floods in, 10, 12, 114; epidemic in, in 1785, 14; responsibility for public health in, 16, 17; sanitation in, 17, 21, 23, 28, 34, 35, 38; location of cemeteries in, 26; history of cemeteries in, 27; inspection of burial sites in, 29; condition of cattle in, 35; smallpox epidemic in, 1797, 39; cofradía in, 45; division of, into districts, 60; urge for use of inoculation in, 112–113; administrative divisions of, 118–119; compared to Monterrey, 149; financial condition of, 164; epidemics in, 185–186; poverty in, 189; socioeconomic classes in, 189; social conditions in, 189–191, 199–200; relation of charity to economic prosperity in, 190; epidemic disease as cause of death in, 197; tensions in social order in, 198; favoring of upper class in, 198; cycle of disease in, 200; mentioned, 25, 33, 200
—, social classes of. *See* lower class; sick-poor
Mier y Trespalacios, Cosme de: in inspection party of Convent of Jesús María, 12–13; on epidemic of 1779, 68; authority of, during epidemic of 1797, 104 and n. 51; deemphasis of, on epidemic of 1797; and identity of smallpox victims, 110; suggestions of, on burial ground for virolentos, 110–111; efforts of, to provide municipal lazaretto, 111;

Lightning Source UK Ltd.
Milton Keynes UK
UKOW04f0425310315

248810UK00001B/5/P